The Memoirs of

Madame Roland

A Heroine of the French Revolution

Translated and Edited by
EVELYN SHUCKBURGH

Moyer Bell Limited
Mount Kisco, New York

Published by Moyer Bell Limited

Translated from the Memoires de Madame Roland, edited by Paul de Roux, published in a new edition. This edition published by arrangement with Barrie & Jenkins Ltd.

Copyright © 1986, Mercure de France
Copyright © 1989, Evelyn Shuckburgh

First Edition
1990

**LIBRARY OF CONGRESS
CATALOGING-IN-PUBLICATION DATA**

Roland, Mme (Marie-Jeanne), 1754–1793.
    [Mémoires de Madame Roland. English]
    The memoirs of Madame Roland /
    translated and edited by Evelyn
    Shuckburgh.— 1st ed.

    p. cm.
Translation of : Mémoires de Madame Roland.

    1. Roland, Mme (Marie-Jeanne), 1754–1793.
2. France—History—Revolution, 1789–1793—Personal narratives. 3. Girondists—Biography. 4. Revolutionists—France—Biography.
I. Shuckburgh, Evelyn, 1909– . II. Title
DC146.R7A3   1990
944.04′1′092—dc20
[B]   89–12870

ISBN 1–55921–014–1   CIP

Printed in the United States of America
Distributed by Rizzoli

CONTENTS

ILLUSTRATIONS

INTRODUCTION

M ADAME ROLAND (née Phlipon) is a controversial figure. In the
nineteenth century she was regarded as a great romantic
heroine. Goethe, Sainte-Beuve, Carlyle and many others admired
her and Stendhal wrote that she was 'the woman he most respected
in the world'. On the other hand a leading modern historian of the
French Revolution has described her as 'a dreadful snob and a
bluestocking ... a sanguinary terrorist.... In short, a very nasty
piece of work.'

A woman writing compulsively about herself while in prison and
under imminent threat of death does not necessarily disclose the
whole truth or present a fair picture. But the reader of these
memoirs will find that they reveal a very strong and unusual
personality with attractive as well as unattractive qualities. One can
well understand why there should be widely contrasting opinions
about her. Her goodness is too good and her hatreds overstated,
and yet it is hard not to have sympathy with her when reading her
polemics. As a typical romantic, she lives in a dream world and
seems to be constantly on stage, as it were, even when talking to
herself in the moonlight.

She does not emerge as an easy person. Her contempt for the
dullness of her own daughter Eudora, her lack of sympathy for the
sorrows of Marie Antoinette and her unfailing self-esteem detract
from our admiration for her spirited behaviour. To our twentieth-
century ears the Plutarchian posing and romantic enthusiasm for
the republics of classical antiquity strike an unrealistic note, and
there is something uncomfortable about the chips on her shoulder.
She is class-conscious both upwards and downwards, resentful of
privilege and touchy about her own status. But there is something
endearing about the openness with which she admits these feelings.
In this, as in the case of other defects, we keep having to remind
ourselves that her own candid pen is the source of the evidence on
which we criticise her.

She may have been vain and deluded, 'palpably impolitic and

ungenerous' as an earlier translator called her, but she had other qualities for which she should receive our sympathy. She was serious-minded and acutely sensitive to spiritual and artistic experience. The reader will find poetical feeling in some of her descriptions of the Paris sky, the joys of friendship, the soothing influence of flowers and the mystery of the heavens. She was high-principled in her personal behaviour as well as in the realm of political theory. Having had a disagreeable sexual experience at the age of twelve, which she describes in detail in the Private Memoirs (to the great indignation of Sainte-Beuve who called the passage 'an immortal act of indecency'), she became very wary of men, or at any rate of young men. She was also wary of her own physical impulses and describes with great frankness how from the age of fourteen she brought them under control. In her adolescence she formed romantic attachments with members of her own sex (one of these, with Sophie Cannet, inspiring courageous fidelity right up to the steps of the scaffold), and strictly intellectual or spiritual relationships with various elderly clergymen. She married a man twenty years older than herself, an upright, cautious, clearly rather boring bureaucrat whom she had to drag to the altar, and with whom her wedding night provided 'unpleasant surprises'. They had one daughter, who was not a success. When, in her early forties and within a few months of death, she fell in love, probably for the first time, with a real man, Buzot, she fought her passion with the same high-principled courage as had always sustained her against other forms of oppression, such as fear, despair and doubt. The guillotine put an end to the agonies of decision with which this particular infatuation confronted her.

Unfailing courage and complete frankness towards herself and others are the outstanding impressions one derives of her character. But of course it is she who is speaking. Her intense self-confidence, combined with an exceptionally serious education, wide reading and beady eye must have made her very formidable to meet and may explain the hatred with which she was pursued at the end. Those who are interested in the history of women's role in public life will find her an unusual example, for those days, of a woman who exercised political influence not indirectly, via the drawing-room or the bedchamber, but by sitting in on conferences of political leaders and drafting State papers herself. Her own views on the role of women, however, and on the purposes of women's education, are far from enlightened in modern terms.

Madame Roland gives some account of her origins at the beginning of the Private Memoirs, which form the second part of this book. She belonged to the class of small tradesmen in Paris who were to play such a prominent part in the Revolution. Her ancestors were artisans or small shopkeepers. Her father, Pierre-Gatien Phlipon, was a master engraver and had the title 'Engraver to the comte d'Artois'. Part craftsman, part artist, he decorated *objets de luxe* such as snuff boxes and watch cases with the help of several apprentices and supplemented his revenue by trading in jewellery. His wife, Marie-Marguerite Bimont, had seven children who all died in childbirth or soon after, except for this one daughter, Marie-Jeanne (known in the family as Manon), born on 17 March 1754. As was customary in those days, the child was sent away to a wet nurse. She returned to her family at the age of two and spent the rest of her childhood with her parents on the Quai de l'Horloge, a few steps from the Pont-Neuf, except for an interlude of two years in 1765–6 when she spent twelve months in a convent and another twelve with her grandmother on the Île St-Louis. All this she describes fully in her Private Memoirs.

From her earliest days she was extraordinarily studious, reading indiscriminately anything that fell into her hands. Plutarch was the first major influence (before she was nine years old) and Rousseau perhaps the last. She absorbed a great deal of controversial religious literature before she lost her faith and of, rationalist and romantic controversy thereafter. She developed a bold and effective style of writing, which she put to good use in a prolific private correspondence with one or two friends[1] and, later, by drafting documents of all kinds for her husband, both in and out of office. The French historian Michelet held that writing was a kind of mania with Mme Roland, and that she shared this weakness with Robespierre. 'Beneath the heroism of the one and the admirable determination of the other', he wrote, 'lay a common fault, a common absurdity one might call it; they were both born scribes. They were at least as preoccupied with style as with the reality of things and they wrote away, day and night, living and dying, in the

---

[1] Her letters to the Cannet sisters, published by M. Perroud in four volumes in 1902–15, were described at the time as 'not only one of the most interesting exchanges of correspondence that the eighteenth century has bequeathed to us but one of the most instructive and perhaps one of the chefs-d'oeuvre of our epistolary literature'.

midst of the most terrible crises and under the very shadow of the knife. The written word was for both of them an obsession.' (*History of the French Revolution*, 1836.) The memoirs illustrate very clearly Mme Roland's faith in the power of the pen. She was constantly issuing stirring appeals and denunciations which had disappointingly little effect upon events. She describes on several occasions how some great manifesto by Roland (probably drafted by herself) was rapturously applauded in the Assembly, ordered to be printed and circulated throughout France, judged to have had a profound effect on public opinion but unfortunately not followed by any action. In her private life her pen was equally active and fearless. Apart from her voluminous personal correspondence she drafted her father's replies (invariably negative and often wounding) to her own suitors and she even agreed to send an anonymous homily to the ne'er-do-well son of her literary friend, M. de Boismorel, urging him to mend his ways. This lifelong practice in the art of persuasive penmanship may explain partly how she found the concentration and detachment to write her memoirs in a noisome prison and under the shadow of death.

There had been no reason to expect, when at the age of twenty-five she married M. Roland, that she would become involved in national politics. Her husband was then engaged in local government business in Lyons, mainly concerning the control of commerce, and in assisting with the compilation of an encyclopedia. Their first contact with political leaders arose out of M. Roland's literary and business correspondence. They met Brissot in this way and, through him, other revolutionary and 'patriotic' deputies to the Estates-General. The Revolution stirred them, as it stirred the rest of their class, into excitable activity and frenetic philosophical speculation. Coming to Paris (on municipal business for the city of Lyons) they established regular contact with the Jacobin, Girondin and other 'left-wing' leaders and Mme Roland began to operate a political salon. But there was still no expectation that they themselves would have an important political role to play. Monsieur Roland had no political experience and no political backing.

Those of us who have forgotten what we learnt at school about the French Revolution may care to be reminded very briefly how matters stood in France at this point. The Revolution may be said to have started in 1788, when Louis XVI was forced, by near bankruptcy and widespread popular discontent, to summon the Estates-General. This ancient institution, based on separate representation of the three 'estates' – nobility, clergy and the 'Third Estate' – had not been called together since 1614. It gathered at Versailles, with great ceremony and in the King's presence, on 5 May 1789. The first overt act of defiance against the established order was the decision of the Third Estate to call itself a National Assembly and to declare (in the 'oath of the tennis court') that it would not disperse until a satisfactory new Constitution had been adopted. Two months of increasing hunger, discontent and disorder culminated in the storming of the Bastille on 14 July. For nearly two years after that (one is apt to forget) Louis XVI remained on the throne, not as King of France but as 'King of the French'. He was not comfortable. He had been forced to move his family and his court from Versailles to the bleak Tuileries palace in Paris, where he was more accessible to pressure from the Assembly and from the mob, and he was obliged relentlessly to sanction decrees which went against his conscience – nationalisation of Church property, suppression of the religious orders, abolition of hereditary titles, etc. Food shortages and financial collapse made France – and especially Paris – almost ungovernable. After eighteen months of it the King, in a despairing gesture, tried to flee the country. He was caught at Varennes, brought back to Paris and suspended from his functions. Three months later he accepted a new Constitution. He was virtually a prisoner, but he was still King. He appointed his own ministers and presided in person over his Council. He was still able to veto decrees of the legislature and did so in several important cases.

The surprising self-confidence and obstinacy displayed by the Court during these months may be explained by the hope they undoubtedly cherished of armed intervention on behalf of the King from outside France. The Assembly certainly had no confidence in the King's loyalty to the new Constitution and suspected (rightly) that he was intriguing with his father-in-law, the Emperor of Austria, for help to restore his full powers. Thus there was continuous conflict between the Assembly and the Court.

Such, very briefly, was the situation at the beginning of 1792, when the Rolands were beginning to be actively engaged with their 'patriot' political friends. In March the King was obliged, under pressure from the Assembly, to dismiss his Chief Minister, Narbonne, and to appoint a new Council of more popular tendency. The man whom he charged to form a government was General Dumouriez, who was believed to be a 'patriot' (though Mme Roland claims that she thought him a twister the first time she saw him) but who had secretly offered his services to the Court and was eventually to defect to the Austrians. Hoping to divide the opposition of the left in the Assembly, Dumouriez invited the Girondins to nominate two ministers. The leaders of the party, among them Brissot, Condorcet and Vergniaud etc., were debarred by an Assembly resolution from accepting ministerial office themselves, so they nominated two men who were practically unknown to the public, Clavière and Roland. Roland thus found himself, quite unexpectedly it seems, appointed Minister of the Interior. A month or so later, through Mme Roland's influence, a third 'patriot', General Servan, was appointed Minister for War.

Madame Roland was now at the centre of political events. She and her husband had been living in Paris for over a year, in an apartment well situated for receiving political friends, and she was acquainted with all the leading activists of the left. Now that her husband was a minister her scope for political activity was very greatly extended. She made the fullest use of the opportunity, and although she says that she never interfered in any of the administrative affairs of her husband's ministry she clearly dominated him. Danton made a sneering reference to the fact in a speech to the Convention. She brought to bear on the affairs of the government an idealistic, romantic, semi-religious enthusiasm derived from the teachings of Rousseau and the Enlightenment. The Revolution was, to her, a purification of the soul of France which, however, should have remained under the inspired leadership of the 'patriots' who had promoted it. She watched it get out of control with the bitter chagrin of the idealist who finds that Man is more vicious than he or she supposed.

Roland's first experience of office lasted only three months. The Girondin ministers had taken a great risk in joining a Cabinet over which they had no effective control. As Dumouriez had predicted, it separated them from many of their fellow 'patriots'. Robespierre and his friends attacked them as collaborators with the Court and they were unable to induce the King to approve measures which they thought necessary for the survival of the Revolution. Eventually they rebelled, and Roland took the initiative in sending the King his famous challenge of 10 June, which had been entirely drafted by Mme Roland. The King at once dismissed the three ministers, who became national heroes, symbols of revolutionary and patriotic resistance to the Court. Madame Roland wrote: 'I had not been proud of his entry into the ministry, but I was proud of his departure.'

They left their sumptuous quarters in the ministry and returned to their private apartment. Roland would have liked to go back to the country at this stage, but his wife had other ideas. She was sure that the pressures in the Assembly would bring her Girondin friends back into office, as indeed they did. On 10 August a new 'Provisional Executive Council' was set up and Roland went back to his ministry. But he no longer had effective authority. Danton, whom Mme Roland could not stand, was now in the ascendant. Worse than that, a new power-centre had emerged: the insurrectionary Commune of Paris, which eventually overawed and destroyed the Assembly itself. The stage was set for the Terror.

Roland was in office this time for about five months. His wife does not tell us very much about this period, except to insist that he was consistently honourable and patriotic. Dramatic and terrible events took place while he was an important member of the government, including the trial and execution of the King, military aggression against Belgium and appalling massacres in the Paris prisons. It is hard to assess Roland's personal responsibility for any of this, for his power was ebbing. He was increasingly overshadowed in the Council by the personality of Danton. The Girondins were advocates of war with the Empire and with Prussia and Mme Roland was one of the most belligerent of their spokesmen. Christopher Hibbert, whose *The French Revolution* (Penguin, 1982) is the best possible background and key to the political content of these memoirs, quotes her as saying 'Peace will set us back.... We can be regenerated through blood alone' – a sentiment which accords ill with her later professions of horror at the shedding of blood. Meanwhile on the home front her influence was behind the unwisely aggressive attitude of the Girondins towards the other deputies of the 'left'. Roland, who believed in economic liberalism and was opposed to taxes and controls, took measures to meet the rising cost of living which were violently unpopular with the public and eagerly exploited by his enemies. Another grievance against him was that he had established a form of propaganda service throughout the provinces of France, the famous *Bureau de l'Esprit public*, in which Mme Roland was probably the leading spirit. In November he made a grave error in opening an iron cabinet of State papers seized from one of the royal palaces without informing the Assembly in advance; he was accused of wanting to destroy compromising documents. By the beginning of 1793 the Rolands had become the favourite target of the revolutionary extremists, the *sans-culottes* as they were called. Their friends in the Assembly, themselves under great pressure over the trial of the King (in which they had voted against the death penalty), were not courageous enough to support them. On the day after the King's execution on 21 January 1793, Roland's isolation and impotence were shown by a vote in the Assembly abolishing the financial provision for his *Bureau de l'Esprit public*. He resigned the next day. But resignation did not save him. His enemies were after him and they were after his wife. The Revolution swept on, killing Mme Roland, her husband, her lover and almost all her friends.

The material in the present volume is translated from the *Mémoires de Madame Roland*, edited by Paul de Roux and published in a new edition by Mercure de France in 1986. This brought together all that survives of what Mme Roland wrote during her incarceration in the Abbaye and Sainte-Pélagie prisons between 1 June 1793 and her execution on 8 November of the same year.

The original text had been written in rough notebooks and smuggled out from time to time by her friends, probably with the connivance of sympathetic officers in the prisons. The collection has no particular shape or structure and was of course never seen as a whole by Mme Roland. There is a great deal of repetition, mainly due to the fact that at one stage, having been told that her notebooks had been thrown on the fire, she rewrote a large part of them. It later transpired that some of the originals had been saved.

After her death her friend, 'the estimable Bosc',[2] collected all the surviving manuscripts (many of which he himself had hidden during the Terror) and published them in the spring of 1795 under the titie *Appel à l'impartiale postérité*. (The original manuscript of 'seven hundred small-sized sheets of greyish paper, compactly filled with Mme Roland's neat and firm handwriting' is now in the

[2] Louis-Augustin-Guillaume Bosc (1759–1828): a friend of the Rolands since 1780; they obtained for him the position of Administrator of Posts in 1792. It is believed to have been Bosc who helped Roland to escape from Paris; certainly he hid Roland for several weeks in a cottage in the forest of Montmorency.

Bibliothèque Nationale.) But Bosc took great liberties with the text. He arranged the material 'so as to give the illusion of a balanced and reasonably well-constructed work. He also made important cuts. All the expressions of her love for Buzot, all scenes he considered too daring (and notably the whole story of her attempted seduction as a child) and all disobliging references to people still alive were removed. The style, too, was corrected, often clumsily.' (From Paul de Roux's Introduction to the 1986 edition.) It was over a hundred years before an integral, unbowdlerised version was made available to the French reader.

Although Mme Roland herself has long been well known in the English-speaking world – and especially in the United States – as a romantic heroine and victim of the French Revolution, there seems never to have been a complete translation of her memoirs into English. An extract from Bosc's original edition was published in London as a political broadsheet in 1795, and over a hundred years later, in 1901, Grant Richards published a translation of the more personal Private Memoirs, still in a heavily bowdlerised form. There is a lacuna here which it seems appropriate to fill during this bicentenary year of the French Revolution. In *Romantic Affinities* (The Bodley Head, 1988) Rupert Christiansen described the memoirs as 'perhaps the prose masterwork of the first revolutionary years' and said it was 'scandalous that at the time of writing, it is unavailable in a modern English translation'. This edition is partly an answer to that challenge.

It would have been superfluous to reproduce all the material in the 1986 collection. Apart from the numerous repetitions, there would be a plethora of names and descriptions of French revolutionary politicians of whom the English-speaking reader has never heard, and an overdose, especially in the first part, of declamatory protest and ephemeral denunciation. A selection has therefore been made which reduces the whole by about a quarter while still leaving all the essential features and providing, it is hoped, a convenient and readable version.

Since this selection is designed for the general reader, no attempt has been made to reproduce the extensive and learned notes and index of Paul de Roux's edition. I have given short biographical notes on most of the characters mentioned, but only for the purpose of clarifying the story and helping the English-speaking reader to enjoy it; I have assumed that historians and students who want more detail will go to the original. With the same purpose I have divided the text into chapters, giving them chapter headings and in some cases introductory notes.

There is a certain logic in the memoirs as a whole, despite their disorderly arrangement, if one looks at them from the point of view of how they were written in those five months of imprisonment. When first arrested Mme Roland was still 'fighting mad'. Her husband and the man she loved had only just been forced to flee from Paris; many of her Girondin friends were still attending sessions of the Convention, though increasingly terrorised by thugs from the Paris Commune, and there was still the possibility that moderate forces from the rest of France might be brought to bear to curb the excesses of the capital. For the first few days or weeks of imprisonment she still thought it worthwhile to address protests to the Convention and write furious letters to the press. Day by day we see these hopes fade. Everything fails. The horrors increase but Mme Roland's character does not allow her to despair. She turns to describing her own past as a relief from what she can now see as her certain doom. The Private Memoirs are the product of a more relaxed, fatalistic pen than the earlier accounts of political struggle and arrest. They have always been highly regarded in France and outside as a unique description of bourgeois life under the *ancien régime*, but they derive a special flavour from their juxtaposition with the last political and personal agonies of their author.

E.S.

BIOGRAPHICAL NOTES

BRISSOT

Jacques-Pierre Brissot (1754–93): born in Chartres. Noted journalist and political writer, praised by Voltaire. After attempting to set up a newspaper in London he had been sent to the Bastille by Louis XVI on charges of sedition. When it was captured in 1789 he was presented with the keys. One of the most influential of the Girondin deputies in the Legislative Assembly and the Convention. Arrested with the other Girondins and guillotined on 31 October 1793.

BUZOT

François Buzot (1760–94): a lawyer, born in Évreux. Married his cousin, who was 'plain and somewhat deformed', in 1784. Deputy to the Estates-General and to the National Assembly where he sat on the extreme left. A frequent attender of Mme Roland's salon in 1791, when she considered him, with Pétion and Robespierre, to be one of the few 'resolute' Jacobins. He withdrew to Évreux as President of the Criminal Court there during the period of the Legislative Assembly, but returned to Paris in September 1792 as a deputy to the Convention. At this point his friendship with Mme Roland turned rapidly into mutual infatuation. She told her husband of her *passion amoureuse* some time before his resignation on 22 January 1793. Buzot escaped from Paris at the time of the arrest of the Girondins but killed himself in June 1794 to avoid arrest.

CHAMPAGNEUX

Luc-Antoine de Champagneux (1744–1807): a lawyer from Lyons, where he met the Rolands in 1785; founded the *Courrier de Lyon* in 1789 to support the ideas of the Revolution; was appointed by Roland to a post in the Ministry of the Interior, 1792; remained there under Garat but was denounced on 2 April 1793 and imprisoned in La Force until August 1794. Two years later his son married the Rolands' daughter, Eudora.

CLAVIÈRE

Étienne Clavière (1735–93): a Genevan who had taken refuge in France in 1782. Appointed 'Minister of Public Contributions' in March 1792 and dismissed the following June with Roland and Servan. Reinstated on 10 August. Imprisoned in June 1793 in the Conciergerie, where he committed suicide.

CONDORCET

Antoine-Nicolas Caritat, marquis de Condorcet (1743–94): philosopher, mathematician, member of the Académie française. Elected to the Convention and joined the Girondins. On their fall he escaped from Paris and wrote his most famous work on the *Progrès de l'esprit humain*. In 1794 he was arrested and took poison to escape the guillotine.

DANTON

Georges Jacques Danton (1759–94): born of well-to-do parents. He practised as an advocate in Paris until the outbreak of the Revolution. Founded and presided over the Cordeliers Club which attracted the more extreme revolutionaries. In August 1792 he was made Minister of Justice at the moment when Roland became Minister of the Interior for the second time. His personality was dominating and his eloquence effective. Madame Roland had a particular dislike of him. He sought to justify the September massacres though he probably took no part in them himself. He is famous for the words 'We must dare, and dare and forever dare' in urging resistance to the Prussians. He voted for the death of the King and was one of the original members of the Committee of Public Safety. He led the deputies of the 'Mountain' (see p. 57) in the Convention and was responsible for the overthrow of the Girondins. He then fell victim to the intrigues of Robespierre, was condemned by the revolutionary tribunal which he had himself set up the previous year, and executed on 5 April 1794 with fourteen others.

DUMOURIEZ

General Charles-François Dumouriez (1739–1823): invited by the King to form a government in March 1792. Resigned after the King's dismissal of Roland and the other two 'patriot' ministers and rejoined the army. After victories at Valmy and Jemappes he suffered reverses and entered into negotiations with the Austrians with a view to restoring the monarchy under Louis XVII. When the Convention sent envoys to dismiss him he handed them over to the Austrians. Having failed to persuade his army to march on Paris he defected to the Austrians.

MARAT

Jean-Paul Marat (1743–93): physician, specialist in eye diseases. Author of *Philosophical Essay on Man* (1773) and *The Chains of Slavery* (1774). An MD of St Andrews University, 1775. In 1789 he abandoned his scientific career for politics. Arrested in that year, he spent three months in prison and then fled to London. Back in Paris in 1790 he went into hiding in dank cellars where he contracted a painful skin disease from which he could obtain relief only by lying in warm water. Took a leading part in the struggle between the Jacobins and the Girondins. After being tried and acquitted by a Girondin government he became the idol of the Paris mob. Was implacable in demanding the King's death. Assassinated while sitting in the bath working on his journal by Charlotte Corday, an enthusiastic Girondin who believed herself to be ridding France of a bloodthirsty monster. The painter David made a famous picture of his death.

MIRABEAU

Honoré Gabriel Riqueti, comte de Mirabeau (1749–91): one of the most powerful personalities of the French Revolution. After a wild and stormy youth, which included three years in prison at Vincennes where he wrote his famous *Lettres de Cachet* attacking prison abuses, he became a deputy for the Third Estate in the Estates-General and was soon one of its dominant figures, foremost in urging defiance of the King. He was widely distrusted and disliked but at the same time had strong popular support. Despite his wild character his political views were pragmatic and he deprecated extreme measures on either side. He hoped to remodel the monarchy somewhat on British lines. It has been suggested that, had he lived longer and had the Court followed his advice, the Terror might have been averted. Madame Roland admired him and regretted his death.

NECKER

Jacques Necker (1732–1804): Swiss financier and banker who came to Paris in his youth and made a fortune. He wrote extensively about the financial problems of France under the monarchy and was appointed Director-General of Finances by Louis XVI (for the second time) in August 1788 when he attempted to cut down the royal expenditure and to reform the chaotic tax system of the country. Louis XVI dismissed him in July 1789 but was compelled to recall him by the National Assembly after the fall of the Bastille. But the problems were beyond him; his advice was not taken and in 1790 he resigned, spending his remaining days in Switzerland writing political tracts. His daughter was the celebrated Mme de Staël.

ORLÉANS

Louis-Philippe, duc d'Orléans (1747–93): born at St-Cloud. Known principally for his support of the popular cause during the Revolution, when he took the name of Philippe Égalité and voted for the death of the King. Despite his populist appeal he was guillotined and many of his followers massacred during the Terror.

ROBESPIERRE

Maximilien François Marie Isidore de Robespierre (1758–94): born in Arras and brought up there by the Bishop. Deputy for the Third Estate in the Estates-General, he soon acquired a dominant position in the Jacobin party. Attached himself first to Mirabeau and on the latter's death to the Marat/Danton group until he was strong enough to destroy them. His disinterest in personal gain earned him from Carlyle the title of 'the sea-green incorruptible'. Helped to create the revolutionary tribunal and after the execution of the King became a member and virtual dictator of the Committee of Public Safety. Largely responsible for the Reign of Terror. Faced with a plot for his own destruction he lost his nerve and absented himself from a crucial meeting of the Convention on 27 September 1794 at which he was openly accused of despotism. Arrested and guillotined the following day.

SERVAN

General Joseph Servan de Gerbey (1741–1808): Minister for War, 1792. Dismissed, with Roland and Clavière, on 13 June and returned to office with them on 10 August. Resigned on grounds of health in October 1792 and was imprisoned for a while in the Abbaye. Survived the Terror.

SILLERY

Brulart de Genlis, comte de Sillery (1737–93): member of the Constituent Assembly and later of the Convention. Accused at the same time as Philippe Égalité and condemned and executed with the Girondins. His wife, better known as Mme de Genlis (1746–1830), had been governess to the children of Philippe Égalité.

— I —
Historical Notes
and
Portraits

1

ARREST

•❦•

Madame Roland was taken to the Abbaye prison on 1 June 1793. As soon as she was settled in she began writing down her thoughts and recollections. Although it was over four months since her husband had resigned from the ministry they had not been able to detach themselves from public life. They, or at any rate she, had continued to be active among the Girondin deputies and had shared in the steady erosion of that party's ascendancy in the Convention. Their own unpopularity had been kept alive by continuous attacks from their former colleagues and rivals, notably Danton, Robespierre and Marat. This partly explains, no doubt, the defensive and self-justifying element in much of what Mme Roland wrote in prison. In the first chapters she is still defiant and unbowed.

Roland himself put a less bold face on misfortune than his wife. His obsession, after his resignation, was to obtain parliamentary approval of his official accounts, so that he might retire to the country. When the crisis came, he escaped from Paris; she disdained to do so.

THE ABBAYE PRISON
JUNE 1793

On the throne today; tomorrow in irons.

THAT IS THE COMMON LOT OF THE VIRTUOUS in time of revolution. When the people first rise up against oppression, wise men who have shown them the way and helped them to recover their rights come to power. But they do not stay there long. More ambitious characters soon emerge, flatter and delude the people and turn them against their true defenders. That is what has happened here, particularly since 10 August. One day, perhaps, when I am feeling more detached I shall take up the story again and describe these events in greater detail. My only purpose now is to set down on paper the circumstances of my arrest – a suitable pastime I think for a solitary person like myself, describing her own experience and expressing her own feelings.

Roland's resignation had not appeased his enemies. He had always meant to weather the storm and face the dangers, but the state of the Council, its inherent and increasing feebleness, particularly marked towards the middle of January, gave him no chance. He quit the ministry because he was not prepared to share the blame for crimes and follies which he could not prevent. He had not even been able to get his views and arguments recorded in the minutes of the meetings when they ran counter to the decisions of the majority.

For this reason, and dating from the day of that pitiful resolution concerning the article 'l'Ami des Lois' which he refused to sign because its second part was, to put it mildly, ridiculous, he never again signed any Council record. That was on 15 January. The Convention was no better; his very name had become a subject of controversy and of derision, and could not be mentioned without uproar. If a member tried to reply to the odious charges made against the minister he was accused of being factious and was shouted down. Pache[1] at the War Ministry was committing error after error through weakness and devotion to the Jacobins, and allowing his agents every sort of licence, but the Convention could not sack Pache because as soon as a voice was raised against him the opposition started baying against Roland. Even if he had prolonged his brave struggle in the ministry, Roland could not have checked the errors of the Council and would only have added to the causes of disorder in the Convention. He therefore handed in his resignation. The saner elements in the legislative body, though entirely convinced of his virtues and talents, did not dare to express an opinion. This weakness was fatal. The Convention needed a just and firm man at the Ministry of the Interior; it was the best support they had and it was inevitable that, once they lost it, they should fall into the hands of extremists. The stage was set for the emergence of the Paris Commune as a rival authority to the national House of Representatives.

Roland had held in check the upstart Commune; he had imposed harmonious and regular discipline on all the elements of his administration; he had seen to the provision of supplies, restored peace in the departments and breathed a sense of order into the public service by means of a fair and energetic administration and

---

[1] Jean-Nicolas Pache (1746–1823): Minister of War, Oct. 1792–Feb. 1793, and Mayor of Paris, Feb. 1793–May 1794.

an enlightened system of communications. They should have supported Roland; but their impotence, which he understood only too well, made this impossible and he had no option but to resign.

He was replaced by the timid Garat,[2] a charming man to meet at a party and a moderately talented writer but a hopeless administrator. Garat's appointment to the Ministry of Justice had already shown what a shortage there was of capable men and how difficult it was for people in responsible positions like Roland to find effective collaborators. Garat should never have set his sights beyond the Ministry of Justice. His poor health and natural dislike of hard work were not too noticeable in that low-key department, but when he moved to the Ministry of the Interior his weaknesses were all too apparent. He had none of the necessary political experience and no knowledge whatever of commerce or of the arts or of the thousand administrative problems involved in this post. Yet here he was, with his ignorance and his idleness, replacing the most active and experienced man in the Republic. It was not long before the machine began to break down. The departments became discontented, food shortages recurred, civil war broke out in the Vendée, the municipal authorities in Paris began to encroach on the administration. Very soon the Jacobins took over the reins of power and the puppet Pache, removed from the War Ministry which he had reduced to disorder, was shunted by the cabal into the Town Hall, where they needed a compliant figurehead. In the Council he was replaced by the fool Bouchotte who was just as submissive but more stupid than he.

Roland had struck a judicious blow against his adversaries by publishing, on his retirement, more detailed accounts of his tenure of office than any minister before him had ever produced. He tried to have these examined and approved by a resolution of the Convention; but this would have meant their recognising the falsity of the accusations levelled against him, the infamy of his detractors and the feebleness of the Convention itself in not daring to defend him. They preferred to continue abusing him without bringing anything to the proof, hoping to rid themselves of an inconvenient witness to the many horrors they were committing. He demanded officially and in public that his report should be examined, and he

---

[2] Dominique-Joseph Garat (1749–1833): Minister of Justice from Oct. 1792 to March 1793; briefly Minister of the Interior after Roland's resignation; later held office under the Empire.

[29]

wrote to the Convention seven times in four months to this end. It was no use. The Jacobins and their supporters continued to scream that he was a traitor. Marat told his followers that for the tranquillity of the Republic it was necessary that Roland's head should fall. A series of conspiracies, failed and renewed, aborted but never abandoned, led ultimately to the insurrection of 31 May in which the good people of Paris, though of course having no wish to massacre anyone, nevertheless did exactly what they were told by their leaders, by the insolent Commune and by the revolutionary committee of crazy Jacobin fanatics and traitors.

Roland had written for the eighth time to the Convention, but it still ignored him. I was in the process of obtaining permits from the municipality to go to the country with my daughter. My domestic affairs, my health and many other good reasons urged me to do this, including the consideration that in the last resort it would be much easier for Roland to avoid pursuit by his enemies if he were alone and not encumbered by his family. It was obviously sensible to reduce the number of ways in which they could get at him.[3]

My permits had been held up in the local section through the intrigues of Marat's fanatical followers, to whom I was suspect. They had just been delivered to me when I was struck down with an attack of nervous colic, with convulsions, the only form of indisposition to which I am subject and which results from the distemper of a lively personality dominating a strong physique. I was obliged to stay in bed for six days. On the Friday[4] I got ready to go out and call at the municipality, but the sound of the alarm gun warned me that the moment was not favourable. It had been obvious for some time that a crisis must come. The ascendancy of the Jacobins certainly did not promise well for true lovers of liberty, but vigorous characters like mine hate uncertainty more than anything else. The degradation of the Convention, its daily acts of cowardice and impotence upset me so much that I found the

---

[3] In a footnote Mme Roland wrote:'This was not my main reason; for though deeply upset by the course of events I had no fear for myself. I was innocent and I was courageous. Injustice could not make me flinch; indeed I took some pleasure in defying the challenge of danger. But I had another reason for leaving Paris which I will perhaps explain one day and which is entirely personal.' She wanted to get away from Buzot and recover from her infatuation.

[4] 31 May 1793, the day on which the first of the two insurrections broke out which led to the proscription of the Girondin deputies.

recent excesses almost preferable; they might at least wake up the departments and force them to take a stand. The alarm gun and the agitations of the day exercised a certain fascination over me, as always happens when I find myself at the centre of great events. I was not particularly disturbed. Two or three people came round to support us and one of them urged Roland to show himself in his section, where he was well liked and where sensible arrangements could be made for his safety. But it was agreed that he should not sleep at home the following night. Apart from this, everyone spoke of the good intentions of the citizens; they had drawn themselves up under arms, it was said, in order to oppose any act of violence. Nobody mentioned that they would simply stand by and let preparations be made for violence on an unprecedented scale.

My blood boils when I hear the Parisians praised for not wanting another 2 September massacre. Good God! Nobody needs you, citizens of Paris, for another massacre. All you have to do is to sit tight, as you did last time. Your help was necessary for collecting the victims and you lent yourselves complacently to their arrest. You were required to give an air of legitimacy to the action of the tribunes who rule you and you approved their crimes. You obeyed their orders and you have sworn fealty to the monstrous authorities they have now set up. You surround the legislative body with your bayonets and force it to vote decrees dictated to it by them. Do not come now boasting that you defend the Convention; you are the ones who bind the Convention in chains, standing by like cowards as its most virtuous and talented members are led to execution. France will hold you accountable for all these crimes. You serve our enemies; you are preparing the disintegration of France! Do you think that proud Marseilles and wise Gironde will forgive the affronts committed against their representatives? Do you think they will ever again co-operate with your criminal city? You, citizens of Paris, are the destroyers of your city; when you find yourselves standing in its ruins you will regret your cowardice.

It was half past five in the evening when six armed men presented themselves at my house. One of them read out to Roland an order of the revolutionary committee by virtue of which they had come to place him under arrest. 'I know of no law', said Roland, 'setting up the authority to which you refer and I shall not comply with orders emanating from that body. If you employ force, I can only offer you the resistance of a man of my age, but I shall protest against it to the last.' 'I have no orders to employ force,' said the man, 'and I shall report your reply to the Council of the Commune. I leave my colleagues here.'

I saw at once that we must denounce this occurrence to the Convention with as much publicity as possible, in order to prevent Roland's arrest or to have him promptly released if it should take place. In a very few minutes I had explained my idea to my husband, written a letter to the President of the Convention and set off. My servant was absent; I left a friend of ours who happened to be in the house with Roland and stepped alone into a hackney coach which I ordered to drive as fast as possible to the Carrousel. The courtyard of the Tuileries was full of armed men and I flew like a bird across the space between them. I was in my morning gown but I had picked up a black shawl and was veiled. When I came to the doors of the first rooms I found they were all shut and that there were guards preventing anyone from entering. They sent me from door to door. I tried to insist, but it was no use. Then I thought of using the sort of language that some follower of Robespierre might use. 'Come now, citizens,' I said. 'Today is a day of destiny for our country! We are surrounded on all sides by traitors! I have important papers here which I must pass on to the President! Fetch me an usher to whom I may entrust them.' The door opened and I found myself in the hall of petitioners. I demanded an usher. 'Wait until one of them comes out,' replied the guards on the inside. A quarter of an hour elapsed. Then I spotted M. Rôze, the man who had brought me the decree of the Convention summoning me to the bar at the time of Viard's ridiculous denunciation – which I had so successfully thrown off.[5] I now asked permission to appear again, explaining the danger in which Roland stood and the threat to the public interest. But, alas, conditions were now very different. Then, I had been an invited guest; now I was a petitioner, much less likely to be heard. Rôze understood the situation and my impatience. He took charge of my letter and went to present it to the Bureau of the Convention and urge that it be read. An hour went by. I strode up and down, gazing into the Chamber every time the door opened, but it was always closed again at once by the guard. From time to time I heard a fearful uproar. Finally, Rôze

---

[5] An adventurer called Viard had accused Mme Roland of corresponding with French refugees in England. He was summoned to the bar of the Convention, where she successfully confronted him (7 Dec. 1792).

reappeared. 'There is nothing to be done at present,' he said, 'the Assembly is in indescribable tumult. The petitioners now at the bar are calling for the arrest of the Twenty-Two.[6] I have just helped Rabaut to get out of the Chamber unseen; they refused to let him present the report of the Commission of Twelve; he has been threatened, several others have escaped and nobody knows what is coming next.' 'Who's in the chair now?' 'Hérault-Séchelles.'[7] 'Ah, then my letter will not be read. Find me a member to whom I can talk.' 'Who?' 'Alas! I know so few of them and those whom I respect are all proscribed. Find Vergniaud[8] for me.' Rôze went to look for Vergniaud and warn him. After a very long time he appeared. We talked for five minutes. He went back to the Bureau, returned again and said: 'In the present state of the Assembly I can give you little hope. If you are admitted to the bar you may, as a woman, receive a little more respect, but the Convention is no longer capable of doing any good.' 'It is perfectly capable,' I cried. 'The majority of the people in Paris are simply asking to be told what to do. If I am admitted I shall have the courage to say things which you cannot safely say. I am afraid of nothing. Even if I cannot save Roland I shall proclaim truths which the Republic ought to hear. Warn your colleagues! A courageous outbust from me may have a profound effect; at least it will set an example.' I was in the state of mind that makes one eloquent. Boiling with indignation, void of all fear, passionate for my country whose ruin I could see before my eyes, conscious that all I loved in the world stood in mortal peril, I felt myself to be at the height of my powers and in a unique situation. Deep emotion, an eloquent tongue, a noble pride, a great cause to defend and the occasion right: this seemed my moment. 'But', said Vergniaud, 'your letter cannot in any case be read for an hour and a half. They are about to discuss a draft bill in six parts and the petitioners are already at the bar.' I was mad with frustration. 'I shall go home', I said, 'to see what has happened there, and come straight back. Warn our friends.' 'Most of them are not here', he said. 'They are brave enough when they do come

---

[6] Twenty-two Girondin deputies against whom a petition had been presented on 15 April by thirty-five Parisian sections.

[7] Marie-Jean Hérault de Séchelles (1759–94): Deputy to the Legislative Assembly and the Convention. Guillotined with Danton in April 1794.

[8] Pierre-Victurnien Vergniaud (1753–93): Deputy for the Gironde in the Legislative Assembly and the Convention. One of the best speakers of the Girondin party. Guillotined on 31 October 1793.

but they have no endurance.' This is unfortunately too true.

I left Vergniaud and rushed off to see Louvet.[9] Not finding him at home, I wrote a note to tell him what had occurred and what I feared and leapt into another coach, ordering it to take me home. The wretched horses were much too slow for me. Soon we ran into regiments of armed men barring our way. I threw myself out of the cab, paid the driver, burst through the ranks and fled. This was near the Louvre. I ran to my house in the rue de la Harpe, near St-Côme. The porter whispered to me that Roland had gone up to the landlord's apartment at the back of the courtyard. I went up there. I was quite out of breath and sweating. They brought me a glass of wine and told me that the bearer of the arrest warrant had come back without having been able to make himself heard at the Commune; that Roland had continued to protest and that the man had asked for the protest in writing and had withdrawn with his followers. After that, Roland had passed through the landlord's apartment and gone out by the back of the house. I went out the same way to find him and to tell him what I had attempted and what I meant to do next. I went to one house, but he was not there and then to another where I found him. From the emptiness of the streets, and the lamps being lit, I assumed that the hour was late but I got ready nonetheless to return to the Convention. I would of course have said nothing about Roland's flight and would have spoken exactly as I had planned before. I was about to leave on foot, not conscious that it was after ten o'clock or that I was out that day for the first time after an illness which required rest and baths. They fetched me a cab. Approaching the Carrousel I saw that there were no armed men there any more. Two cannon and a few men stood before the entrance of the Palais National. I went forward; the Convention had risen.

Imagine this! A day of insurrection, when the sound of the tocsin had scarcely ceased to rend the air, when two hours previously 40,000 armed men had surrounded the Convention and petitioners were threatening members at the bar of the house. Why was the Convention not in permanent session? Had it then been entirely subjugated and agreed to do all that it was told? Was the revolutionary power now so mighty that the Convention dare not oppose it? 'Citizens,' I said to a bunch of *sans-culottes* standing

[9] Jean-Baptiste Louvet (1760–97): Deputy from the Loiret; author of *Amours du chevalier de Faublas*. He lived in the rue St-Honoré.

around a cannon, 'did everything pass off well?' 'Marvellous well,' they replied. 'They were all embracing one another and singing "La Marseillaise", over there under the tree of liberty.' 'Then were the men of the right reconciled?' I asked. 'Faith, they had no choice, they had to see reason', they retorted. 'And the Commission of Twelve?'[10] 'Kicked into the ditch'. 'And the Twenty-Two?' 'The municipality is to arrest them.' 'But has it the power to do that?' 'Of course, isn't it sovereign? Just as well too, so it can sort out the f... traitors and defend the Republic.' 'But what about the departments, will they be content to see their representatives treated so?' 'What do you mean? Paris does nothing without the consent of the departments; they said so in the Convention.' 'But to know the departments' opinion there should have been primary assemblies.' 'What about the tenth of August? Didn't the departments approve what Paris did then? They'll do the same again, you see! Paris is their salvation.' 'Their ruin, more like,' I said.

Having fired this parting shot at an old *sans-culotte*, no doubt well paid for indoctrinating dupes, I crossed the courtyard and found my cab. A charming little dog rubbed up against my leg. 'Is the poor creature yours?' asked my coachman, with a gentle tone rare in his sort, which struck me particularly. 'No, I don't know him,' I replied gravely as if we were speaking of a person. I was already thinking of other things. 'Please put me down at the colonnades of the Louvre,' I said. I wanted to consult a friend about the best way of getting Roland out of Paris. We had not gone twenty paces when the cab stopped. 'What is it?' I asked. 'He's escaped, stupid animal,' said the driver. 'I wanted him for my little boy to play with. Here, come here, little one,' he called. I remember that dog very well; it was comforting to have a friendly man, a father and a good fellow, as my driver at that hour. 'If you can catch him', I shouted, 'you can put him in the cab and I will hold him for you.' The man was delighted. He caught the dog, opened the door and put it in with me. The poor beast seemed to feel that he had found a refuge; I was much licked and fawned upon. I remembered that story by the poet Sa'di about the old man, tired of people and disgusted by their passions, who made his home in a forest and found amongst the animals an affection and gratitude for his attentions which he had never had from his fellow men.

---

[10] The Girondin-dominated Commission of Twelve had been set up to investigate the behaviour of the Commune and the troublesome sections.

P. had just gone to bed.[11] He got up and I outlined my plans to him. We agreed that he would come to my house the next day after seven o'clock and that I would show him where he could find Roland. I got back into my cab. It was stopped by the sentinel at the checkpoint of the Samaritaine. 'Don't worry,' said my driver very quietly, turning on his seat, 'it's the usual thing at this time of night.' The sergeant came up and opened the door, 'Who's there?' 'A woman.' – 'Where have you come from?' – 'From the Convention.' – 'That's right' muttered the coachman, as if he was afraid they would not believe me. 'Where are you going?' – 'Home.' – 'Have you no baggage?' – 'Nothing, look.' – 'But the session's over.' – 'I know, unfortunately for me; I had a petition to present.' 'But a woman, at this hour? It's impossible. Most imprudent!' 'Perhaps it is unusual; it's certainly not pleasant for me. I had the strongest possible motive.' – 'But, Madame, a woman, all alone!' – 'How alone, Sir? Do you not observe Innocence and Truth, my travelling companions? What more is necessary?' – 'I must accept your explanations.' – 'And you do well to do so, Sir,' I said in a softer tone, 'for they are true.'

The horses were so tired that the coachman had to lead them by the bridle up my street. I arrived, paid the coachman and had climbed eight or ten stairs when a man who had somehow got through the gate without the porter seeing him stepped out behind me. He asked me to conduct him to Roland. 'To his apartment, certainly, if you have anything useful to communicate, but to Roland himself, impossible.' 'I just wanted to say', he whispered, 'that they've decided to arrest him tonight.' 'They will be very clever if they succeed,' I said. 'I am glad to hear it,' he replied, 'I am an honest citizen and a friend.' 'Thank you,' I said, and went on up, not knowing what to think.

Now why, I might be asked, did I go back to my house in these circumstances? It is a reasonable question, for I too had been publicly attacked and there was every possibility of a hostile move against me. To give a true answer I should have to develop fully the state of my feelings at that time and enter into details which I prefer to reserve for another occasion. So I will restrict myself to

---

[11] Pierre Pasquier (1731–1806): painter in enamel, member of the Academy of Painting and Sculpture, friend of Roland who made him a 'Guardian of the Museum'. Denounced for this reason by David as a 'friend of Roland' and imprisoned for some time.

describing the conclusions I reached.

I have a natural dislike of any act which is out of character with the open, proud and courageous conduct of an innocent person. The effort of eluding injustice is to me more burdensome than enduring it. In the last two months of Roland's ministry our friends often pressed us to leave the house and once or twice they persuaded us to sleep away from home. But it was always against my will. Assassination was then the fear, but my feeling was that to violate the private home of a public figure was a very grave step for a criminal to take, and that if there were villains capable of attempting such a crime it might not be altogether a bad thing for the enterprise to succeed; in any case, I thought, the minister ought to stay at his post. Death at his post would cry out for vengeance and provide an object lesson to the Republic; whereas an assassination in the by-ways, though of equal value to the perpetrators, would inspire less horror in the public and give less glory to the victim. I realise that this will sound absurd to anyone who values his life above everything; but in time of revolution anyone who attaches importance to his own life is likely to attach none to virtue, honour or his country. So I refused to leave home in January. Roland's bed stood in my chamber so that we should share the same fate and I had a small pistol under my pillow, not for fear of assassination but to protect my honour if need be.

Once we were out of office the obligation was not the same and I thought it quite right that Roland should avoid the fury of the mob or the grasp of his enemies. As for myself, their interest in harming me could not be so great; to kill me would entail odium which they would not want to incur, while to arrest me would hardly serve their turn and would not be such a great misfortune for me. I reckoned that if they had any sense of shame and wanted to respect the formalities, interrogate me and stage a trial, I would have no difficulty in confounding them; indeed it might give me a chance to enlighten people whose minds had been poisoned against Roland. If, on the other hand, they wanted to renew the massacres of 2 September, then all the honest deputies would be similarly in their power and all would be lost in Paris. In that case, I would rather die than witness the ruin of my country; I should consider it an honour to be counted amongst the heroic victims. It was also possible that having gratified their hatred against me they might become less violent against Roland, who might still render great service in other parts of France if he could be saved from this crisis.

Thus there were but two prospects: either I risked nothing worse than prison, and a trial which I might turn to the advantage of my country and of my husband; or I should perish, but in such extreme circumstances that life would already be hateful to me.

I have a young daughter. She is charming, but nature has made her cold and indolent. I nursed her, I brought her up with all a mother's love and care and set her such examples as, at her age, will not be forgotten. She will be a good wife, with reasonable talents. But her dullness and lack of spirit will never give me the joy for which I had hoped. Her education can be completed without my help; her existence will be a consolation to her father. She will never know my lively affections nor my pains nor my pleasures. And yet, if I was to be born again and allowed to choose my qualities, I would not want to change; I would ask the gods to make me again exactly as they have done.

After Roland's resignation from the ministry I lived so retired from the world that I hardly saw anyone. The owners of one house where I might have hidden were away in the country; in another there was a sick person whose presence made it difficult to admit another guest. The house where Roland was concealed could not have received me without great inconvenience and it would have been too noticeable and therefore impolitic for us to be together. It would also have been painful to me to abandon my faithful servants. So I went back into my apartment, calmed their fears, kissed my little girl and took up my pen to write a letter to my husband, which I had intended should be delivered at dawn.

I had hardly sat down when I heard a knock on the door. It was about midnight. A large deputation from the Commune presented itself and called for Roland. 'He is not at home,' I said. 'Where is he then?' asked someone with the insignia of an officer. 'I do not know whether your instructions authorise you to ask me such questions,' I replied, 'but I do know that I am not obliged to reply. Roland left his house while I was at the Convention. He had no opportunity to inform me of his movements and I have nothing more to say.' The party withdrew in high dudgeon. I saw that they left a sentinel at my door and placed a guard on the house. I assumed that there was nothing for it but to brace myself for the worst. I was dead tired. I had supper served, finished my letter, gave it to my faithful maid and went to bed.

I had been fast asleep for an hour when my servant came into my room to announce that the gentlemen from the section requested me to step into the salon. 'I know what that means,' I said. 'Come along, my girl, let's not keep them waiting.' I jumped out of bed and dressed. My maid came in and was surprised that I had taken the trouble to put on more than a dressing gown. 'One must be decently dressed to go out in the street,' I said. The poor girl stared at me and burst into tears. I walked into the salon. 'We have come, *citoyenne*, to place you under arrest and to seal up your apartment.' 'Where is your authority?' 'Here,' said a man, drawing from his pocket a *mandat* from the revolutionary committee to conduct me to the Abbaye prison. It gave no grounds for the arrest. 'I tell you,' I said, 'as Roland told you before, that I know nothing of this committee, that I do not comply with its orders and that you will not get me out of here except by force.' 'Here's another order,' interjected hastily a little man with a mean face and an insolent voice, and he began to read out a decision of the Council of the Commune ordering the arrest of Roland and his wife, again without any statement of grounds. While he was reading I deliberated whether I should try to resist or not. I could, for example, appeal to the law prohibiting nocturnal arrests. If they cited the law which authorises the municipality to seize suspected persons, I could retort by questioning the legality of the municipality itself; for it had been dissolved and recreated by an arbitrary power. But, but ... this arbitrary power had in a sense been sanctioned by the citizens of Paris. A 'law' was now little more than a word which was being used to deprive people of their most widely recognised rights. Force was now the master and if I compelled them to use it these brutes would stop at nothing. Resistance was useless and could weaken my position. So, 'How do you mean to proceed, gentlemen?' I asked. 'We have summoned the Justice of the Peace of the section and the men you see here are a detachment from his forces.'

The Justice of the Peace then arrived. They went into my drawing room, placing seals everywhere, on the windows, on the linen cupboards. A man wanted to put a seal on the forte piano. When it was pointed out to him that this was a musical instrument he pulled a footrule from his pocket and measured it as if he had some fairly good idea where it might go. I insisted on taking out the contents of my daughter's wardrobe and I made up a small night case for myself. Meanwhile, fifty people, a hundred people, were pouring in and out continuously, filling the two rooms, surrounding everything and providing ample cover for any ill-intentioned person who might wish to remove something – or to plant something. The air was filled with stinking breath; I had to stand by the window of the antechamber in order to breathe. The officer did not dare order the crowd to withdraw; he addressed to them from time to time a little plea to which they paid no attention. I sat down at my desk and wrote a letter to a friend describing my situation and recommending my daughter to his care. As I was sealing the letter, M. Nicaud (the man who had brought the warrant from the Commune) stopped me. 'We must read the letter, Madame, and know the name of the person to whom it is addressed.' 'I agree to read it to you, is that sufficient?' 'You had better say to whom you are writing.' 'I will do nothing of the kind,' I said. 'Considering my present situation and the danger attaching to my name I have no intention of revealing to you those whom I call my friends.' I tore up the letter. As I turned away, they collected the pieces together and put them under seal. I could not help laughing at such stupid officiousness; there was no name and no address.

Finally, at seven o'clock in the morning I left my daughter and my people, having exhorted them to calmness and patience. I felt more honoured by their tears than grieved by my own wrongs. 'You have people there who love you,' said one of the commissioners. 'I have never had any about me who did not,' I replied, and went down the stairs. At the gateway I found two rows of armed men leading all the way from the foot of the staircase to the carriage, which was waiting on the other side of the road, and a crowd of onlookers. I advanced slowly and sedately, watching these cowardly or deluded people. The armed men followed the vehicle in two ranks. A few of the unhappy rabble, attracted by the spectacle, stopped in my path to stare, and one or two women cried 'to the guillotine'. 'Shall we close the carriage windows?' the commissioners obligingly enquired. 'No thank you, gentlemen,' I said. 'Innocence, however sorely oppressed, will never adopt the posture of the guilty. I am not afraid of anyone's looks and ask for no protection.' 'You have more character than many men and you await justice calmly,' they said. 'Justice!' I cried. 'If justice were done I should not be here in your power. But if this iniquitous procedure leads me to the scaffold I shall mount it calmly and firmly, as I now proceed to prison. I weep for my country; I blush for my mistake in thinking that France was ready for liberty, for happiness. But I value life; I have never feared anything but sin, I despise injustice and death.' The poor commissioners understood very little of all this and probably thought it typical aristocratic talk.

Now we arrived at the Abbaye, scene of those bloody events which the Jacobins, for some time now, have been so loudly clamouring to repeat. Five or six camp beds, occupied by as many men, in a dark room, were the first things I saw after passing through the gate. Men stood up in a flurry of agitation. I was made to climb a narrow and filthy staircase, where we found the keeper of the prison in quite a clean little room. He offered me a chair. 'Where is my room?' I asked his wife, a large, plump person. 'I was not expecting you, Madame, and I have nothing prepared. But you may stay here while you wait.' The commissioners went into the next room, obtained the receipt for their warrant and gave some verbal instructions. I learned later that these were very severe and were several times repeated but never written down. The keeper knew his job too well to follow to the letter anything for which he did not have written authority. He is an honest man, active, obliging, doing his duty with as much justice and humanity as possible, 'What would you like for breakfast?' he asked. 'Some milk and water,' I replied. The commissioners now withdrew, observing that if Roland was innocent he should not have run away. This set me off. 'It is incredible to me', I said, 'that anyone should suspect that man, who has done so much for liberty. It is hateful to see a minister slandered and persecuted whose conduct has been so open and his accounts so clear. An Aristides in justice, a Cato in severity, his very virtues have made him enemies. If they turn their boundless animosity against me I shall defy them and gladly sacrifice myself. But Roland must preserve himself for the good of his country; he can still render her great services.' A shamed acknowledgement was all they could manage. They left. I ate my breakfast and was then taken to the room which had been hastily prepared for me. 'You can stay here all day, Madame, and if I cannot find you a room for tonight, as I am very crowded, I will make up a bed for you in the salon.' The keeper's wife who so addressed me then added some kindly words about how sorry she always felt when people of her own sex arrived there. 'For they are not all serene and calm like Madame,' she said. I smiled and thanked her and she locked me in.

2

IN PRISON

The first letter Mme Roland wrote from the Abbaye prison was to her friend, Bosc. 'Here I am, safely housed so long as it shall please God. As always, I shall be on sufficiently good terms with myself not to mind the change too much. ... With warmest greetings in life and death.' Bosc rallied round at once. He entrusted the little Eudora to some old friends, the Creuzé-Latouches, and managed to get Roland out of Paris. On the following night Mme Roland heard the tocsin sound for another insurrection and on 3 June she read in the paper that the Convention, under threat of artillery, had decreed the arrest of about thirty of the leading Girondin deputies, including Buzot. Buzot managed to escape, and about three weeks later she heard that he was in Normandy, trying to raise the departments there against the Convention. She managed to be in touch with him by letter. Roland in the meantime had gone into hiding in Rouen.

So HERE I WAS, IN PRISON. I sat down on the bed to collect my thoughts.

I would not exchange the moments which followed for what others might consider the happiest of my life. I shall never forget them. They have enabled me to appreciate, in a critical situation and confronted by a stormy future, how precious is the power of a clear conscience and true courage. Up to that moment I had been carried along by events in a whirl of emotion and excitement. How sweet now to apply the test of reason to my actions. I recalled the past and calculated the future. And although, listening to my innermost soul, I may have detected some excessive emotionalism, I heard nothing there to make me ashamed, nothing which did not justify my courage or which I did not feel capable of mastering. I committed myself, as it were voluntarily, to my destiny whatever it might be; defied its rigours and settled into that frame of mind in which one concentrates exclusively on the present without a thought for the future.

But this unconcern about my personal position I did not even attempt to extend to the fate of my country or my friends. I waited for the evening paper and listened to the shouting in the street with an impatience I cannot describe. In the meantime I made enquiries about my new way of life and what facilities I should be allowed. Should I be able to write, could I see anyone and what expenditure would be required here? These were my first questions. Lavacquerie (the keeper) told me of the verbal instructions he had been given. He also explained that he had discretion as to carrying out such orders; they could if necessary be regarded as not having been received. I wrote to my maid to come and see me; it was agreed that she should ask for the keeper's wife, without mentioning my name, and that no one else should be told.

It is curious to see how, every now and again, events reward a man for his labours. When Roland first came to the Ministry of the Interior he found that the state of the prisons had been horribly neglected. He looked with pity at those squalid habitations, built originally for criminals but too often occupied by innocent people, and considered that they ought to be kept salubrious and if possible comfortable even for the former. He created a special post for the surveillance of the prisons. The incumbent was expected to visit regularly, to provide the minister with an accurate list of those detained and of the orders under which they were held, to note their grievances and to transmit these promptly. He offered the modest salary of 1,000 écus, which he thought sufficient for a good man who would appreciate the value of having humanitarian duties, and he appointed Grandpré,[1] a man of sensibility, very conscious of suffering, perfectly suited in his feelings and experience for dealing with the unfortunate. Grandpré carried out his duties to perfection; I recall an incident relating to him which deserves to be recorded.

On 1 September of last year he became aware of disturbances threatening the prisons. Early in the morning he visited them all. At the Abbaye, as in others, he found a crowd of people who had just come in, having been arrested during the latest domiciliary raids, and held as I am held today under arbitrary and unmotivated warrants. There was an atmosphere of agitation and fear; orders from the Commune had prohibited all communication with the outside world. Grandpré invited these people to write notes to their friends. He waited for two hours and carried out the letters which he delivered to the section, enabling at least some of them to

---

[1] A friend of Sophie Cannet, appointed by Roland as prison inspector.

be saved in time. For in the meantime the report of a massacre was spreading like the dread murmur that precedes a storm. Grandpré went to the Ministry of the Interior and waited for the rising of the Council which was being held in the office of Roland, its president. Danton came out first; Grandpré approached him, described with some heat the imminent dangers and insisted on the need for a distinction to be made at once between the different types of prisoner. Danton cut him off with an oath, shouting at the top of his voice and with a madman's gesture, 'I don't give a damn for the prisoners. They can go to the devil.' The bystanders (for this took place in the second antechamber) were horrified that a Minister of Justice could express such views. They did not know that, as has subsequently emerged, clandestine meetings were being held in Danton's office where lists of prisoners were produced, orders given to lock up the victims and a number of them set aside for dispatch in a manner which would give the impression of a 'people's verdict'. Roland had already put in a requisition for army reinforcements; he now tried again, and again issued orders to the constituted authorities to prevent excesses. In vain. He was himself the object of an arrest warrant which the conspirators did not dare to carry out. He denounced the crimes of these dreadful days with untiring courage and his letter of 3 September to the Assembly is authentic evidence of that austere probity which so enraged his enemies.

My first visitor at the Abbaye, the very day of my arrival, was Grandpré. He was struck to the heart. I have never witnessed more touching or more honourable concern. 'You must write to the Assembly,' he said. 'Have you not thought of that?' 'No; but how could I get it received and read?' 'I will do what I can,' he said. 'Very well! then I will write.' 'Do so and I will be back in two hours.' He went away and I wrote as follows:

CITOYENNE ROLAND TO THE NATIONAL CONVENTION

THE ABBAYE PRISON
1 JUNE 1793

Legislators!
I have today been dragged from home, from the arms of my twelve-year-old daughter, and I am detained in the Abbaye prison by virtue of an order which gives no grounds for my arrest. The order emanates from a revolutionary committee. The commissioners of the Commune, who accompanied those of the committee, showed

me another warrant, by the 'General Council', which likewise stated no grounds. I am simply presumed guilty. I was hauled off to prison in a public fashion, surrounded by an imposing force of armed men and a crowd of bemused spectators, several of whom consigned me unhesitatingly to the scaffold. No one has given the slightest indication to me or to anyone else why I am considered a criminal. And that is not all. The bearer of the orders of the Commune carried them out only inside my apartment and in order to obtain my signature to his *procès verbal*; as soon as I left the house I was handed over to men from the revolutionary committee. It was they who bought me to the Abbaye and it is on their *mandat* that I entered it. I attach a certified copy of this *mandat*, signed by a single unidentified individual. Seals were placed all over my apartment. While this was being done, that is to say from three in the morning until seven, a large crowd of citizens filled my apartment. If any of them had wanted to plant incriminating material in my library, which was open to all, there would have been ample opportunity.

Yesterday, that same committee tried to serve a warrant of arrest on the ex-minister, whom the law makes accountable only to you and who has not ceased to beg you to pronounce judgment on his administration. Roland protested against the warrant and after the men who brought it had withdrawn he left home in order to forestall a criminal mistake. This took place while I was out of the house, having gone to the Convention to tell them what was happening. I delivered a letter to the President – quite uselessly, as it was not read – asking for *justice* and for *protection*; I now make the same request with even greater right, for I am under restraint. I demand that the Convention give a ruling. If you confirm my arrest, then I invoke the law which requires a statement to be made of the offence and an interrogation to be conducted within twenty-four hours. Finally, I demand the Convention's decision on the accounts of the irreproachable minister now subjected to unheard-of perse-cution, whose case appears likely to give a terrible example to the world of virtue proscribed by blind prejudice.

If my crime is to have shared his rigid principles, his courageous energy and his ardent love of liberty, then I plead guilty and await punishment. Pronounce, legislators! France, Liberty, the fate of the Republic and your own survival depend on justice being done today. You are the guardians of the law!

After the agitations of the previous night I was completely exhausted. I was given a room the same evening and got into it at ten o'clock. When I saw the four dirty walls, the pallet in the centre without curtains and the window double-barred, and became aware of the stink which anyone accustomed to a clean apartment always finds so disagreeable, I realised that this was in truth a prison and that I must not expect any comfort. On the other hand, the space was reasonably large, there was a chimneypiece, the bed cover was passable and they had given me a pillow. All things considered it was not too bad. I lay down determined to stay in bed as long as possible. It was ten o'clock in the morning when Grandpré arrived. He looked no less distressed than on the previous evening and even more anxious. He glanced round the squalid little room, which had already become tolerable to me because I had slept in it, and there were tears in his eyes. He asked me how I had slept. 'I kept being woken up by the noise, but each time it stopped I went back to sleep, despite the tocsin which I think I heard this morning. Listen! is that not the tocsin sounding now?' 'I thought so too; but it is nothing.' 'Whatever will be, will be. If they kill me it shall be in this bed; I am so tired, I shall await my destiny here. Is there any new move against the deputies?' 'No. But I have brought your letter back. Champagneux and I thought you should soften the opening passages; here is what we propose instead. And we thought that you should also write a line to the Minister of the Interior so that he can take note officially of your letter. This will give me more grounds for insisting that it be read.'

I thought for a minute or two and then said, 'If I thought that my letter in its present form would be read, I would leave it unchanged even if it meant the failure of my plea. For there is no justice to be expected from the Assembly. The truths which I have expressed are universal; they must be said openly and the departments must hear them. However, I do see that the opening passage might prevent the letter being read, so it would be stupid to leave it in.' I substituted what they had proposed for the first three sentences. 'As for bringing in the minister', I said, 'I see that this would make the *démarche* more regular. Garat does not deserve a letter from me, but perhaps I can do it without lowering myself.' I then wrote the following lines:

To the Minister of the Interior

The Ministry of which you are in charge, citizen, gives you authority to supervise the execution of the laws and the duty of denouncing their violation. In the name of justice I request that this petition, which I present as a victim of oppression, be passed by you to the Convention.

[46]

I got up at midday and began to consider how I should settle myself in my new quarters. There was a common little table which I covered with a white cloth and put near the window to serve as my desk. I decided to eat off the corner of the mantelpiece so as to keep my work-table clean and orderly. Two large head-combs nailed to the shelves did service as coat-hangers. I had in my pocket Thomson's *Seasons*, a poem which I love for many reasons. I made a note of the books which I should need; first of all Plutarch's *Lives*, which at the age of eight I used to take to church instead of my prayer book but had not seriously looked into since; the English *History* of David Hume, together with Sheridan's dictionary, to improve my knowledge of English. I would have preferred to follow Macaulay[2] but the friend who had lent me the first volumes of that author was certainly no longer at home and I would not have known where to look for it, having already failed to find it in the bookshops. I smiled to myself at my plans, for there was a tremendous commotion outside; the roll-call was constantly being called and I had no idea what was going on. 'They shall not prevent me from living to the full, right up to the last moment,' I told myself. 'If they come they will find me much happier with my clear conscience than they are themselves; I shall meet them face to face and go to death as if it were to sleep.' The wife of the keeper came to invite me to her room, where she had laid a place for me so that I could dine in fresher air. I went over, and there I found my faithful maid! She threw herself into my arms, sobbing aloud. I was overcome with tenderness and grief. I felt guilty at being so calm, when I thought of the distress of those who were attached to me. In my mind's eye I pictured the anguish of X, or Y, and I felt indescribable heartbreak. This poor girl, how many tears I have caused her, how little I deserve such devotion! In ordinary life sometimes she is blunt with me, but only when she thinks I am neglecting my own happiness or my health. When I suffer, it is she who groans and I who comfort her.

And so it must be now. I explained to her that if she was always in tears she would be much less helpful to me, that she was more useful outside the prison than within and that, all in all, I was not so miserable as she supposed. This was the truth. Whenever I have

[2] Mrs Catharine Macaulay (née Sawbridge, 1733–91): historian and controversialist; author of the *History of England*, in eight volumes, which appeared 1763–83 and, in a French translation, 1791–2.

been ill I have felt a special kind of inner calm which comes, no doubt, from my philosophical way of thinking and from my determination always to make a virtue of necessity and never to rebel against fate. From the moment I go to bed, all obligations seem to vanish and anxieties have no further hold; my sole duty is to lie there and to stay there resignedly. I let my imagination run free. I call up agreeable feelings, happy memories and pleasant associations. No more struggle, no more calculation, no more argument; all is left to Nature and with the peacefulness of Nature I suffer patiently or rest content. I find that prison has much the same effect. I have nothing to do here but to exist, and what harm does that do me? I am not such bad company!

I was soon told that I had to move; there were so many new arrivals. The room I had been given could take more than one bed, so if I wanted to be alone I must go into a much smaller room. More disturbance as a result. The window of this cubby-hole looks out, I think, over the sentry who guards the front entrance of the prison. All night long I heard raucous voices shouting 'Who goes there? – Kill him! – Officer! – Patrol!' The buildings were lit up and it was clear from the continuous patrols that some sort of uprising was expected or had taken place. I rose very early in the morning and put my house in order: that is to say, made my bed, cleaned out my little room, tidied up my surroundings and my person. I knew that I could have asked for these things to be done for me, but I also realised that however much I were to pay for such services they would be a long time coming and very superficial. There was everything to be said for doing them myself; and the small presents which I was able to offer to the staff would be more appreciated if they were unearned. I waited impatiently for the great key to turn in the lock of my door, so that I could ask for the morning paper. It was brought to me; and there it was, the fatal news: an order of arrest had been issued against the Twenty-Two deputies. The paper slipped from my hands and I cried out in despair 'France is lost!'

So long as I had thought myself alone, or nearly so, under the yoke of the oppressor I had been able to preserve a proud and tranquil optimism for the defenders of liberty. But not now. Folly and crime have triumphed; the country's representative institutions have been violated, its unity torn apart. All that was notable for probity, force of character and talent is now proscribed. The Paris Commune dominates the legislature; Paris is lost, the flames of civil war are lit; the enemy will profit from our disunity, there will be no more liberty for the north of France and the whole Republic is delivered over to internecine war and strife. Farewell, our sublime illusions, our generous sacrifices, our hopes, our happiness. Farewell, beloved country. When I was a child of twelve, I wept that I had not been born in Sparta or in Rome; and in the French Revolution I thought I saw the unexpected triumph of principles upon which I had been nourished. Liberty, I said to myself in those days, has two sources: high morality, which makes wise laws, and enlightenment, which teaches us our rights. From now on, there will be no more degrading inequalities, I thought; nothing can now prevent human improvement; the general good will support and guarantee the happiness of the individual. Oh, those shining illusions, those seductive dreams! The terrible corruption of an immense city has swept them away. Life, which I never greatly valued, has become hateful to me now that these hopes are gone. Let the madmen do their worst. What are you waiting for, anarchists, brigands? You outlaw truth, you spill the blood of the virtuous; the very earth beneath your feet will swallow you up in blood. The course of events should have warned me how it would turn out. But I still could hardly believe that the great majority of the Convention would not be held back by the dangers of what they were doing. I cannot help being amazed at this act, which sounds the death-knell of the Convention itself.

An icy indignation now lies like a blanket over all my feelings. Indifferent as ever to my own fate, I preserve a faint hope for others and I await events with more curiosity than hope. I live now only for facts, not for feeling. I soon heard that the steps taken to enforce the decree of arrest had given rise to great anxiety about the prisons, which explained the turn-out of the guards and all that shouting in the night. It also seems that the citizens of the Unité section[3] were reluctant to obey the summons to surround the Convention; they all stayed at home to guard their properties and to keep an eye on the prison in their section. I then understood why Grandpré had looked so alarmed. He explained next day that he had been to the Convention to get my letter read and that for eight solid hours he and a few other deputies had vainly urged my petition on the Bureau. It was clear that I should never obtain my hearing.

I saw it reported in the *Moniteur* that my section, the section of Beaurepaire, had made a statement in my favour even after my

[3] The section in which the Abbaye prison was situated.

arrest. I therefore wrote to them in the following terms:

> Citizens! I learn from the newspapers that you have placed Roland and his wife under your protection. I did not know this when I was seized from my home. On the contrary, the man who brought me the orders of the Commune claimed that the armed men he had with him belonged to the section and they were so described in his *procès verbal*. The moment I was locked up in the Abbaye I appealed to the Convention and wrote to the Minister of the Interior asking him to forward my appeal. I know that he did this, and that the appeal was received. But it was not read. I have the honour to enclose a certified copy. If the section feels that it would be honourable to intervene on behalf of an innocent person, it could send a representative to plead my case at the bar of the Convention. I submit this matter to the wisdom of the section. I make no plea. Truth has only one tongue; an upright citizen will not beg for favours; and innocence scorns to grovel.
>
> P.S. It is now four days since I was arrested and I have not yet been interrogated. I note that the warrant contained no grounds for the arrest but stated that I should be interrogated the following day.

Several days passed in which I heard no news. I still had not been interrogated. On the other hand I had received numerous visitations from functionaries with mean faces and dirty ribbons across their stomachs, some claiming to belong to the police and others to I know not what. Huge *sans-culottes* with unwashed hair and fussy little bureaucrats came to enquire whether the prisoners were satisfied with their treatment. I expressed myself to them all with the energy and dignity appropriate to an innocent victim. Two or three of them, I noticed, understood what I was saying though not daring to support me. I was having dinner when someone came to announce that a group of five or six more had arrived. One man spoke on their behalf. I could tell before he had opened his mouth that he was an empty-headed windbag.

'Good morning, *Citoyenne*.' 'Good morning, Sir.' 'Are you satisfied with these premises? Have you any complaints regarding your treatment, or any requests to make?' 'Yes. I complain of being here; I demand to be released.' 'Is your health affected? Are you perhaps bored?' 'I am well and I am not bored. Boredom is a malady of empty souls and resourceless minds. But I know what justice is and I protest against having been arrested without charge and detained without interrogation.' 'Ah! But in time of revolution there is so much to do; one cannot attend to everything.' 'A woman to whom King Philip once made that reply answered, "If you have no time to do me justice you have no time to be King." I say the same to you.' 'Adieu, *Citoyenne*.' 'Goodbye, Sir.' And off goes the windbag, unable to cope with the argument. These men seem to have come here just to see what I look like in my cage. It would be hard to find stupider people.

I have mentioned that I made enquiries about the conditions of life here. I do not set great store by what are called the amenities of life. I make use of them gladly but always with moderation, and if they are not conveniently to hand I can easily do without. Purely in a spirit of orderliness I needed to know my expenses here and to settle them appropriately.

They told me that Roland, when he was at the ministry, decided that the allowance of five livres per day for the expenses of each prisoner was excessive, and reduced it to two livres. But the great rise in the price of food, trebled over the past few months, made this totally inadequate. All the nation was prepared to supply was the four walls and some straw, so that twenty sous were deducted right away to cover the keeper's room charges – that is, the bed and any furniture there might be. From the twenty sous remaining, the prisoner has to pay for light, heat if he needs it and his food. It is not enough. One is free in theory to add whatever one likes to one's expenditure. I do not like spending a lot on myself and I get some pleasure from voluntary privation. I thought I would find out how far I could reduce my needs by willpower. I took it step by step. After four days I cut down my breakfast and substituted bread and water for coffee and chocolate. I arranged that for the midday meal I should be given one plate of ordinary meat with some greens, and in the evening a few vegetables. No dessert. I drank beer at first, to break myself of wine, and then I gave that up too. In the meantime, as this dieting had a moral purpose and since I have no use for pointless economy, I began to set aside a sum of money for the unfortunate down-and-outs, so that when I ate my dry bread in the morning I should have the pleasure of knowing that thanks to me they could add something to theirs at night. Even if I stay here six months I hope to emerge plump and healthy, needing nothing but soup and bread and having earned some blessings incognito. In a rather different spirit I also gave a few presents to the staff of the prison. Anyone who is, or appears to be, severely economical in his own expenditure must be generous to others, and particularly to those who are dependent for their livelihood on his spending. I require neither services nor goods; I bring nothing in and I employ nobody. Obviously I shall be a most unsatisfactory prisoner from the point of view of the staff who make their little profits from the commissions and purchases entrusted to them. I must pay for not making use of these people. My own independence – and their affection – must be bought.

I received visits from Champagneux and Bosc. The former, father of a large family and a staunch believer in liberty, had upheld the principles of the Revolution from the very beginning in his popular journal, the *Courrier de Lyon*. He was a sensible, upright man and hardworking. Roland had called him in to run the first division of the Ministry of the Interior and it was one of the best appointments he made. He had been equally successful in his choice of other heads of department, notably Le Camus,[4] active and straightforward, and Fépoul,[5] a man of unusual ability. In fact, the government departments had never been more ably staffed and it is only because of this that Garat today is able to hold down an office which is far beyond his powers. He is well aware of this; he said that he could not carry on if he was forced to make staff changes. It will not save him, of course, because no number of talented subordinates can make up for lack of character in a minister. The greatest fault of all in a man who seeks to govern is weakness, especially in times of factional strife. Men like Garat and Barère,[6] who as ordinary individuals might very well be considered intelligent and worthy, are quite unfitted to govern any state. Their half measures are fatal. They are so keen to be conciliatory that they approach any challenge sideways on, so to speak, and land themselves inevitably in confusion and catastrophe. Conciliatoriness in a statesman ought to be confined to the way he conducts his business; I mean he should treat the people he employs with respect and should know how to take advantage of the enthusiasms and even the faults of those with whom he works. But when it comes to his principles and his actions they should be rigorous, ruthless and swift. No obstacles and no secondary considerations should make

[4] Gabriel-Étienne Le Camus: a friend of the Rolands from Lyons. Appointed head of a division in the ministry by Roland, Aug. 1792.
[5] Guillaume-Charles Faypoult (*not* Fépoul): another head of a division in Roland's ministry. Survived the Revolution to become a préfet under the Empire.
[6] Bertrand Barère de Vieuzac (1755–1841): member of the Constituent Assembly and of the Convention; member of the Committee of Public Safety.

him compromise with principle or deflect him from his aim.

Roland has exceptional vision and greatness of soul and prodigious energy. If he had only had a little more subtlety in his manner he could easily have ruled an empire. His faults harm only himself; his abilities are infinitely precious to the administration.

Our old and trusted friend Bosc came to see me on the first day of my detention. He hastened to conduct my daughter to Madame Creuzé-Latouche, who agreed to look after her and bring her up with her own children. This was the act of a true friend; there was no home where I would feel happier to see her established, no more loving foster parents possible than Creuzé and his wife.

Who, then, is to be pitied in all this? Only Roland! Roland, whose accounts they refused to examine; Roland, who is persecuted, proscribed, forced to hide himself like a criminal; Roland, who must fear for the lives of any who protect him and bear in silence the incarceration of his wife, the sealing-up of all his possessions. There can be no comfort for Roland, no possible compensation for all that he has suffered. ...

The animals in the fable habitually tremble before the lion of the forest, but when he is sick they creep up one after the other to insult him. Just so, when a man of virtue has been laid by the heels or his reputation undermined by his enemies, a rout of second-rate people, fired by ignorance and malice, will turn upon him. Issue no. 526 of the *Thermomètre du jour* of 9 June gives an example of this. Under the heading 'Interrogation of Philippe d'Orléans' we find recorded a series of questions amongst which appears the following accusation:

'... of having taken part in clandestine meetings at night *chez* the wife of Buzot, in the faubourg St-Germain, at which were present Dumouriez, Roland and his wife, Vergniaud, Brissot, Gensonné,[7] Gorsas,[8] Louvet, Pétion,[9] Guadet[10] etc.'

---

[7] Armand Gensonné (1755–93): Deputy from the Gironde to the Legislative Assembly and to the Convention; guillotined on 31 Oct. 1793.
[8] Antoine-Joseph Gorsas (1752–93): member of the Convention, where he joined the Girondins and shared their fate in Oct. 1793.
[9] Jérôme Pétion (1756–94): Mayor of Paris in 1791; committed suicide with Buzot at St-Émilion after Mme Roland's execution.
[10] Marguerite-Élie Guadet (1758–94): Deputy from the Gironde in the Legislative Assembly and the Convention. Guillotined in Bordeaux in June 1794.

What utter villainy, what brazen impudence! Every one of the deputies mentioned here voted for the exile of the Bourbons. Never for one moment had these fierce defenders of freedom considered d'Orléans a possible leader; they always regarded him as a dangerous puppet. They were the first to fear his vices, his money, his connections and his popularity; they were the first to denounce his faction and to pursue those who appeared to be his agents. Louvet singled them out in his polemic against Robespierre, a most valuable piece which like all his writings will be cherished by history. He traced their progress to the electoral college out of which Philippe d'Orléans emerged as a deputy. Buzot, whose tireless energy always upset the intriguers, took the first suitable occasion to demand that *all* the Bourbons be banished. He regarded this as essential from the moment when the Convention decided to put Louis on trial.

Neither Roland nor I ever met d'Orléans. I even managed to avoid inviting Sillery to my house, though I was told that he was a good and sensible man, because his relations with d'Orléans made him suspect to me. ... As to the so-called clandestine meetings at Mme Buzot's apartment, nothing could be more absurd. I had seen a great deal of Buzot at the time of the Constituent Assembly and had remained in friendly correspondence with him. I had an admiration and affection for him on account of his pure principles, his courage and his good manners. He often came to the Ministry of the Interior. I went only once to his wife's apartment after their arrival in Paris for the Convention and they had no sort of relationship with Dumouriez.

I was so indignant at this rubbish that I took up my pen and wrote to Dulaure, editor of the *Thermomètre du jour*, a decent man but weak, whom I had met once, just at the moment when he was being seduced by the Mountain.[11]

CITOYENNE ROLAND TO DEPUTY DULAURE, EDITOR OF THE *THERMOMÈTRE DU JOUR*

THE ABBAYE PRISON
9 JUNE 1793

If I was still capable of being surprised by anything, citizen, in these days of oppression, I should tell you that I was astonished at the absurdities printed in your issue of today under the heading

[11] Or Jacobins – see p. 57.

'Interrogation of Philippe d'Orléans', which chance has brought to my attention. It is scarcely credible that the men who were the first to fear, denounce and persecute the d'Orléans faction should now be represented as having founded it themselves!

Time will no doubt eventually throw light on this iniquitous accusation, but in the meantime I think you owe it to your sense of justice to publish, alongside the tendentious questions in the 'interrogation', the replies which must have been given. Then the public will be able to judge how much credence to give to the suspicions which have been raised.

Your readers will no doubt be aware that the persons named in this 'interrogation' are at present subject to libellous abuse and persecution and that most of them are under restraint by virtue of a decree extracted from the Convention by force and fraud. I myself have been in detention now for eight days, under a warrant that gives no grounds for my arrest. I have not been interrogated and I have not been able to make the Convention listen to my case. When eventually they were informed of my complaints they voted to move to the orders of the day on the pretext that it was no business of theirs! So, upstart and arbitrary authorities commit an outrage, the official authorities turn their backs and the victim may not even complain to the Convention. There is no court of appeal left except the legislative body, and yet one is not allowed to address them. They are prepared to interest themselves in some prisoners detained by a tribunal in Marseilles, but I, held here by a revolutionary committee, have no rights. And yet the Commune keeps repeating in the newspapers that the Paris prisons contain nothing but murderers, thieves and counter-revolutionaries. Citizen! I know you; I believe you to be an upright man. You will regret this one day. I am sending you some papers which I beg you to read. I ask you to find space in your paper for the letter which I failed to get read in the Convention. You must see that you owe me this in all fairness. If you do *not* see it then of course it is no use my insisting.

P.S. Neither Roland nor I have ever even met Philippe d'Orléans. I must add that I have always heard the deputies named in the 'interrogation' (quoted in your paper) express the same contempt for that person as I feel myself, and that if at any time we discussed him, it was solely to note what a danger he represented to the true friends of liberty and to agree on the necessity for his banishment.

Since I have mentioned Dumouriez I will say what I know and what I think of him. But this takes me back to Roland's first term of office and leads me to explain here how this austere man came to be appointed to a post to which the King seldom summons anyone of his type. I shall take things a little further back and use the leisure of my captivity to record past events about which I should probably not otherwise have written....

3

WIFE OF THE MINISTER

•───•

*The Legislative Assembly met for the first time on 1 October 1791, shortly
after the King had accepted the new Constitution. The majority of the
deputies held moderate opinions and wanted to maintain a constitutional
monarchy. But on the benches to the left of the President sat a large number
of vigorous and eloquent deputies of more republican inclination. (The terms
'left' and 'right' in politics date from this Assembly.) The largest group on the
left were the Girondins, so-called because a number of their leaders came
from that part of south-west France. These were the men to whom Brissot
introduced the Rolands when they came to Paris. Their romantic admiration
for Rousseau and for the Romans suited Mme Roland's style.*

*The other main group on the left was the Jacobins, so-called because they
met in a convent which belonged to the Dominican Order, called in France
the Jacobin. They, too, at this stage advocated constitutional reform of a
moderate kind. Roland joined the Jacobin Club when he first arrived in Paris
and served on their 'correspondence committee'. Later, under the leadership
of Robespierre and others, they became more extremist and it was they who
organised the Terror. Their power ended in 1794 with the execution of
Robespierre.*

*One of the criticisms of Mme Roland is that she stirred up animosity
between the Girondins and the Jacobins (who, under the Convention, became
known as the Montagnards, or the Mountain, because they occupied the
highest seats in the hall). Her personal distaste for Danton played a part in
this; she 'evidently found his overt sexuality disturbing' (Hibbert, op. cit.)
and bitterly resented the fact that he outshone and outmanoeuvred her
husband.*

WE ARRIVED IN PARIS on 20 February 1791. I had not seen my
home for five years. I had followed the progress of the
Revolution and the work of the Assembly and I had studied the
character and qualities of its principal members. I went to all the
meetings. I saw the powerful Mirabeau, the astonishing Cazales, the
audacious Maury, the astute Lameth, the cold Barnave. I observed
with some distress that the deputies on the benches of the right

possessed the sort of superiority always enjoyed in an Assembly by men who are accustomed to lead and who have the advantages of an educated accent and a distinguished manner. But I could also detect in the men of the left powers of reasoning, true courage and philosophical enlightenment which, backed by their administrative and legal experience, could have given them victory if only they had stuck to their principles and remained united.

Brissot came to see us.... He gave us the names of the deputies with whom he was in closest touch, either as old colleagues or through their common concern for the public good. Seeing that I was properly established and had a sizeable apartment, well situated in town for all these people, it was agreed that the group should meet at my house four times a week in the evening.

This arrangement suited me very well. It meant that I could keep in touch with public affairs, in which I was so deeply interested; it gave scope to my taste for political argument and for studying men. I knew the proper role of my sex and never exceeded it. The conferences took place in my presence but I played no part in them. I sat at a separate table, outside the men's circle, and I always had some work for my hands or wrote letters while they were talking. But however many letters I might write (and on occasions it was as many as ten in a session), I did not miss a word of what was being said. Sometimes I had to bite my tongue to prevent myself putting a word in.

What struck me most, and pained me most, was the sort of disorganised and unserious talk in which quite sensible men are prepared to spend three or four hours without deciding anything. If you looked at it in detail, you could say that you had heard admirable principles and ideas expounded and new horizons opened. But when you considered the net result you saw that not a single course had been set, not a single conclusion reached and no fixed objectives established towards which each man could be asked to direct his efforts.

In my impatience I could sometimes have boxed the ears of these sages, whose honourable souls and pure intentions I learned every day to admire. Excellent dialecticians, learned in philosophy, wise in theoretical statesmanship, they knew nothing whatever about leadership or of how to manage an Assembly and they habitually wasted their time in pure cleverness and wit.

I did witness in this way the birth of one or two good decrees which passed into law. But before long, the coalition with the minority of the *noblesse* weakened the left and brought about the evils of constitutional revision. Only a small number of resolute men were left who were prepared to stand for principle, and in the end these were reduced practically to Buzot, Pétion and Robespierre. The latter seemed to me at that time to be an honest man. I forgave him his foul language and boring delivery on account of his principles. But I did notice that he always kept very quiet at meetings where anything confidential was being discussed. He would listen to all opinions but rarely gave his own or took the trouble to explain his thoughts.... His timidity, his sheer fright in time of danger, struck me particularly at the time of the King's flight and the affair of the Champ de Mars. But I felt quite sorry for him; nature had made him so timorous that he needed a double dose of courage to support a dangerous cause. I did not reckon then that popularity with the mob, which he was already courting, would give him the necessary leverage to offset his weaknesses and sustain his ambition in the battle against the Court.

Roland's mission had kept him in Paris for seven months. By mid-September he had completed his work for Lyons and we left town. We spent the autumn in the country seeing to our grape harvest.

One of the last acts of the Constituent Assembly had been to suppress the Inspectors. We had to decide whether to stay in the country or spend the winter in Paris. Two considerations inclined us towards Paris: Roland would be able to press his claims to a pension after forty years of service, and could at the same time pursue his research for the encyclopedia surrounded by scholars and artists rather than in a cultural desert.

So in December we went back. The Constituents had gone home. Pétion had moved to the Town Hall and was entirely preoccupied with his problems as Mayor. There was no longer a rallying point and we saw much less of Brissot. Our attention was concentrated on our own affairs; Roland made plans for a journal of the practical arts and we sought in the pleasures of study a distraction from public affairs, which seemed to us to be in a very bad way. A few deputies from the Legislative Assembly met from time to time in the Place Vendôme, where one of them lived, and Roland was invited to join them. But it was too far away and he seldom went. One of our friends who attended frequently told us in mid-March that the Court was in a state of nerves and was looking round for some move which might restore its popularity.

He said it was quite possible that some Jacobin ministers might be appointed and told us that the 'patriots' were now busy trying to ensure that if that were to happen the choice should fall on serious and capable men. They were afraid that the whole thing might be a trap, and that the Court might be hoping that extremists would be put forward, so that they could then discredit the opposition. Our friend added that some of the colleagues had been thinking of Roland, whose position in the academic world, administrative experience and reputation for justice and firmness offered a consistent picture. Roland was seeing a good deal of the Jacobins at that time, and was employed in their 'correspondence committee.' This idea seemed to me pretty insubstantial and made no great impression on my mind.

But on the evening of the 21st Brissot came to see me and repeated the same story in more positive terms, asking whether Roland would consent to take on this responsibility. I replied that when the first overture had been made it had seemed to me that Roland, though he saw the difficulties and possibly the dangers, would not be reluctant to meet such a challenge. I asked for time to look more closely at the idea. When it came to it, Roland had no hesitation; he was confident that he could be useful to his country. A reply to that effect was sent to Brissot the following morning.

On Friday 23, at eleven o'clock in the evening, Brissot appeared at my house with Dumouriez, having just emerged from the Council, to tell Roland that he had been appointed Minister of the Interior and to congratulate him. They remained for a quarter of an hour and agreed to meet the following day for Roland to take the oath. After they had gone I said to my husband, speaking of Dumouriez, whom I had never seen before, 'There is a man with a shrewd mind and a false mien, deeply to be mistrusted, I am sure. He professed great satisfaction with the patriotic choice which he was charged to announce to you, but I would not be at all surprised if one day he sacrificed you.' One look at Dumouriez had been enough to show me such incompatibility between him and Roland that I thought they could not possibly work together for long. On the one side stood the epitome of uprightness and honour, with no trace of the courtier's arts or of time-serving, and on the other a highly intelligent roué and buccaneer, with no respect for anything but his own interests and his glory. It was not hard to conclude that such characteristics must repel one another.

It did not take long for Roland, with his energy, passion for hard work and sense of order, to classify in his head all the sectors and functions of his ministry. But the ingrained habits and conservatism of his departmental heads made his work very painful. He had to be constantly on the watch to prevent mistakes and was in a state of perpetual struggle with his officials. He could see that staff changes would be necessary but was wise enough not to make them until he had familiarised himself with the whole scene and was ready with suitable replacements....

The first time Roland appeared at Court the simplicity of his clothes, his round hat and the laces on his shoes astonished and scandalised the lackeys. These creatures have no existence outside etiquette and believe that the salvation of the Empire depends on preserving it. The Master of Ceremonies went up to Dumouriez with a worried look and a deep frown and, indicating Roland out of the corner of his eye, said in a low voice, 'Imagine, my Lord, no buckles on his shoes!' – to which Dumouriez replied with comic gravity 'My dear sir, all is lost!'

The Council met four times a week. The ministers agreed to dine together in one or the other's home on the days of session. I received them every Friday....

When my husband was at the ministry I made it a rule not to make or to receive social calls and not to invite any women to meals. This was no great sacrifice for me. As I was not living permanently in Paris I had no extensive circle of personal friends. I had never frequented high society anywhere because I enjoy a studious life, hate wasting my time in gossip and am bored by fools. Being accustomed to spending my time within the domestic circle I shared in Roland's work and cultivated my own tastes. This severe regime enabled me to preserve my way of life and at the same time to protect my husband from the crowd of hangers-on who always surround a man in a high position. I had no real social circle; twice a week I invited to dinner ministers, deputies and others with whom my husband needed to be on good terms. They always talked business in front of me because I did not interrupt and was not surrounded by indiscreet friends.

Of all the rooms in our large apartment I had chosen for our daily use a small parlour forming a study where I had my books and a desk. Friends or colleagues who needed to talk confidentially to the minister, instead of going to his rooms where he was surrounded by his officials and by the public, would often come to me and ask me to call him in to my study. Thus without any need for intrigue or unseemly curiosity I found myself at the centre of affairs. Roland used to enjoy telling me about his conversations afterwards in private with the confidence which has always existed between us; so that our knowledge and our opinions were, so to speak, held in common. It would also happen that friends who merely had a piece of information to impart or a word to say to the minister would come to me, knowing that I was always at home, and ask me to pass the message on to him.…

During the course of July, seeing the situation deteriorating as a result of the perfidy of the Court, the movement of foreign troops and the feebleness of the Assembly, we began to look about and to consider where Liberty, so evidently threatened, might find refuge. We spoke often with Barbaroux[1] and Servan about the excellent spirit in the Midi, the energy of the departments there and the facilities which that part of France might provide for the foundation of a Republic should the Court succeed in subjugating the north of France and Paris. We got out the maps; we drew the line of demarcation. Servan studied the military positions; we calculated the forces available and examined the means of reorganising supply. Each of us contributed ideas as to where and from whom we might expect support.

We were all agreed that after a revolution which had aroused such high hopes we must on no account fall back into slavery; we must establish a free government somewhere, even if it be in only part of France. 'That', said Barbaroux, 'will be our last resort, if the men from Marseilles with whom I came up here are not sufficiently supported by the Parisians to defeat the Court. But I still hope that we shall have a Convention which will give a Republic to the *whole* of France.' We understood very well, without his being more explicit, that he was preparing an insurrection. Indeed something of that sort seemed inevitable, considering that the Court's supporters were making preparations which clearly showed that they meant to impose their own solution. It will be said that they were acting only in self-defence; but the idea of attacking the monarchy as such would not have occurred to anyone, nor would it have been

---

[1] Charles-Jean-Marie Barbaroux (1767–94): Deputy from Marseilles to the Convention; after escaping arrest in 1793 he was captured in Bordeaux and executed in June 1794.

supported by the people, if the King had sincerely backed the Constitution. Even the most avowed republicans, though they saw its faults, wanted nothing more at this stage than the Constitution and would have been prepared to wait for time and experience to improve it.

Amongst a corrupted people, especially in large towns, revolution throws up a whole class of unscrupulous adventurers seeking fortune at any price and by any means. A specially bold and tough individual can quickly make himself the leader of these elements. A gang is formed, its ranks swollen with dupes and malcontents, and before long it is infiltrated by cleverer men, politicians and so on, who turn the agitation to their own advantage. So it is with patriotic societies, groups of men gathered together for the discussion of their rights and their interests; and so it is also, on a vaster scale, with the great institutions of the State. It begins with a few ardent spirits seeking in good faith to serve the public. Philosophers join in, hoping to contribute to the overthrow of tyranny and the triumph of noble principles. Great truths emerge and are exchanged, generous sentiments are aroused and widely expounded; hearts and minds are stirred to action. But soon the fine principles are taken over by publicity-seekers and demagogues. These men overstate the truth in order to draw attention to themselves, strike the imagination with exaggerated colours, flatter the passions of the crowd which always admires extremes and turn the people against their true friends.

Undoubtedly many people of this sort had infiltrated the popular movement, ready to take bribes from the Court and to betray it if it should prove the weaker party. The Court affected to believe that anyone who opposed its views must be of this stamp and was pleased to lump them all together as factious persons. The true patriots were not sufficiently alert to the danger presented by these men; perhaps they thought that they could use them. In their hatred of despotism they did not see that, while it is permissible in politics to have good things done by bad men or to take advantage of excesses done in a good cause, it is infinitely dangerous to honour such men for any of their actions and not to punish them for their crimes.

Everyone has heard of the Revolution of 10 August. I know no more about it than the public, for although I was well informed on great events so long as Roland was a public figure and followed them with interest even when he was no longer in office, I have

never been familiar with what one might call the political in-
fighting, just as he himself had never operated at that level.

Recalled to the ministry at that time, he had brave new hopes for
liberty. 'But it is a shame, we used to say, that the Council should
be tarnished by the presence of the man Danton, who has such an
evil reputation.' Friends to whom I whispered this thought took the
line that he had been useful in the Revolution, that the people loved
him, and that there was no point in making an enemy unnecessar-
ily. They thought we must make the best of him as he was. This was
all very well, but it is easier to avoid giving a man power than to
prevent him from abusing it. That is where the patriots started to
go wrong. The moment the Court was defeated, a first-rate Council
should have been formed in which all the members, irreproachable
in their conduct and distinguished by their abilities, would have
imposed proper policies on the government and earned the respect
of foreign powers. To give a place to Danton was to inject into the
government the type of person I have just described: the sort who
torments an administration when not employed by it but discredits
and degrades it when he is. But who would have thought of this at
that time? Who would have dared to express such views and to
press them in high quarters? It was the Assembly, or its
Commission of Twenty-One, which made the choice. There were
many men of merit in that Assembly but not a single leader, not one
man of the Mirabeau class, able to weld the collective will into a
single instrument of action and to make himself obeyed. ...

Roland's first concern was to put into operation the reforms which
he saw to be necessary in his own ministry. He surrounded himself
with hard-working and enlightened men of principle. If he had
done nothing else he would have performed a great service to that
part of the administration. He wrote at once to all the departments
with the vigour and authority which derive from reason and truth
and with the eloquence of true sentiment. He depicted for them the
new destinies of France in the light of the Revolution of 10 August;
and he urged all parties to unite their efforts in favour of justice to
prevent extremism, of liberty to ensure the happiness of all and of
good order without which these benefits cannot be ensured. He
begged them to support the Legislative Assembly as the authority
responsible for expressing the popular will. Any administrative
bodies which showed hesitation were suspended or dissolved.
Business was speeded up, and this, coupled with active and

Manon at the age of twelve.

'My father's apartment . . . looked out over the busy, ever-changing traffic of the Pont-Neuf'; the Rolands' apartment seems to have been in one of the buildings on the left, at the back. A view of the Pont-Neuf and the Samaritaine by Raguenet, c. 1760.

M. and Mme Phlipon, Manon's parents; eighteenth-century French School portraits.

Manon in her teens; a nineteenth-century portrait by Jules Goupil.

Brissot.

Vergniaud, by Raffet.

Desmoulins, by Boze.

Danton; a portrait attributed to David.

Robespierre, by David.

Manon aged nineteen; an engraving by her father.

Composing the famous letter to the King; a popular print of the nineteenth century.

widespread correspondence, reinvigorated the country, restored confidence and gave new life to the general scene.

Danton scarcely let a day go by without coming to see me. Sometimes it was for the Council; he would then arrive a little early and come to my apartment or he would stay behind after the meeting, usually accompanied by Fabre d'Églantine.[2] Sometimes he would invite himself to supper on a day when I was not normally receiving, in order to discuss some matter with Roland. No one could have shown more zeal, a greater love of Liberty or a stronger desire to agree with his colleagues in her service. I used to look at his repulsive features and although I told myself that one must not judge by appearances, that I knew nothing certain against him and that the most honest of men must be allowed two faces in a time of turmoil, I could not read into that face the image of an honest man. I have never seen features which reflected so clearly the licence of brutal passions; an astonishing audacity emanated from them, partly hidden by an air of vulgar joviality, an affectation of frankness and bonhomie. I have a lively imagination and when people impress me I tend to see them performing actions which suit their character. I can never look for any length of time at a physiognomy which is a little out of the ordinary without clothing the owner with the uniform of some profession or giving him a role which fits my idea of his nature. My imagination has often figured Danton with a dagger in his hand, inciting by voice and gesture a gang of assassins more timid or less ferocious than himself, exulting in his crimes and demonstrating his depraved inclinations with a gesture worthy of Assur-bani-pal. I really defy any skilled painter not to be able to find in the person of Danton the necessary ingredients for such a picture. As for Fabre d'Églantine, kitted out in a monk's robe and armed with a stiletto, weaving a plot to slander and undo some rich man whose fortune he covets – he is so perfectly fitted for the part that anyone wanting to portray a typical villainous *tartufe* need only paint his portrait in that outfit.

These two men did their best to make me chatter by talking patriotism at me. I had nothing to keep quiet about or to dissimulate on that subject. I am always prepared to expound my principles, not only to those who I believe share them but equally

[2] Philippe Fabre, known as Fabre d'Églantine (1750–94): dramatist; inventor of the revolutionary calendar; friend of Danton; executed with the Dantonists in 1794.

to others whose motives I suspect of being less pure. In this I show my confidence in the former and a proper pride vis-à-vis the latter. I disdain to conceal my opinion even on the pretext or with the hope of better penetrating the minds of others. I try to draw men out with discretion. I judge them by comparing their deeds with their words. I reveal my whole self and never leave any doubt as to who I am. ...

Danton and Fabre stopped coming to see me towards the end of August. I dare say they had taken the measure of Roland and his friends and felt like keeping out of our way while they went round justifying the September massacres. They had no doubt concluded that Roland was an upright man who would have no part in their type of enterprise and that his wife could not be used to influence him. They probably saw that she, too, had principles and a woman's instinct for recognising false knaves; and they will have conjectured, I little doubt, that she could on occasion use her pen. In short, they will have regarded us as a principled and talented couple, highly threatening to their ambitions and fit only to be destroyed. All this has since been shown to be only too true.

One of the first measures proposed by the Council was to send commissioners into the departments to enlighten the people about the events of 10 August and above all to encourage defence preparations and raise recruits for our armies at the frontiers. When the question of selecting these men came up, Roland asked for a twenty-four-hour delay in which to make proposals. Danton leapt to his feet. 'I will undertake the whole thing,' he cried. 'The Paris Commune will supply true patriots for this job.' With fatal indolence the Council authorised him to find the men and the next day he turned up with the commissions all complete, ready to be filled in with the names suggested by himself and signed. There was no discussion, no examination; they just signed. So now you had a swarm of unknown adventurers, tavern brawlers, fanatic patriots and riff-raff making profit out of the public disorder, united only in their loyalty to Danton whose coarse behaviour and licentious doctrines they adored. These were the men who were to represent the Council in the departments of France.

This operation has always seemed to me one of Danton's greatest coups and the most humiliating setback for the Council. You need to take account of the pressure on ministers, each fully engaged in his own departmental business, in such tempestuous times, to understand how honest and capable men can behave with such levity. The fact is that the ministers of the Interior, of the War Department and even of the Marine were over-burdened with work and too absorbed in the details of their departments to have time for political reflection. The Council should have been composed of men whose sole duty was to think, not to administrate. Danton's ministry had the least work, and in any case he paid little attention to his duties there; the clerks kept the wheels turning and he provided his signature. His whole time and attention were devoted to plotting and intrigue in furtherance of his own power and fortune. He was constantly at the War Ministry, slipping men of his confidence into the armies, giving them personal interest in purchase and supplies. He neglected no opportunity to advance these men, dregs of a corrupt society risen to the surface like scum in the shake-up of political life and buoyant for a few brief moments. Thus he built up his credit and formed his faction, soon to become irresistible and still paramount today.

Foreign armies were advancing on our territory with alarming speed. Men who aspire to lead the people and have studied how to stir them up know very well that terror is one of their most potent weapons. ...

The news of the fall of Verdun broke like a bombshell on 1 September and created panic. The rumour-mongers said that the enemy were approaching Châlons and needed only three days to reach Paris. The public, who judge these matters by distance alone and overlook what is needed for the advance of an army, its provisions, its baggage, its artillery and the thousand other requirements which distinguish its progress from the speedy posting of a private traveller, imagined foreign troops already burning and sacking the capital. Everything was done to exaggerate the dangers and to inflame opinion, and the Assembly was easily persuaded to take panic measures which made matters worse. Raids on private houses on the pretext of looking for arms or suspected persons, which had been common enough since 10 August, were now given general sanction and took place in the middle of the night. Innumerable new arrests and unheard-of persecution were the result.

The Commune, consisting for the most part of men who had nothing to lose and everything to gain by the Revolution, felt the imperative need to commit new crimes in order to cover up the old.

They solemnly declared the fatherland to be in danger, hung black flags of distress on the towers of the city churches and sounded the alarm guns. They summoned the citizens to gather in a mass demonstration in the Champ de Mars on 2 September to 'rally around the altar of the nation' all those who were zealous to rush off and defend her frontiers. At the same time they ordered the barriers to be closed. Nobody noticed the contradiction between these two dispositions. Then they sparked off rumours about conspiracies in the prisons amongst the aristocrats (or the rich) of whom there were huge numbers in custody. Their infamously provocative line was that the citizens could not be expected to leave their families and homes and go off to war, leaving behind them these ravening wolves who would at once fall upon everything they held most dear.

At the first signs of agitation the Minister of the Interior, who was generally responsible for public order but had no forces at his command and no powers, wrote urgently to the Commune, in the person of the Mayor, pressing for action and vigilance. Not only that, but he warned Santerre, the Commander of the National Guard, to strengthen his posts and to have particular care for the prisons. When he heard that there was a special threat to the prisons he wrote formally asking that they be carefully guarded.[3] This was all he was entitled to do, but to give it more effect he had his formal request printed and posted up at every street corner, thus warning the citizens to keep guard for themselves in case the Commander should neglect his duty.

At about five o'clock in the evening of Sunday 2 September, at about the same time as the prisons were surrounded, a crowd of 200 or so men turned up at the Ministry of the Interior, calling for the minister and demanding weapons. I heard their shouting from my private apartment. I went out and could see them from the window overlooking the main courtyard. In the antechamber I was told what was going on. Roland was absent, but this was not accepted by the demonstrators who were determined to see him. Our staff were doing their best to prevent the crowd from coming

[3] Paul de Roux comments: 'Unfortunately all trace of these appeals has disappeared. It looks as if Roland did not react to the events until the evening of 3 September (twenty-four hours after the massacres) when he declared to the Assembly that ... the executive had been unable either to foresee or to prevent the excesses. There is every reason to think that the only letters he sent to Pétion and Santerre were those dated the afternoon of 4 September.'

upstairs, repeatedly assuring them that the minister was not there. I gave orders that ten of them should be invited up. When they came I asked them politely what they wanted. They said that they were honest citizens, all ready to set off for Verdun, but they had no arms; they had come to see the minister and demand weapons. I explained that the Minister of the Interior had never had arms at his disposal and that they should address themselves to the War Ministry. They replied that they had already been there and had been told there were no arms. They said all the ministers were f... traitors and that they must see Roland. 'I am sorry he is not at home,' I said, 'because he would convince you. Come and search the building with me; you will see that he is not here and that there are no arms, and when you reflect you will see that there is no reason why there should be. Go back to the War Ministry or make your just complaint to the Commune. If you want Roland to speak to you, go to the Marine building where the whole Council is in session.' They withdrew. I went onto the balcony overlooking the courtyard and from there I could see a man in his shirt sleeves waving a sword and yelling out that all the ministers were traitors. My ten friends mixed with the crowd and eventually persuaded them to retire, drums beating. They took the *valet-de-chambre* with them as a hostage and made him run around the streets for an hour or so and then let him go. I got into a coach immediately and drove to the Marine to warn my husband. The Council had not yet begun but I found a number of ministers and deputies assembled there waiting for the ministers of War and of Justice. I told them the story. They made various comments, but most of them thought it was a natural result of the prevailing conditions and of the public agitation.

What was Danton doing? I did not know until several days later, but I must record it here. He was at the Town Hall with the so-called Watch Committee from which the numerous orders of arrest had been issuing these last few days. He had staged a public reconciliation with Marat after a pretended breach of 24 hours. He went up to Pétion's office, took him aside and said to him in his usual coarse tone 'What do you suppose they have thought up now? They have made out a warrant for the arrest of Roland!' 'Who have?' asked Pétion. 'That crazy committee. I have taken the warrant. Look! Here it is. We cannot allow them to behave like that. Good God! Against a member of the Council!' Pétion took the warrant, read it and handed it back with a smile. 'Let them do it,' he said, 'it will have a good effect.' 'A good effect?' replied Danton, looking curiously at the Mayor. 'No! I cannot allow it; I will make them see reason.' And the warrant was never executed. But who can doubt that the 200 men who invaded the Ministry of the Interior that day were sent by the authors of this warrant? Who can doubt that it was the delay caused by Roland's absence from his office that made them think again? And who can fail to see, in Danton's approach to the Mayor, the action of a conspirator who is trying to find out the likely effect of a coup, or to take credit for having prevented it if it fails or is unexpectedly delayed?

The ministers emerged from the Council after eleven o'clock; we heard only next morning of the horrors committed during the night and which were still being committed in the prisons. Appalled by these abominable crimes, by our own inability to prevent them and by the evident complicity of the Commune and the General commanding the Guard, we decided that the only course open to a responsible minister was to denounce them publicly with the utmost vigour, challenge the Assembly to put a stop to them and arouse the indignation of all good men, taking the risk of assassination if need be. 'The truth is', I said to my husband, 'that a courageous decision is as conducive to safety as it is to justice. Terrorism can be suppressed only by firmness. Even if it were not a moral duty it would be political prudence to denounce these atrocities. The men who commit them hate you anyway, since you have tried to check them; you must make them fear you and impose your will.' Roland wrote to the Assembly his letter of 3 September, which became almost as famous as his letter to the King. The Assembly received it with enthusiasm, ordering it to be printed, distributed and posted up. They applauded it with the boldness that weak people often show when they witness a courageous act: they would not be capable of it themselves, but it raises their spirits and gives them hope....

But the massacres continued. At the Abbaye they lasted from Sunday evening until Tuesday morning; at La Force, longer; at Bicêtre, four days, and so on. I am now in the first of these three prisons myself and that is how I have heard the gruesome details; I dare not describe them. But there was one event which I will not pass over in silence because it helps to show how all this was linked and premeditated. In the faubourg St-Germain there was a warehouse where they put prisoners for whom there was no room in the Abbaye. The police chose the Sunday evening just before the general massacre to move prisoners from this depot to the prison. The assassins were lying in wait; they fell upon the coaches, five or six in number, broke them open with swords and pikes and slew the men and women within, screaming there in the open street. All Paris witnessed these terrible scenes, carried out by a small number of butchers. (At the Abbaye there were barely fifteen of them, but the only defenders of the gate, despite all the demands made to the Commune and to the Commander of the Guard, were two men of the National Guard.) All Paris saw it and all Paris let it go on. I abominate this city. It is impossible to imagine Liberty finding a home amongst cowards who condone every outrage and coolly stand by watching crimes which fifty armed men with any gumption could easily have prevented.

The forces of law and order were badly organised, and still are, because the power-hungry brigands were careful to oppose any form of discipline which might restrain them. But does a man need to receive orders from his officer and march in column of fours when it is a question of rescuing people who are having their throats cut? The fact is that the reports of conspiracies in the prisons, however improbable, and the constant propaganda about the people's will and the people's anger, held everyone in a sort of stupor and gave the impression that this infamous performance was the work of the populace, whereas in reality there were not above 200 criminals. It was not so much the first night that astonished me, but *four days!* And the ghoulish sightseers coming to watch the spectacle! I know of nothing in the annals of the most barbarous nation to compare with these atrocities. Roland's health was impaired. Such was the effect of nervous tension that his stomach could take no nourishment and the obstruction of his spleen broke out in a rash. His skin was yellow and he had no strength; he could neither eat nor sleep, but he worked incessantly. I remember seeing poor, sensitive Gorsas[4] in tears at his condition, begging him to moderate his indignation. He was not yet aware that there had been a warrant out for his own arrest. I knew it, but was careful not to tell him for fear of adding to his distress. Someone told him of it a week later. It has to be admitted that he subsequently spoke of this personal predicament in a way which

---

[4] It must be recorded, however, that the 'sensitive' Gorsas had written in his *Courrier des 83 départements* that the September massacres were 'a necessary act of justice'.

enabled his enemies to suggest that his opposition to the executions was due to fear for his own neck. The truth was that his genuine horror of the atrocities had been enhanced merely by righteous indignation at being thought a possible victim himself....

Marat now began to revile us. I must explain that the Assembly had placed funds at the disposal of the Minister of the Interior for the printing of publicity material. Marat (who after 10 August had seized four presses from the Royal Printing House for the use of his own people, to replace four which he had previously been ordered to hand back) at once wrote to Roland asking for 15,000 livres to enable him to publish propaganda material. Roland replied that this was too great a sum for him to authorise without knowing what it was for; but that if Marat would send him the manuscripts he would leave it to the Council to decide whether they were suitable to be published at the public expense. Marat replied in a surly fashion, as he knows very well how, and sent along a pile of manuscripts the mere sight of which made one tremble. There was a treatise on 'Shackles of Slavery'[5] and I know not what else, all typical of Marat's outpourings.

I had sometimes wondered whether Marat was a real person; I now realised that there was nothing imaginary about him. I mentioned to Danton that I would like to meet him (for one must know these monsters) and I was curious to see whether he was a genuine fire-eater or just a windbag. Could Danton not bring him along? Danton excused himself; he clearly thought it would be useless and possibly disagreeable, Marat being an eccentric who would not respond to such an invitation. I could see that he would do nothing to satisfy my curiosity even if I were to insist, so I let it drop.

The Council's decision was that Marat's manuscripts should be handed over to Danton, and that they should arrange matters between them. This was truly a case of cutting the Gordian knot instead of untying it. The Minister of the Interior obviously could not have used public funds to subsidise such an extremist; but at the same time he did not want to make an enemy of the man. The Council should have given a straight refusal. By passing the decision to Danton they helped him to bring this mad dog under his

[5] Not published in France until 1792. An English translation had appeared in Edinburgh in 1774.

personal control, to savage and bite whomever it might please him to point to. Marat later had the impudence to attribute the request for the 15,000 livres to d'Orléans, complaining of the minister having refused it and naming me personally in one of his broadsheets. 'That is pure Danton,' I said to my husband. 'He is trying to attack you and begins by prowling around your family. He imagines that I shall be provoked into replying and that he may cast ridicule on the public figure to whom I am married. These people may have their own opinions about my abilities, but they have no understanding of my spirit. They can slander me to their hearts' content, they won't make me budge, or complain, or even care.'

Roland made his report on the state of Paris on 22 September. It was accurate and vigorous. He described the disorders which had taken place and pointed out the disastrous weakness of the public authorities and the growing exercise of arbitrary power by revolutionary committees. He gave credit to the Commune for its part in the events of 10 August, but argued that to prolong revolutionary methods was bound to be counter-productive. Tyrants are overthrown in order that justice and order may prevail, but anarchy is incompatible with both. He also explained the absolute necessity of obtaining accounts from the Commune, for which he had so long pleaded in vain.

The feeble Assembly applauded the speech and ordered it to be printed but gave no instructions and put nothing right. There is no more painful situation than that of an upright and steadfast man, at the head of a department where he seems to hold power and does in fact have great responsibility, witnessing day by day scandalous abuses which he can do nothing to prevent and on which the legislative body to which he is responsible cannot or dare not take a stand. The only effective way of restoring order in Paris would have been to dissolve the Commune, order the election of a new municipality, reorganise the forces of public order and provide them with a new commander chosen by the sections. Short of this it was futile to appeal to the law. I would rather have seen Roland serve his country as a simple deputy than as a member of an indolent Council and a minister in a government of inaction. ...

4

PORTRAITS
AND ANECDOTES

•◆•

The material to which Mme Roland gave this title was written between 8 and 31 August to replace what she believed had been lost. It consists of pen portraits of contemporary politicians, most of them unknown to the English-speaking reader, and of gossip relating to their political and private lives. In this selection I have concentrated on Buzot, because he was the man with whom Mme Roland fell in love, and on Brissot as the most important of the Girondin leaders with whom the Rolands had associated. A long diatribe against Danton, much of it covered elsewhere in the memoirs, has been omitted.

SAINTE-PÉLAGIE PRISON
8 AUGUST 1793

I HAVE NOW BEEN INCARCERATED for more than two months because I am married to a man who has shown himself to be upright in a time of revolution and incorruptible as a minister. For five months he tried in vain to have his accounts audited and his record cleared. The investigation had been completed but as nothing was found to his discredit they would not make their report and proceeded to slander him. Roland's energy, widespread activity and sharp pen had earned him a formidable reputation, or at any rate a reputation which the envious affected to believe formidable in their desire to undo him; for his integrity was hateful to them. They tried to arrest him at the time of the insurrection of 31 May, when the national representatives were humiliated and the decemvirate took over, but he escaped. In their fury they then seized me. But they would probably have done that anyway; they are well aware that, although my name may not carry as much weight, my character has no less strength than his. They wish to destroy me almost as much as they do Roland.

I devoted the first period of my captivity to writing; I wrote so rapidly and in such an excellent frame of mind that by the end of the first month I had enough manuscript to fill a whole volume. It consisted of detailed comment, under the title Historical Notes, on all the events and all the personalities connected with public life that my position had enabled me to know. I wrote with the freedom and energy which characterise me; I depicted with ease, and with a frankness quite above all personal considerations, what I had experienced and what I had felt. I believed that whatever might happen to me, this would be my moral and political testament. The circumstances lent it originality and it had the quality – and the freshness – of reflections set down in the heat of events.

When I had completed the task, bringing the story down to the most recent past, I entrusted the manuscripts to a friend. But the storm broke suddenly over his head. Seeing himself about to be arrested he thought only of the dangers and threw my manuscripts in the fire.[1] I must admit that I would rather have been thrown in the fire myself. This loss caused me more distress than anything else I have suffered. I am in despair. My end is very near; any day I may be slaughtered, or hauled before some tribunal where the tyrants get rid of troublesome people. These papers were a consolation to me. I hoped that they would justify my memory and the memory of so many worthy people. The death of Lauzun's spider in the Bastille[2] was not a crueller blow.

However, one must never give up and I shall now devote my leisure to jotting down, in no particular order, whatever comes into my head. These scraps will certainly not replace what I have lost but they will help to remind me of it and one day perhaps, if I am spared, I shall be able to fill them out.

BUZOT

Buzot is a man of elevated character, proud spirit and fiery courage; sensitive, ardent, but sometimes also melancholy and slothful. It must be admitted that on occasions he gets carried away. He is a passionate observer of nature and loves philosophy. He deserves domestic happiness; he would forget the whole world if he could live in quiet, virtuous communion with a soul-mate worthy of

[1] It was not Champagneux who burned the notebooks, but someone in his household, perhaps one of his sisters.

[2] Antonin de Caumont, duc de Lauzun. It seems that as a prisoner in the Bastille under the *ancien régime* he found consolation in the company of a spider, and that the governor walked in one day and crushed it. The story does not appear to be widely known today.

himself. In public life he recognises no rules but those of the strictest equity, and defends them at all costs. Easily roused against injustice, he challenges it without fear and will never compound with crime. Benevolent, susceptible to the tenderest affections, capable of sublime enthusiasm and of the most generous resolve, he loves his fellow men and is a devout republican. But he judges individuals severely. He is hard to please in friendship and accords his confidence to very few. This reserve and the energetic freedom with which he expresses himself have given him a reputation for pride and made him enemies amongst lesser men. Buzot is the gentlest man on earth to his friends and the toughest enemy of rogues. Although he is still young, the maturity of his judgement and the probity of his conduct earned him the admiration and confidence of his fellow citizens. He justified both by his devotion to the truth and by the firmness and perseverance with which he spoke it. Second-rate men, who depreciate anything that they cannot obtain themselves, called his foresight dreaming, his warmth passion, his powerful thoughts diatribes, his opposition to all forms of excess disrespect for majority opinion. He was accused of *royalism* because he believed that morality is necessary in a republic and should be upheld; of *slandering Paris* because he abhorred the September massacres; of *aristocracy* because he wanted the people to be allowed to exercise their sovereignty in the trial of Louis XVI;[3] and of *federalism* because he called for equality between all the departments of France and spoke against the municipal tyranny of the usurping Paris Commune. These were his 'crimes'. He also had his eccentricities. With a noble presence and elegant bearing, he preserved in his dress that care, neatness and decency which indicate an orderly mind, good taste and propriety and an honest man's respect for the public and for himself. ...

Buzot professed the morality of Socrates and preserved the good manners of Scipio. What a scoundrel! So the brigands led by ... Danton declared him a traitor to his country, razed his house to the ground and confiscated his goods, as once they banished Aristides and condemned Phocion. I am surprised that they did not order his name to be forgotten: that would have been more consistent with their views than to keep it alive with epithets attached which all the evidence refutes.

---

[3] After proposing an appeal to the people, Buzot voted for the death sentence 'with profound sorrow' and called for a reprieve.

They cannot efface Buzot's conduct in the Constituent Assembly nor suppress his wise motions and vigorous interventions in the Convention. Whatever may have been the swing of opinion in the faithless press, the principles upon which Buzot based his actions are still valid. He often improvised; he was not a hard worker, but he never failed to raise his voice against perverse systems harmful to liberty. His report on the *garde départementale*,[4] which has been so criticised, contains arguments which have not been refuted; that on the draft law against provocation to murder contains sound political sense and philosophy true as nature, strong as reason; his proposal relating to the banishment of the Bourbons, founded in justice, is written with elegance and feeling; his opinion on the trial of the King, packed with facts and argument, has none of the pathos and irrelevance with which this subject has been treated by so many speakers; and finally, his Letters to his constituents, from 6 to 22 January, offer future readers a true delineation of his character. A few more fighters like him might have given the Convention the necessary impulsion; the trouble was that the other men of ability, reserving themselves simply as orators for grand occasions, paid too little attention to the daily battle and seriously underestimated the tactics of their less talented adversaries. . . .

BRISSOT

Roland's relations with this celebrated man, about whom so many people still have a false or unclear opinion, are so bound up with the political life of each that it may be of interest to know how they were formed, what cemented them and what results they produced.

We lived in the district of Lyons, spending two winter months in that fine city, the autumn in the country and the rest of the year at Villefranche, devoting ourselves to study and to domestic cares, happy in the performance of voluntary work and charity. Roland was engaged on the *Encyclopédie méthodique* when he received from Brissot, whom we had never met, a copy of one of his works, I do not remember which. It was inscribed by the author as a mark of his esteem for Roland, whose publications, he wrote, reflected principles similar to his own on Liberty, on commerce, and on the sources of public welfare and prosperity.

---

[4] This was Mme Roland's pet idea of placing at the disposal of the Assembly a force recruited from all the departments of France.

Roland received this civility with the natural delight of an author whose writings have been appreciated and praised. In Brissot's work he recognised good sense and honesty and his reply was well calculated to establish confidence between the two men, who evidently looked on many things in the same light. A short while after that, one of our friends living in Paris with whom we were in regular touch wrote to say that he had met Brissot and had found him to be a philosopher whose simple life, high moral purpose and easy nature in no way contradicted his writings. This friend had evidently been much edified by Brissot's family life and attracted by his mind, and saw a great deal of him. He wrote to us often about him, and became the channel for a number of letters which Roland and Brissot exchanged with one another after their first literary contact. Then came the Revolution. Brissot threw himself into the midst of it with all the impetuosity of a man whose writings had helped it into being, who saw in it a means of regeneration for mankind and believed that it might justify his great hopes for the happiness of his fellow men.

We were detained in the country at that time by a serious illness which Roland only just survived, and we heard the details of what was happening in the capital from two friends who welcomed the Revolution with fervent hope and blind faith. I had hated kings since I was a child and I could never witness without an involuntary shudder the spectacle of a man abasing himself before another man. Roland and I, proud, energetic and deeply feeling, now talked of nothing but reform of the abuses which had so long offended us. We made plans, pointed the way, foretold the glorious future. Brissot was writing ceaselessly; he sent us everything. He started a journal and we passed all our ideas to him. I was normally responsible for Roland's correspondence, and I now found the task all the more agreeable. My fiery letters so pleased Brissot that he often used them in writing pieces for his journal (*Le Patriote français*), where I would discover them with surprise and pleasure. Our correspondence grew and bound us in friendship. More than eighteen months went by, in which we got to know one another and to become friends without ever having met. Perhaps only those who have experienced the emotions aroused by a revolution can appreciate the power they have of uniting people who have similar feelings. These political upheavals create a moral fermentation, in which opposing elements are separated off and homogeneous ones intimately merged.

In February 1791 Roland was specially deputed by the Commune of Lyons to represent its interest in the Constituent Assembly. We came to Paris with all possible eagerness. I had followed, through the published documents, the proceedings of the Assembly and the various opinions of its members. I had studied the character and the abilities of the leading men and I could hardly wait to see how far their persons would bear out the judgements I had formed.

I heard – but far too seldom – the astonishing Mirabeau, the only man in the Revolution who had the genius to sway men and to magnetise an Assembly; a great man in his abilities (though he had his faults), he stood head and shoulders above the rest and was the unquestioned master whenever he took the trouble to command. He died soon after. I thought at the time that this was timely for his reputation and for the cause of freedom, but subsequent events have taught me to regret him more. We needed the counterweight of such a man to oppose the depredations of a pack of curs and to save us from the domination of swindlers. ...

Needless to say, we had not been long in Paris before we met Brissot. He came to call on us. Nothing is more fascinating than the first encounter of people who are closely linked by correspondence but have never set eyes on one another. You look with curiosity to see whether the features of the face correspond to the physiognomy of the soul and whether the person's appearance confirms the opinion you have formed. Brissot's plain manners, his openness, his relaxed nature seemed to me to be in perfect harmony with the austerity of his principles; but I did detect a sort of lightness, both of intellect and of character, which sat ill with the gravity of a philosopher. This has always pained me in him and his enemies have not failed to take advantage of it. The better I have known him, the more I have valued him; there could not be a happier combination of total disinterestedness with zeal for the common good. But his writings are more effective than his person. Lacking a certain dignity, he does not inspire the same authority as his writings command through their rationality and truth. He is the best of men: good husband, loving father, faithful friend, virtuous citizen. His company is as agreeable as his character is easy. But it must also be said that he has a self-confidence amounting to imprudence, with the gaiety and ingenuousness of a schoolboy. It was his destiny to live among wise men and to be mocked by the unrighteous.

He is a well-informed political writer who from early youth has studied social conditions and thought about how to improve the human lot. He is an expert on Man but knows very little about men. He is aware that evil exists but cannot believe that anyone who looks him straight in the eye can be a villain. When he does recognise a bad man he treats him as if he were mad and to be pitied. He cannot hate: one might say that any feeling so vigorous as that is too strong for his sensitive nature. He knows a lot and he writes easily: he will dash off an article as another might copy out a song. In some of his writings, despite their serious content, there is hastiness and a touch of levity and his boisterous energy gives him the air of interfering in everybody's business. People looking for something of which to accuse him say that he is an intriguer, but that is hardly the word for a man who never thinks of himself, is incapable of looking after his own interests and is not ashamed of poverty or afraid of death. He devoted all his time to the Revolution with no other aim than the public good. He made nothing out of the journal which he edited with so much care and was content to let his partner make a small fortune from it.

His wife was as retiring as he, but more hard-headed. She admired her husband's devotion to the cause and would help him when she could, but basically she thought France unworthy of liberty and that anyone who attempted to promote it was wasting his time. Ever since their marriage she had had her eyes on the United States as the country most suited to their tastes. They felt sure that they could set themselves up there with limited means, and Brissot had been over to prospect. They were on the point of emigrating when the Revolution caught him in its toils.

Brissot had been born in Chartres, where he was a school-fellow of Pétion. They became more closely acquainted in the Constituent Assembly and it was there that he introduced us to Pétion and to the other like-minded deputies. ...

I loved political life, its talk, its intrigues. I had been well prepared for it by my habit of hard work, my study of history, my taste for philosophy and my devouring passion for human relationships. I do not mean the petty intrigues of a court or the sterile controversies of gossips and fools, but the true art of politics, the art of ruling men and organising their happiness in society. I do not often talk of it, because discussion of this kind does not suit a woman. Women who pronounce on affairs of state always sound to me like yesterday's newspaper. But no subject, to my mind, is more worthwhile. I occasionally discuss politics with my close friends, but otherwise I let the men do the talking. I particularly enjoy listening to old men who imagine that every word they say is a revelation to the listener and who think that all I am capable of is stitching a shirt and adding up figures.

I was not always satisfied with the committee.[5] Not that its meetings ever seemed useless, for there was always interesting talk; but they seldom led to any conclusion. ...The French are no good at discussion. They have a sort of levity; they skip from subject to subject without proper order and never pursue anyone's thesis to a conclusion. They are not good listeners ... Their attention is easily diverted; a single word will make them laugh and then the theme of the discussion may be lost in pleasantries.

I have had the same impression in the National Assembly, in the Jacobin Society and in smaller groups. Such people are not serious enough to be free. Bind them in chains of flowers and they will play happily. But of course times may now have changed. The national character has altered dramatically in the last twelve months and misery may compel us to be serious. But I fear that we may first have to pass through a period of ferocity whose results no one can foretell.

ROBESPIERRE

Robespierre's behaviour during the sessions in my house was extraordinary. He spoke little, sneered a great deal and threw out sarcastic asides, but never gave a straight opinion. If there was any coherent discussion he would take pains to appear in the Assembly the following day and make use of what he had heard his friends say. They sometimes reproached him about this. He would excuse himself with a joke and they would overlook it as the product of an insatiable *amour propre*. But it did undermine confidence. If they wanted to follow some agreed course of action, and to allot tasks to one another in pursuit of it, they could never be sure that Robespierre would not give the game away and upset the whole thing by trying to take the credit for himself. I thought then that Robespierre was a genuine libertarian and I attributed his faults to excessive zeal. He had a kind of reserve which could either have

[5] The group of deputies of the left with whom the Rolands were associated.

[81]

been lack of self-confidence or over-suspicion of others. I did not like him, but I did put his reserve down to timidity. It is easy enough, when one is prejudiced in a person's favour, to interpret the worst signs as signs of grace. No confident smile ever rested on Robespierre's lips: they were almost always curled in a bitter, envious sneer intended to pass for disdain. He was a very poor orator. His trivial tone of voice, unpleasant expressions and atrocious delivery made his utterances infinitely tedious. But he defended his principles with heat and obstinacy and had the courage to continue doing so when there were very few others still on the side of the people. The Court hated and abused him; patriots were obliged to support and encourage him. I respected Robespierre for these qualities, and showed it, and even at times when he came rarely to the little group he occasionally invited himself to dinner.

I had noticed how terrified he was on the day of the King's flight to Varennes. I found him that afternoon at Pétion's house, where he was muttering nervously that the royal family could not have taken this step unless they were sure of having friends in Paris ready to murder all the patriots. He did not expect to live another twenty-four hours. Pétion and Brissot on the contrary were arguing that the King's flight was his undoing and that advantage must be taken of it. They thought that, after this, public opinion would be even more convinced of the Court's perfidy and of the King's disloyalty to the Constitution. The time had come, they said, for a more root-and-branch solution; opinion should now be prepared for the idea of a Republic. Robespierre, sneering as usual and biting his nails, asked what was meant by a Republic. That was the point at which they thought of founding a newspaper entitled Le Républicain. (In the event it ran for only two issues.)

The arrest of Louis XVI delighted Robespierre. He thought that it solved all the problems and he ceased being afraid for his life. But the others were not so pleased: they feared that it would bring the curse of intrigue back into the government and that the excitable and fickle populace, once they saw the criminal brought to book, would no longer feel it necessary to support the true friends of freedom. They were quite right. The reconciliation between Lafayette and the Lameth Brothers[6] brought into being another

---

[6] Charles and Alexandre de Lameth: Deputies for the *noblesse* in the Estates-General; they both survived the Revolution.

right-wing combination which could be opposed only by really effective popular opposition. The patriots have always relied on the power of their pens and their brains. They have never had a grass-roots following, and whenever any truly popular force came forward to support them they were inclined to welcome it without looking too carefully into its origins. So it was now. There was an interested party, Philippe d'Orléans, lurking in the background. He was being so vigorously attacked by the aristocrats that the patriots were tempted to think that he might be useful in the common cause, not realising what a dangerous ally he could be.

It is very difficult, if not impossible, to make a revolution without becoming emotional. The obstacles are so great that leaders have to be in a sort of perpetual frenzy in order to overcome them; they will seize hold of any support and all too easily lose their ability to judge which friends might be dangerous ... In isolation d'Orléans presented no threat, but his name, his connections and his wealth gave him great influence. There is no doubt he was secretly encouraging much of the popular agitation. Genuine democrats suspected this but considered it to be part of the leverage necessary to shift the inert mass of the *ancien régime*. They thought that so long as they themselves took no part in his intrigues they could safely make use of them in the public interest. They also imagined that d'Orléans was more interested in humiliating the Court that had spurned him than in seeking power for himself.

The Jacobins drew up a petition to the Assembly calling for the condemnation of the King. They had been put up to this by Laclos, an intimate supporter of d'Orléans, who suggested a final article providing for the retention of the monarchy in terms which would have served the personal ambitions of d'Orléans. Brissot, when asked to support the resolution, refused to accept this last article, but it appeared nevertheless in the version which was printed and distributed in the name of the Jacobin Society. However, when they all met the following day to finalise their petition they learned that the National Assembly had already determined the fate of the King. So they sent their commissioners to the Champ de Mars to inform the crowds gathered there that the petition was withdrawn. I happened to be there. There were not more than two or three hundred people scattered about round the 'altar of the Republic' and they were being harangued by speakers from various 'fraternal societies' carrying pikestaffs with slogans hostile to the King. When it was announced that the Jacobins' petition was withdrawn there was a loud demand that all zealous citizens should meet next day to prepare another. At this point the partisans of the Court decided to use force: in a quick and unexpected move they declared martial law and attempted to impose it, leading to what has been justly called the 'Massacre of the Champ de Mars'. ...

I have never seen anything like Robespierre's terror on this occasion. There was talk of putting him on trial, probably to intimidate him, and of some plot being hatched against him and the other authors of the Jacobins' petition. Roland and I were seriously worried about his safety. We had ourselves driven to his house, deep in the Marais, at eleven o'clock at night in order to offer him asylum.[7] But he had left home. So we went to Buzot's house to enlist his help.... Buzot behaved in all this with the utmost rectitude and courage. He is the epitome of probity as well as being very caring by nature. I had already singled him out in our little circle for his breadth of vision and confident manner. He lived not far from us. His wife was a good woman, though not worthy of him, and we saw a lot of them. When Roland had successfully completed his mission regarding the debts of the city of Lyons and we went back to Beaujolais after seven months in Paris, we kept in touch with Buzot and with Robespierre. The correspondence with Buzot was the more extensive: we had more in common, and a more solid basis for mutual understanding. Our friendship became intimate and unbreakable. ...

[7] This story is contested by Robespierre's biographers.

5

FIRST TERM OF OFFICE

23 March – 13 June 1792

•◆•

L OUIS XVI SHOWED THE GREATEST FRIENDLINESS to his new ministers. This King was not quite what his critics like to pretend. He was certainly not the imbecile they make him out to be, but neither was he honest and straightforward as his friends claimed. By nature he was a perfectly ordinary man who would have done quite well in an obscure station. Unfortunately his character had been ruined by the experience of kingship: he was fatally inadequate in a position where only the highest virtue and genius could have saved him. Having been brought up close to the throne and taught from his earliest youth to dissimulate, he had acquired certain useful tricks for dealing with men. He knew how to prevent people from seeing more of his intentions than he thought fit, and everyone found that very clever. You would have to be born a fool to seem stupid in such a situation. Louis XVI had an excellent memory and was very active. He was never idle and he read a lot. He carried in his head all France's treaties with foreign states; he knew French history and he was the best geographer in his kingdom. He had an extraordinary memory for names and had no difficulty in matching them with the faces of members of his Court or in remembering anecdotes connected with each individual. He extended this faculty to cover all the figures who emerged during the Revolution. It was impossible to recommend a man for any employment without finding that the King knew something about him, based on a few facts. But having no high principles, no intellectual conviction and no strength of character, he suffered from having had his outlook narrowed and his feelings falsified, if I may so express it, by religious prejudice and jesuitical modes of thought.

Great religious ideas, the belief in God and the hope of immortality, consort very well with philosophy; they give it a firm base and are its crowning glory. No statesman can ignore these forces with impunity. If the human race had no illusions it would need to create them for its own consolation. But the religion offered by our priests is based on childish fears and sets superstitious practices above good works. It also supports all the maxims of despotism on which its own authority depends. Louis XVI was afraid of hell-fire and of excommunication: this could not fail to make him a bad king. If he had been born two hundred years earlier and had had a sensible wife, he would have been no better remembered than so many other rulers who have come and gone without doing any good or any harm. But it was his misfortune to approach the throne in the midst of the excesses of Louis XV's Court, surrounded by financial disorder and corrupt advisers. He was carried along by a giddy, self-indulgent and frivolous woman who combined Austrian arrogance with an affectation of youth and nobility, and who had herself been corrupted by the vices of an oriental court in which her mother had set her a dreadful example. Louis XVI, too feeble to control a régime already heading for ruin, hastened their common destruction with mistakes innumerable.

Necker was a man who cultivated a bombastic tone both in politics and in his personal style, a mediocre man who was admired only because he had such a high opinion of himself and expressed it so freely. He had no foresight whatever. As a financier he could just about count the money in his purse and he went around talking of his own merits in the way in which a loose woman talks of her chastity. Necker was a bad pilot for the storms ahead. France seemed to be entirely drained of men. The absence of any real leadership has been the most distinctive feature of this revolution; nothing but pigmies are to be seen. It is not that there is any lack of wit, enlightenment, knowledge, accomplishment or philosophy: these qualities have never been so common, as if the torch were emitting a final blaze before going out altogether. But where can one find that *greatness of soul* which Jean-Jacques [Rousseau] has so well defined as the first attribute of the hero? Where do we find a complete man, combining true understanding of the present with a far-sighted vision of the future? Hardly anywhere, however far one looks.

Louis XVI, forever floating between his fear of annoying his subjects and his inability to govern them, summoned the Estates-General instead of regulating his expenditure and putting his Court in order. Having thus opened the gate to reform, he attempted to stifle it by applying the royal authority to which he himself had just created a forum of opposition. This simply invited resistance. If he had had the sense to give up a part of his authority with good grace he could have retained the other part and might even have been able to recover his position entirely. But he had not the wit. He descended to a level of miserable intrigue suited to the second-rate advisers whom he chose and whom his wife protected. If he had only been satisfied with the powers reserved to him under the Constitution, he could have enjoyed a comfortable rule. Having failed to prevent this Constitution from being established, he could nevertheless have saved himself if he had shown good faith and tried sincerely to make it work. But he constantly undermined the arrangements which he was professing to support. This two-faced behaviour inevitably led to suspicion and finally to defiance.

When he took patriotic ministers into his Council he set himself out to gain their confidence. In this he succeeded so well that for three weeks I saw Roland and Clavière charmed by the King's disposition, dreaming of a rosy future and flattering themselves that the Revolution was at an end. 'Good God!' I said. 'Each time I see you two go off to the Council with that confident look on your faces I feel sure that you must be going to commit some folly.' 'But I assure you', replied Clavière, 'that the King knows it is in his interest to support the new laws. It is clear from everything he says that he is convinced of this.' And Roland added: 'If he is not sincere on this he must be the biggest liar in the kingdom. You can't pretend to that extent.' To which I replied that I could not believe in the loyalty to the Constitution of a man born and bred in the practice of despotism and whose recent behaviour showed such instability. The flight to Varennes was my great argument.

The Council's meetings at that time were conducted in a fairly orderly fashion compared with what they later became. But the procedure was quite puerile considering the grave issues with which they had to deal. Any minister who had papers for signature on which no general discussion was needed called on the King at a fixed hour before the Council met. When these individual sessions were over they all proceeded to the Council Chamber, where proclamations that needed to be discussed were laid on the table and the Minister of Justice presented decrees for the royal sanction. Finally they got down, or should have got down, to the consideration of government policy on internal order, relations with foreign powers, peace and war, etc. As to current orders and regulations, they did no more than glance at the text and discuss the timing.

The King let his ministers do the talking, read the *Gazette* or the

English newspapers and wrote letters. He paid attention only when invited to approve decrees. He never rejected these outright but always made difficulties. He would never accept a decree first time round, but remitted it to the next meeting, when he would arrive with his opinion made up, giving the impression that he had been guided by the discussion.

He usually avoided great political issues, turning the conversation to current topics or to some subject which concerned a particular minister. If the subject for discussion was war, he talked about travel; if diplomatic relations with another country, he discussed the manners and habits of that country or asked questions about places in it; if domestic matters, he would concentrate on some detail of agriculture or industry. He questioned Roland about his writings, Dumouriez about his adventures and so on. The Council was like some coffee-house where they amused themselves with chatter. No record was kept of the deliberations and there was no secretary to make one. They emerged after three or four hours having done nothing but affix a few signatures; and they did this three times a week. 'But it is pitiful!' I cried with exasperation when Roland came home and told me what had passed. 'You are all in a state of euphoria because you have not been scolded and he has even been quite polite to you. It seems to me that each one of you does whatever he likes in his own department. I am afraid you are all being fooled.' 'But things are going quite well,' he replied. 'Yes, and time is being lost. I would rather you spent three hours alone thinking about grand strategy than waste your time in this sort of useless chatter.'

France's enemies were preparing themselves and war had been declared. This step had been endlessly debated and the King seemed to have accepted it, though with extreme reluctance. He delayed the decision for a long time and seems only to have been persuaded by the opinion, which had long been known, of the majority of the Assembly and the whole of his Council. The continuation – and the spread – of religious unrest soon forced him to agree also to the corrective measures which Roland had for some time been advocating. Meanwhile foreign troops were boldly advancing on our territory and there was great alarm. The Minister of War had an idea for the disposition of forces which the Assembly had greeted with enthusiasm and voted for on the spot.

Two draft decrees, one for the establishment of a camp of 20,000 men to the north of Paris and the other for dealing with the priests,[1] became critical at this time. The Court saw in them a threat to its own secret designs, which included local risings supported by the clergy and the advance of foreign enemies. The King was determined to refuse his sanction but too clever to say so at once. On various pretexts he avoided the issue for more than a fortnight. Roland and Servan pressed him vigorously, because each felt the importance and the necessity of the law for his own particular department. Everyone could see the national interest, and the six ministers were united on the point. But in the meantime Dumouriez, whose joviality was so popular with the King and whose way of life brought him into close contact with the Court, was several times summoned to see the Queen. He had a grudge to repay and he was keen to rid himself of colleagues whose austerity did not suit his style. He entered into a secret agreement with the Court which soon bore dramatic fruit.

I find it hard to describe my agitation at that time. I was passionate for the Revolution. I thought that the Constitution, whatever its faults, must be made to work. I burned with zeal for the prosperity of my country. Public affairs had become a torment to me, a moral fever which left me no rest. The King's procrastination over the two decrees proved his lack of good faith: of that Roland was now at last convinced. There was only one choice for an honourable minister: he must resign if the King still refused consent to the measures necessary to save the kingdom.

For the conscience of a timid man, this simple decision would perhaps have been enough. But to a citizen of Roland's stamp it was not just a question of leaving a post where he could no longer do any good: he must make his gesture openly and vigorously, so as to enlighten public opinion about the evils which had led to it and turn his resignation to good account for the Republic. Roland and I had already begun to despair of the weakness of his colleagues. While the King was still hesitating we had the idea of sending him a collective letter, setting out all the arguments already put forward in the Council and tendering the resignation of all the ministers if His Majesty would not accede to their demands. We thought that a written protest of this kind, signed by all the ministers, would force the King's hand or expose him in the eyes of all France. I had sketched out the letter, after agreeing its broad lines with Roland, and he put it to his colleagues for their approval. They were all in

[1] A proposal to exile refractory priests.

favour of the general idea but on the execution there was every sort
of difference. Clavière wanted various phrases taken out; Duranthon[2] wanted delay; Lacoste[3] was in no hurry to sign. A step of this
kind can be effective when it results from a flash of united feeling;
the failure of our first attempt to obtain this warned us not to repeat
it, and we were thrown back on the idea of an isolated move. Since
the Council had not enough character to make a common
pronouncement, it was incumbent on the man who felt himself
above these events to take the rôle upon himself. It was no longer
a question of offering his resignation, but of fighting dismissal. It
was a moment for confrontation.

I drafted the famous letter....

*The consequences of this action had been described by Mme Roland in a
previous section of her memoirs. The passage is placed here in order to
give chronological continuity to the narrative.*

Roland took the letter with him to the Council, meaning to read it
aloud; but on that day the King, pressed again about the decrees,
stopped discussion by inviting each minister to send his opinion in
writing, signed; and then passed rapidly on to other business.
Roland came home, added a short covering note to his letter, and
had it delivered into His Majesty's hands on 11 June in the
morning. The next day, 12 June, at eight o'clock in the evening,
Servan arrived with a delighted expression on his face.
'Congratulate me,' he said, 'I have had the honour to be sacked.'
'My husband is likely to join you before long,' I replied, 'I am only
sorry that you should be ahead of him.' He then told me that he had
waited upon the King that morning in order to discuss some
confidential matter and that the King had lectured him about the
camp for 20,000 men and had turned angrily from him. He also
said that Dumouriez had just come from the War Office where he
had taken possession of the minister's portfolio by virtue of an
order which he carried on his person. 'Ah! Dumouriez,' I said, 'he
must be playing a double game, and it does not surprise me.' On the
three previous days he had had long conferences at the Tuileries
with the Queen. When Roland heard the news he summoned all his
colleagues (except Dumouriez) to meet him.

[2] Antoine Duranthon (1736–93): Minister of Justice, April–July 1792;
guillotined at Bordeaux, 20 Dec. 1793.
[3] Jean de Lacoste (1730–1820): Minister of Marine, March–July 1792.

His advice was that they should not wait to be dismissed but that those who shared Servan's opinions should say that they would resign unless the King brought him back. They should also demand the dismissal of Dumouriez. I have no doubt that if the four ministers had done that, the Court would have had difficulty in replacing them. Lacoste and Duranthon would have taken courage and the affair would have made a striking impact on the public. As it was, it turned out very differently.

The ministers arrived; they had a discussion but reached no decision except to meet again at eight o'clock the following morning. Roland was to draft them a letter. I would never have thought, if I had not seen it with my own eyes, that good judgement and firmness of character were such rare commodities and that so few men are fit to govern. As for expecting these qualities to be combined with honesty, it is asking for the moon. I am not surprised that men of superior understanding who govern nations usually have such a low opinion of humanity; it seems an almost unavoidable consequence of knowing the world too well. Men responsible for the happiness of nations need an extraordinary fund of philosophy and magnanimity to avoid these faults.

The ministers arrived at the rendezvous next morning. They were doubtful about the letter and ended by deciding that it would be better to go and talk to the King. This struck me as being a form of evasion; no one speaks with as much force as he writes to someone he is accustomed to looking up to. It was decided to go and find Lacoste, who had not turned up, and get him to join them. Hardly had they all sat down in the Ministry of Marine when a message arrived from the King ordering Duranthon to present himself, alone, at the Palace immediately. Clavière and Roland said they would await his return at the Chancellery. They did not wait long. He came back with a long face and slowly drew from his pocket an order from the King for each of his colleagues. 'Hand it over,' said Roland, laughing, 'I see that we have lost the initiative.' It was their dismissal.

When he got home I said to Roland 'This is good news. But we must not wait for the King to announce it in the Assembly. As he has ignored your advice we must quickly make your position clear to the public. You wrote to the King in the first place; now you must boldly send a copy to the Assembly.' My husband liked this idea and it was done. The Assembly honoured the three dismissed ministers by declaring that they carried with them the nation's regrets and ordered the letter to be printed and sent to the departments. I am convinced, and I think the event has confirmed, that this letter did much to enlighten France. It set out so forcibly and clearly what the King ought to do in his own interest that the only conclusion to be drawn from his rejecting it was that he had no intention of maintaining the Constitution. ...

I pause here for a moment to relieve the doubts and to correct the opinion of those who think that any credit given to me must be at the expense of my husband, or that I had an influence in public life which I never did have. The habits and tastes of a studious life made it natural that I should take a share in my husband's work. Before he ever became a public figure I used to write with him, just as I took my meals with him: the one thing was as natural as the other. Since I lived only for his happiness I devoted myself to whatever gave him the greatest pleasure. If he wrote about the mechanical arts I did so too, though the subject bored me. He liked to be well informed, so we did research together. He enjoyed sending literary contributions to academies; we would work on them jointly, or each of us make a separate draft, compare the two and pick the better one or combine them. If he had written sermons, I would have written sermons too. Then he became a minister. I never involved myself with the administration in any way, but if a circular was required, or an instruction, or any other important public paper, we put our heads together as we had always done. I was steeped in his ideas and teeming with thoughts of my own. It was I, usually, who took up the pen because I had more leisure than he, but since our principles and spirit were the same we ended up by agreeing in our methods too. My husband lost nothing by being interpreted through me. There was nothing I could express, in point of justice or reason, that he was not capable of realising and sustaining by his character and conduct. I could give a fairer picture than he could of his achievements and his intentions. Roland without me would have been no less good an administrator; his energy and his experience are all his own, as is his probity. But with me he has made more mark, because I have been able to inject into his writings a combination of strength and gentleness, reason and sentiment such as perhaps only a woman can provide whose sensitive soul is matched with a practical mind. I delighted in writing pieces for him which I thought would be useful, and when I saw them in print it gave me greater pleasure than if I had been known to be the author. I am avid for happiness and I find it most in the good which I can do; I have no need for fame. Nothing suits me better than acting as a sort of Providence in the background. Carpers are welcome to regard this confession as an impertinence; those who know me will see it as typical of my sincerity. ...

I have mentioned that, in aligning himself with the Court against his colleagues, Dumouriez was taking revenge for an injury. This is how it came about.

Dumouriez had chosen as his principal assistant, and had appointed Director-General of the Ministry of Foreign Affairs, one Bonnecarrère,[4] bearer of the cross of St Louis (which Dumouriez had obtained for him), a good-looking young man with the reputation and habits of an intriguer. I have met him only once, when Dumouriez brought him to dinner, and I was no more attracted by his good looks than I had been by those of Hérault de Séchelles. 'These fine fellows', I said to a friend, 'seem to me poor patriots. They appear to love themselves more than they love the general good and I can never resist the temptation to prick their vanity by failing to notice the merits of which they are so proud.'

I had several times heard this appointment criticised by serious men, deputies, the sort who used to believe in honour and are nowadays held in contempt on that account. It was urged that patriot ministers ought to be particularly careful, when making appointments of this kind, to make sure that there is absolute probity in all parts of the administration. I know that some gentle remonstrances were made to Dumouriez at the time, and that he brushed them aside with praise of Bonnecarrère's intelligence and talents. (His wit, resource and artfulness cannot be denied.) But then there began to be talk of a financial deal, managed by Bonnecarrère, under which 100,000 livres were deposited with a notary, partly for the benefit of Mme de Beauvert. She was Dumouriez' mistress, a loose lady, the sister of Rivarol, who moved in corrupt and immoral aristocratic circles. I forget the details of the affair and the people concerned, but they were well known at the time. It was agreed that Dumouriez must be spoken to and persuaded to dismiss Bonnecarrère. He must be told that unless he preserved – or at least appeared to preserve – the decencies he could

---

[4] Guillaume Bonnecarrère (1754–1825): he had been dismissed in 1791 from the Jacobin Club, where he had held the positions of President and Secretary.

no longer remain in the ministry. Gensonné, who knew Dumouriez well, and Brissot, to whom Bonnecarrère's failings had been denounced, agreed to speak to him at our house in the presence of Roland himself and three or four other colleagues. And so, having dined at my table and retired to the study where I usually worked, they confronted Dumouriez. Roland, with the gravity of his age and of his character, allowed himself to insist on the seriousness of the affair as affecting the whole government. Dumouriez was not accustomed to this sort of pressure or to being criticised in this way. He tried to pass it off lightly, but when pressed became angry and left in high dudgeon. From that moment he ceased seeing these deputies and would not meet them at my house. Reflecting on his behaviour, I told Roland that, though I was not used to intrigue, I thought that, the world being what it was, it was time to undo Dumouriez if they did not want to be undone by him. 'I know very well', I said, 'that you would not stoop to such a game but you must realise that Dumouriez is bound to try and rid himself of men who have censored him so roughly. If you give a man a lecture and it does not come off, you must either suppress him or expect to be suppressed yourselves.'

Dumouriez, who loved Bonnecarrère, told him at once all that had passed. Then followed a typical intrigue. Bonnecarrère, who had access to the Queen through his relations with certain of her ladies, suppressed the evidence of his financial deal. The famous decrees came up for the King's approval and Dumouriez, though he was in favour of the measures themselves, managed to convince the Court of his loyalty and eased the way for the sacking of his patriot colleagues, partly by suggesting successors and partly by himself accepting the Ministry of War. He did not keep this appointment long, for the Court, glad enough to keep him for the time being in order not to be seen to get rid of all the patriot ministers at the same time, dismissed him shortly afterwards. But he was clever enough to avoid complete disgrace and obtained employment in the army at his serving rank.

The patriots themselves still imagined that they could make use of his talents in the military sphere. One of the great problems facing the government after 10 August had been finding good candidates for public office, particularly in the army. Under the *ancien régime* only members of the nobility had been accepted as officers, so that military knowledge and experience were confined to that order. The people were naturally concerned at seeing the force responsible for defending the Constitution commanded by officers who were opposed to it. They could not judge, as more experienced leaders could, how much confidence was to be placed on this man's character, that man's loyalties or principles. Demagogues exaggerated their fears and stimulated their suspicions. As throughout history, from Hippo the tub-thumper of Syracuse down to Robespierre the Parisian chatterbox, these professional carpers will always abuse those in authority and covet the highest places for themselves.

When Roland came back into office he thought it was in the public interest that he should be reconciled with Dumouriez. Each in his own way, after all, was expected to serve the Republic. 'The uncertainties of politics', he wrote, 'are as varied as those of war. I find myself again in the Council, you command the armies. You may now wipe out the errors of your ministry by glorious achievements in the field. You were led into an intrigue which made you play false with your colleagues and were betrayed in your turn by the Court which you had tried to accommodate. You remind me of those *preux chevaliers* who would often commit small villainies which they were the first to repent but would fight like tigers when honour was at stake. This behaviour may not accord well with republican austerity, but it is the consequence of habits which we have not yet shaken off. You will be forgiven if you bring home victory. You will find me ever ready, in the Council, to support your enterprises when they are aimed at the public good; I have no personal feelings when the national interest is at stake, and I shall cherish you as one of the saviours of my country if you devote yourself sincerely to its defence.' Dumouriez sent a worthy reply and proceeded to fight worthily. He repulsed the Prussians. I remember that there was some hope at that time of detaching them from the alliance and some negotiations to that end took place, but nothing came of it. After the enemy had evacuated our territory he came to Paris to prepare the operations against Belgium. Roland saw him in the Council and I received him to dinner, once only, with a number of others. When he entered my apartment he looked somewhat embarrassed and offered me, rather clumsily for so self-assured a man, a charming bouquet of flowers. I smiled and said that fortune played some strange tricks and that I did not suppose he ever expected to be received by me again in this same apartment; but that I gratefully accepted the flowers he offered me, coming so fitly from the hand that had conquered the Prussians. He suggested that we should go to the Opéra after dinner. I saw at once that he was typical of the sort of general who wants to show himself off in the theatre and looks for paper crowns whenever he has won an engagement.

Someone asked me whether I would not go too. I avoided answering because it does not suit my character or my reputation to appear in public with Dumouriez. But when the company had gone, I suggested to Vergniaud that he should come with me and my daughter to my box. When we arrived, the embarrassed box attendant told me that the minister's box was occupied. 'But that is not possible,' I said, for I knew that entry tó the box was by a ticket signed by my husband and I had not given one to anyone. 'The minister insisted on entering,' she said. 'No, it cannot be him, open the door and let me see who it is.' Three or four *sans-culottes* were standing about outside the door, 'Mustn't go in there,' they said, 'the minister is there.' But the woman said she had no choice and opened the door. Inside I saw the gross figure of Danton and Fabre and three or four dowdy-looking women. The play had begun and they were looking at the stage. Danton was leaning over to the neighbouring box and I just caught sight of Dumouriez there, talking to him. I quickly withdrew without any of them having seen me and closed the door. 'You are right,' I said to the box attendant, 'it is an ex-Minister of Justice. I will leave him to his impertinence rather than have a scene with him. I have no place here.' And I walked out, reflecting that Danton had at any rate saved me the embarrassment of finding myself so close to Dumouriez. I heard afterwards that Danton and Fabre constantly accompanied Dumouriez to shows where he was foolish enough to display himself. I myself never saw him again. This is the extent of our relations with a man they now accuse us of aiding and abetting in his treason.

Dumouriez is energetic, vigilant, amusing and brave, just made for war and for intrigue. He is a capable officer and even his jealous colleagues thought him the only one of them fit to command a great army. But in character and in morality he was more suited to the old Court than to the new régime. He has imagination and courage but lacks stability and self-control. He can hatch a plot but he is too indiscreet to keep it to himself. In short, too hot-headed to be the leader of a party.

I am sure that Dumouriez did not go to Belgium with the intention of betraying his country; he would have served a

Republic or a King with equal enthusiasm if he could have seen glory and profit in it for himself. But the rotten decrees of the Convention, the appalling behaviour of the commissioners and the follies of the executive destroyed our cause in that country. Everything was in turmoil there and he had the idea of changing course. He tied himself up in his own contrivances through imprudence and immaturity.

Dumouriez must have been very good company at male revels and with women who have no morals: he still carries about with him a sort of juvenile petulance and gaiety, a lively and unrestrained imagination. When he is with reserved women like me there is something forced in his politeness. He amused the King at Council meetings with outrageous stories at which even his graver colleagues could not help laughing, occasionally interspersing them with bold and witty home truths. What a difference between this man, vicious as he was, and Luckner,[5] who was for a while the hope of France. I have never seen anything so second-rate in my life. An old soldier, half besotted, witless, spineless, a sort of nobody whom the most primitive monkey could lead by the nose! Bad language, a taste for wine, a few oaths and a certain intrepidity had made him popular in the army where mercenary automata will always fawn on anyone who claps them on the back, treats them with familiarity and has them punished from time to time. I once had him to dinner during Roland's first ministry and had to endure his conversation for four or five hours. 'Poor France,' I said next day to Gaudet when he asked me how I had found Luckner, 'Poor France! You must certainly be done for if we have to go looking beyond our shores for such a creature to protect our future.' I know nothing about tactics and Luckner may well have understood the technicalities of his job, but I do know that nobody can be a good commander if he has no reasoning power and no intelligence.

Since my husband's promotion gave me the opportunity to meet a great many people and especially people concerned with important affairs, the thing that has struck me most has been their universal mediocrity. It passes all imagination. You see it at every level, from the clerk who needs brains only to understand the question, some sense of order and enough style to write a letter, to

[5] Baron Nicolas de Luckner (1722–94): born in the Palatinate: entered at an early age into the service of France; Lt-General, 1763; Marshal of France, 1791; C.-in-C., Army of the North, 1792; guillotined 4 Jan. 1794.

the minister in charge of government, the general commanding the armies and the ambassador negotiating with foreign powers. I would never have believed that my countrymen were such poor creatures. The experience has certainly given me confidence; up until then I had been as modest as a convent schoolgirl. I always assumed that anyone bolder than me must also be cleverer than me. Really! I am not surprised that I was much sought after. They could see that I was worth something. Yet I was quite sincere in respecting other people's *amour propre*.

With such a dearth of quality, and the Revolution having successively done away with anyone who by birth, fortune, education or circumstance was in any way superior to the general level, it is hardly surprising that we have fallen step by step under the dominion of crass ignorance and shameful incompetence. . . .

6

SECOND TERM OF OFFICE

10 August 1792 – 22 January 1793

•◆•

W HEN ROLAND, CLAVIÈRE AND SERVAN WERE BROUGHT BACK the government was completed by the addition of Danton, whom I have described elsewhere, and by the appointment of Monge[1] to the Marine and of Le Brun[2] to Foreign Affairs. It was extremely difficult to find suitable men for public office in those circumstances. Anyone who had had the remotest connection with the Court either directly or indirectly was automatically ruled out by public opinion. Even a man like Servan was only just acceptable because of the clear evidence of patriotism which he had recently displayed. Those who had to make the choice were ill equipped to do so; most of our legislators had been in public life a very short time and had little experience of men or of affairs. There was a long and painful argument in the Committee when Monge's name came up. He had worked with Condorcet at the Académie and his patriotism was well known. He was a mathematician and an academic, a virtuous citizen and a respectable family man. The rival candidate was Meusnier, another mathematician and member of the Académie: but someone remembered having seen him 'kowtow to aristocrats', so the choice went to Monge.

Monge was a stolid, hearty man who had started life as a stonemason in Mézières. Father Bossut had taken him up, subsidised him to the tune of six livres a week and introduced him to mathematics. He had come up in the world, but being accustomed to handling intractable materials and inflexible figures he had little understanding of men or of administration. I always found him heavy and tiresome, and when he was trying to be agreeable he reminded me of a bear in the Berne bear-pit clumsily entertaining the passers-by. He filled his ministry with incapable officials and

---

[1] Gaspard Monge, comte de Peluse (1746–1818): celebrated mathematician; Minister of Marine, 10 Aug. 1792–April 1793.
[2] Pierre Lebrun-Tondu (1763–93) was arrested on 2 June 1793 and guillotined on the following 27 Dec.

allowed the Marine to become completely disorganised. To do him justice, he knew that he was no good and wanted to resign, but as they could find none better they persuaded him to stay. When Pache became a minister Monge fell completely under his thumb and from having been a man with a degree of decent feeling he became, as it were, Maratised and defended the most bloody and atrocious Terror.

When he was at the Ministry of Foreign Affairs Le Brun passed for a wise man because he had no enthusiasms of any sort and for an able man because he was a competent clerk. He knew his diplomatic business pretty well and could draft a reasonable dispatch or letter. In normal times he would have been very well suited to that department, where the work is minimal and what there is is most agreeable. But he lacked the intelligence and enterprise which were so badly needed at the time of his appointment. He knew little of what went on in neighbouring countries and he appointed to foreign courts second-rate men who were hardly fit to cross the antechamber of any important person. He had no idea how to conduct the sort of counter-intrigue which might have given pause to our potential enemies. Nor did he understand that a great nation must endow its official representatives abroad with a certain grandeur if it wants to make itself respected. 'What are you actually *doing?*' Roland sometimes asked him. 'If I were in your place I should already have set all Europe in motion and established a French peace without having to resort to arms. I should have made it my business to know what was going on in all the Courts of Europe and to be exercising my influence there.' Le Brun never made haste over anything. They have just, in August 1793, arrested Sémonville in Switzerland, on his way to take up a diplomatic post in Constantinople which he should have occupied eight months ago. Le Brun's most recent appointments give a sufficiently clear picture of his character and spare me the need to describe him further. He nominated as minister plenipotentiary in Denmark no less a nonentity than Grouvelle,[3] Secretary to the Council, about whom I must now say something.

Grouvelle was a pupil of Cérutti.[4] All he learned from him was to compose little aphorisms which he called philosophy. He was a

[3] Philippe Grouvelle (1758–1806).
[4] Cérutti (1738–92): former Jesuit; Deputy from Paris in the Legislative Assembly.

mediocre man, cold and vain. He had been the last editor of the *Feuille villageoise* which became as flabby under his direction as he was himself. He had also been a candidate for some ministry or other and was appointed Secretary to the Council on 10 August. The appointment was made in conformity with a constitutional law, the non-observance of which had been so strongly criticised by Roland that the King had finally decided he must conform to it. Roland had hoped that if a regular record were kept of its deliberations the Council might become more serious and orderly in its work. He thought it would be helpful to a determined minister that his opinions should be recorded; it might also, he thought, be of interest to posterity and it would certainly be useful to any minister who might subsequently need to justify his record. But the best institutions are useless so long as the men who operate them are able to pervert them. Grouvelle had no idea how to write minutes and in any case most of the ministers did not want their remarks to be remembered. All the secretary has ever been able to do is to record decisions taken, without any account of motives or any mention of contrary opinions. Roland never once succeeded in having the grounds of his objection recorded, even when he had entered a formal reservation against some decision. Grouvelle repeatedly intervened in the discussion, making officious points which added greatly to the difficulties. Roland was once so annoyed by this that he told him he was forgetting his place. 'Am I then to be no more than an inkstand?' replied the pretentious secretary. 'That is all you should be in this place' returned Roland severely. 'Every time you join in the discussion you are forgetting your proper function, which is to write the record. All you seem to have time for is to scribble insignificant notes on odd pieces of paper which when transferred to the record give no idea whatever of the government's operations. The records of the Council ought to serve as the archives for the executive.' Grouvelle was piqued. He did not improve or change his methods; no doubt they suited most of the ministers. A salary of 20,000 livres was attached to his job, but he thought he ought also to have an apartment in the Louvre large enough to house himself and his clerks. He applied for this to the Minister of the Interior. You can imagine how scandalous Roland thought this was and how vigorously he refused it. 'Your clerks? For work which I myself could do better than you in a few hours! I do not object to your employing a copyist to save yourself the trouble of sending out dispatches and summaries of discussion; but twenty thousand livres should be enough to cover that, *and* to house yourself and him. In fact it is an indecently high payment for the position you occupy.' Certainly Grouvelle has the right to be no friend of Roland and I suspect it is a right which he is exercising fully.

As for myself, I thought his ridiculous pretensions intolerable. These little men made of vanity, without character and without virtue, whose wit is all jargon, their philosophy all show and their opinions all second-hand, seem to me to be moral eunuchs. I despise and detest them as cordially as certain women hate and despise other women. And there he is, a minister representing our great nation at the Court of a foreign power whose respect – and neutrality – is so important for France. I do not know the inner secret of this nomination, but I would wager that Grouvelle, half dead with fear at the unpleasant state of affairs here, begged Le Brun to send him out of the country in one way or another; and that Le Brun, the Minister for Foreign Affairs, packed him off as an ambassador as he would have packed him off as a travelling salesman if he himself had been a merchant. It was a private arrangement in which the interest of the Republic counted for nothing except for the title it conferred, the privileges it offered and the damage France will suffer from being badly represented.

The choice of an envoy to the United States was more wisely handled. Brissot is blamed for the part he took in it, but in fact it was greatly to his credit. Bonnecarrère had been nominated – I am not sure at what stage. Brissot remarked to several members of the Council that if we wanted to maintain a good understanding with the United States and do credit to our young republic over there it was important that we send to America someone the Americans would respect and like. From this point of view, Bonnecarrère simply would not do. He was an amiable roué of the *beau monde* and a gambler. Whatever else might be his talents and his intelligence he was not the man for the important role of our ambassador to that nation.

Brissot made no personal claim; he is the last man on earth to press anything for himself. He suggested Genest[5] who had just spent five years in Russia, was well versed in diplomacy and had all

[5] Edmond-Charles Genet (*not* Genest): Chargé d'Affaires in St Petersburg, 1789–92; Minister Plenipotentiary and Consul-General in Philadelphia, 1792–4.

the moral stature and experience that would appeal to a serious people.

This suggestion was carefully examined and was seen to have every possible advantage. Genest was chosen. If that is intrigue, then it is to be hoped that all intriguers are like Brissot. I met Genest, asked to see him again several times and should always be happy to meet him. He has a sound, enlightened mind and a very pleasant and refined nature; his conversation is instructive and agreeable without pedantry and without affectation. Gentleness, truth, grace and reason are inherent in his character and in addition to all this he speaks good English. That an ignoramus like Robespierre and a madman like Chabot[6] should declaim against such a man, calling him a friend of Brissot and demanding that the one be recalled and the other put on trial, just adds to the proofs of their wickedness and ineptitude.

In Roland's second ministry, as in the first, I was determined to receive no woman at my table and I kept strictly to this resolve. I have never had a very extensive circle of acquaintances and women have never played a large part in it. Apart from my closest relations the only people I saw were those whose tastes or occupations interested my husband. I sensed that at the ministry I could easily have become involved in a very tiresome and even dangerous entourage. I found that Mme Pétion had taken a strong line about this at the Town Hall and I thought that it would be no less creditable to follow a good example than to set one. So I had no company and made no visits; it saves a lot of time, which was in itself an advantage for a busy person. Twice a week only I gave a dinner: once for my husband's colleagues and other deputies and the second time for a variety of people, either deputies or senior officials or others connected with public life. My table was neat and in good taste, with no profusion and no luxurious decoration. The atmosphere was relaxed. We did not stay long at table because I provided only one course and did the honours myself. The usual number of guests was fifteen but occasionally we had eighteen and once as many as twenty. Those were the dinner parties which popular orators on Jacobin platforms transformed into sumptuous orgies where I, a modern Circe, corrupted all who had the

---

[6] François Chabot (1759–94): former Capuchin monk; Deputy to the Legislative Assembly and the Convention; accused of corruption in connection with the Compagnie des Indes; executed with the Dantonists.

misfortune to attend. After dinner we talked for a while in the salon and then everyone went back to his business. We had sat down to table at about five in the afternoon and by nine o'clock everyone had gone. Such was the court in which I had set myself up as queen, my notorious hotbed of conspiracy.

On other days, when we had no visitors, my husband and I were often alone together. Dinner was apt to be very late on account of our engagements, so my daughter dined in her own room with her governess. One of these days, when truth is allowed to be heard again, those who knew me will confirm what I say. I shall probably not be here any longer, but I shall depart from this world in full confidence that my detractors and their lies will be forgotten and that I may sometimes be remembered with pity.

I have already named the most notable of the people I entertained, but I must also mention Paine.[7] He had been given French citizenship as one of the celebrated foreigners whom the nation felt proud to adopt, being noted for his writings which had played a large part in the American Revolution and might have helped to bring about a similar revolution in England. I cannot form an absolute judgement of him because he could speak no French though he understood it and I was in much the same position with English; so that although I could follow his conversation with others I could hardly engage him in one myself. But I did form the impression that, like so many authors, he was not worth so much as his writings.

The daring of his opinions, the originality of his style, his audacious way of casting unpleasant truths in the faces of those he was exposing naturally caused a great sensation. But I would judge him more adept at setting things alight than at preparing the foundations for government. He can illuminate a revolution but hardly helps to construct a constitution. Grand principles are evoked, blinding truths, intoxicating in a political club and rousing in a tavern; but for cold committee work and for the day-to-day problems of the legislator I find Williams[8] infinitely more helpful.

Williams, too, had been granted French citizenship but he was

[7] Thomas Paine (1737–1809): English publicist and defender of revolutionary ideas; was given French citizenship by the Legislative Assembly on 25 Aug. 1792 and elected a member of the Convention.
[8] David Williams (1738–1816): one of the leaders of the Unitarian Movement in England; was declared a French citizen by the Legislative Assembly but paid only one brief visit to France in 1792.

not nominated to the Convention where he would have been more useful. However, the government invited him to visit Paris, where he spent several months and had many discussions with working deputies. He was a serious thinker and a true philanthropist. He seemed to me to concentrate on the ways of making men happy, whereas Paine was more concerned with the abuses that made them miserable. From the first moment he attended sessions of the Assembly I found him worried by the lack of order in the debates, upset by the pretensions of the tribunes and doubtful whether such men in such conditions could possibly establish a reasonable constitution. Having seen what our Revolution has brought us to, he was, I think more attached than ever to his own country, to which he eagerly returned. 'How can men debate if they will not listen?' he asked me. 'You French do not even take the trouble to preserve decent outward forms, which are so important in any assembly. Frivolity, carelessness and filthy clothes do not recommend a legislator. These things are not to be under-rated: they are visible day by day and they affect opinion.' What would he say, God help us, if he saw the deputies since 31 May, dressed like navvies in trousers, vest and bonnet, their shirts open to the navel, swearing and gesticulating like drunken *sans-culottes*? He would think it quite natural that the people should treat them like varlets and that the whole lot of them, tainted with violence and excess, should fall under the rod of the first despot to enslave them. The face of Paine reminds me sometimes of the comparison which the Romans made of Sulla's face with a mulberry sprinkled with flour. Williams on the other hand could play his part with equal dignity in Parliament or in Senate. . . .

I must say a word about the famous *Bureau de l'Esprit public* for which Roland has been so criticised. It has been totally misunderstood.

When Roland came back into office on 10 August he felt that the most important need was to inspire the administration with a single purpose, so that it would follow a uniform course and ensure the success of the Revolution. He sent a circular to this effect to all the local authorities and administrative units in the country. It was effective. The Assembly decided that the system should be extended and in the absence of any organised public information service placed a sum of 100,000 livres at the disposal of the Minister of the Interior for distributing appropriate material of his choice. Roland, being a careful and economical man, took great care over the disposal of these funds. He devoted a large portion of them to reputable journals which were already established, sending free copies to popular societies and clubs, clergy and private individuals who expressed a wish to promote the interests of the State. Some of these societies, and many of the individuals, when they saw the government taking an interest in providing an information service, were encouraged to write to the minister asking for this or that document which had been approved by the Convention but which had not yet reached them. The minister deputed one section in his office to deal with this correspondence and to supervise the dispatch of the material. That is all there was to it. The whole set-up, about which there has been such an uproar, amounts to no more than that – a simple mechanism for carrying out the Assembly's decree. Roland was so careful that at the end of six months he had spent only about 34,000 livres out of the 100,000 allocated to him and he drew up a strict account of the payments, with details of the material sent out or acquired. The trouble arose from the fact that Roland, in his ministerial capacity, occasionally used this channel for sending out instructions to the provincial authorities, and because these were so cogent and so well received his enemies feared that he would acquire too much popularity and power.

Of course if that had been a genuine objection Roland could easily have limited his use of this channel to strictly public-relations matters. But it was a mere excuse. They were jealous of his success and started a regular campaign of accusation and vague insinuation of which, at first, he did not take sufficient note. When he did begin to defend himself his lucid and convincing explanations enraged them yet more. They began to speak of him as a public enemy and it became an open struggle between the faithful public servant standing boldly at the helm and a pack of envious trouble-makers determined to overthrow him. So long as he saw any prospect of survival he held firm. But when his own friends and his party failed to support him, he resigned.

His accounts were the despair of his enemies. Having examined them and found them unassailable they took care to ensure that they were not presented to the Assembly. Redoubling their efforts to destroy him, they began to direct their animosity and their lies against me too. We were accused of having set up an instrument for the corruption of public opinion; but not a single concrete fact, not a single word or phrase was adduced to support the accusation. Roland's fame in the future will be at least partly based on the wise things he wrote and distributed at this time.

7

RELEASE AND RE-ARREST

I WAS NEARING THE END OF THE TWENTY-FOURTH DAY of my detention in the Abbaye. I had occupied all this time in study and in writing, compiling my Historical Notes which I am sure must reflect the high spirits in which I wrote them. The insurrection of 31 May and the outrages of 2 June had filled me with indignation, but I was confident that the French departments would not tolerate these things and that their demands, backed if necessary by force, would ensure the triumph of the good cause. So long as I had this hope it did not matter to me that I might so easily fall victim at any moment to personal malice or to some madman's fury in the last convulsions of a dying tyranny. ...

I was aware that some new horror was in preparation for me. A gross libel had been printed in the pages of *Père Duchesne* and they were brazenly shouting it outside my window. This is the foul rag which Hébert,[1] of the Paris Commune, employs every day to poison the people's minds, filling them with lies like water from a bucket. The story was that the author had visited me at the Abbaye and that, having gained my confidence by pretending to be a rebel from La Vendée, he had extracted from me a confession of Roland's contacts – and those of Brissot's friends – with the insurgents in that department and with the English government. This ridiculous tale was seasoned with all the usual venom of *Père Duchesne*. Nothing was spared, not even physical distortion. I was described as a counter-revolutionary and a toothles hag who would do well to repent her sins before expiating them on the scaffold. The newsmongers, on instructions no doubt, hung about the

---

[1] Jacques-René Hébert (1759–94): editor of *Père Duchesne* and one of the most influential members of the Paris Commune. Guillotined on 24 March 1794.

neighbourhood all day and incited the crowd in the neighbouring market to utter the most blood-curdling threats against me. I took up my pen and wrote some lines to that coward Garat[2] who thinks himself a sage because he is always on the winning side and takes no account of truth or justice. I wrote that he should be ashamed of a government which allowed an innocent person, already under lock and key, to be exposed to the unbridled ravings of the ignorant mob. I had no hope of converting him but I was happy to send him my last farewell in the hope that it would tear at his heart like a vulture.

At about this time I had a visit in my cell from a brave and good woman bringing me news of my best friend [Sophie Grandchamp] and offering to pass messages back for me. I was deeply touched and we were both in tears. It was as if an angel had come down to comfort me in my captivity and for a while I was almost able to forget my misery. But on 24 June, at midday, the keeper's wife came to tell me that I was wanted in her room by an administrator of the prison. I was ill and in bed, but I got up and went to her quarters. There was a man there walking up and down, and another man writing. Neither of them seemed to notice my arrival. 'Is it me you asked for, gentlemen?' I said eventually. 'You are *Citoyenne* Roland?' 'Yes, that is my name.' 'Please take a seat.' And the one continued to write while the other walked about. I was wondering what this comedy was in aid of when the man sitting at the table said 'I have come to set you free.' I do not know why, but this announcement moved me hardly at all. 'I should be greatly obliged to be let out of here,' I said, 'but I must also be allowed to go home; there are seals on my apartment.' 'The administration will see to that right away,' he replied. 'I am writing out the order and will require another signature for the keeper's authority to discharge you.' Then he rose and with a smooth smile said casually 'Do you know where your husband is?' I smiled at this question and thought it too indiscreet to deserve an answer. I became bored with his conversation and retired to my room to get myself ready. I thought at first that I might have my dinner quietly and not leave until the evening; but then I reflected that it would be stupid to stay in prison when there was nothing to stop me leaving. And besides, the keeper came to ask whether I was making my arrangements and I could see that he was keen to get hold of my room. It was a minute,

2 See note on p. 29.

unpleasant cubicle, with damp walls and coarse gratings and it lay alongside the butcher's yard where all the dogs of the establishment did their business. Its only advantage was that it could hold only one bed, so one could be alone, and for this reason it was usually offered to new arrivals and to people who particularly wanted privacy. Lavacquerie said that he had never seen it occupied by anyone so contented as me; he liked the way I brought books and flowers into it and said that he would henceforth call it the pavilion of Flora. I did not realise that its next occupant was to be Brissot (I had no idea that he was nearby) or that later on it would be occupied by that herione, worthy of a better age, Charlotte Corday[3] and after her by the effeminate Abbé Fauchet.[4] My poor maid, who had come to see me, wept with joy as she packed my bundle. They made me show them the order of my release which stated that nothing had been found against me. I settled my bills, distributed a few small gifts to the poor and to the prison staff and on my way out I met one of the hostages, the prince de Linanges.[5] He very politely congratulated me on my release and I replied that I wished him similar fortune as surety for the release of our commissioners and for the sake of peace. Then I went down and ordered a hackney cab. I was surprised to find that the administrator had not left the prison and that he came all the way to the gate to watch me get into my cab. I ordered it to take me home, where I intended to leave a few things and then go on to the worthy people who had adopted my daughter. I got out of the cab with a light step – I have never been able to come down from any vehicle without jumping – and passed through the gate like a homing pigeon, calling out gaily to the porter, 'Morning, Lamarre!' I had not gone up four steps of my staircase when two men stepped out from behind me. 'Citoyenne Roland?' 'What do you want?' I asked. 'We arrest you in the name of the law.'

I need not describe what I felt at that moment. I made them read out the order and decided immediately what to do. I came down the stairs and rapidly crossed the courtyard. 'Where are you going?' 'To my landlord, where I have business; follow me.' The landlord's

[3] Marie-Anne-Charlotte de Corday d'Armont, who assassinated Marat on 13 July 1793.
[4] Claude Fauchet (1744–93): Bishop of Calvados; member of the Legislative Assembly and of the Convention; guillotined 31 Oct. 1793.
[5] One of the hostages taken in revenge for the four commissioners of the Convention whom Dumouriez had handed over to the Austrians.

wife opened the door herself, laughing to see me home again. 'Let me sit down and recover my breath,' I said. 'There is nothing to laugh about. They have let me out of the Abbaye but now I am arrested again. It was a cruel deception. They are taking me to Sainte-Pélagie. I place myself under the protection of my section. I know what they feel; please send a message to them.'

The son of the house[6] leapt to his feet and was off. He was an honest young man and he was indignant. Two commissioners from the section arrived at once. They took note of the warrant, drew up their *procès verbal* of objection and asked me to go with them to the Town Hall where they would register their protest and argue my case. I could not refuse. I had written notes for a few friends, to advise them of my new destination and I now took farewell of the landlord's family, leaving them astonished and distressed.

When we got to the Town Hall I was put into a small antechamber with the inspectors who had been ordered to guard me. The commissioners went into the police office and from behind the door I heard a prolonged argument which eventually became heated. I was very uncomfortable and ill at ease. I could not see why an innocent person should be made to play the part of a criminal awaiting sentence, under the eyes of all the people passing through the antechamber. Eventually I lost patience, rose and opened the door to the office, 'Excuse me, gentlemen, but may I have the privilege of hearing this discussion about myself?' 'Go away,' cried a little man whom I recognised as Louvet, the policeman who had interrogated me so incompetently at the Abbaye. 'But I shall not disturb you, I shall not ask to speak. I simply want to be present.' 'Get out, get out! *Gendarmes*, take her out!' You would have thought the office was under siege simply because a well-behaved woman wanted to hear what they were saying about her. I had to withdraw for fear of being thrown out. A little later I became aware of various comings and goings and of signals being passed. A cab was ordered and finally a superintendent asked me to follow him. I went back to the door of the office, opened it wide and shouted 'Commissioners of the section of Beaurepaire, I give you notice that I am being abducted.' 'We can do nothing to prevent it,' they replied. 'but the section will not forget you and we will see to it that you get a proper interrogation.'

[6] Alexandre-Pierre Cauchois: his devotion to the Rolands led to his being condemned to death on 15 March 1794 by the revolutionary tribunal.

'It will certainly be interesting', I said, 'to see how, after having been set free at one o'clock *because there was no case against me*, I have become a suspect on the journey between the Abbaye and my home and am now to face new charges.' Jobert,[7] another police officer as violent as Louvet but heavier and more stupid, made a pompous speech defending the administration. He admitted that my first arrest had been illegal and said that they had had to set me free in order to be able to arrest me again legally. This was a give-away, and I was about to profit by it. But bullies do not like to be contradicted. There was such an uproar and so much fury that not an inch of space was left for reason. I withdrew from the scene and was conveyed to Sainte-Pélagie.

Under the *ancien régime* this place had been occupied by an order of nuns who where supposed to look after the victims of *lettres de cachet* and whose morals were more than suspect. It was remote and isolated, in a very undesirable quarter. Hundreds of priests had been massacred there in September. I was not at all reassured by my new abode. While they were signing me in, a man of sinister appearance opened my bundle and poked about in it. I noticed this just as he was putting some papers from it on to the keeper's table (they were newspapers). I was surprised and indignant at this action, which is illegal. I protested that a man should open a woman's nightcase with such indecent curiosity. They ordered him to desist, but he turned out to be the turnkey of the corridor in which I was to be lodged and I was destined to see his horrible face twice a day. They asked me whether I wanted a room with one or two beds. 'I am alone, and want no company.' 'But it will be a very small room.' 'Never mind.' They looked, but there was no single room available and I was put into one with *two* beds. It was six feet by twelve so that with two very small tables and two chairs there was no space left. I was told that I should have to pay 15 livres a month in advance and twice that for the two beds. But as I wanted only one and would have preferred a single room I said I would pay for only one. 'But is there no water jug or other vase?' 'You can buy them,' the man said eagerly. I also bought a desk, paper and pens and settled myself in. The woman in charge came to see me to tell

---

[7] Augustin-Germain Jobert: merchant; member of the Commune; a municipal officer and police administrator. Later compromised in the trial of Marie Antoinette but acquitted by the revolutionary tribunal. Executed with the other members of the Commune, July 1794.

me the local arrangements. I learned that the State does nothing at all for the prisoners here. 'How do they live then?' 'There is a portion of beans and a pound and a half of bread per day, but you will not be able to eat either of them.' 'It is certainly not what I am used to, but I like to face up to things; I will try them.' I did try them, but whether it was the general discomfort or the lack of exercise or what, my stomach would not take the prison diet and I had to have recourse to Mme Bouchaud's cooking. She had offered to feed me and I accepted. It was clean and economical compared with what I could have got from an eating house, so far away and in such a district. A cutlet and some spoonfuls of vegetables for dinner, some greens in the evening; no dessert, nothing for breakfast but bread and water. That is what I ordered and that is what I had had at the Abbaye. I record this so that it may be compared with the charge made soon afterwards to the section of the Observatoire that I threw money about in Sainte-Pélagie, corrupted the keeper and junketed with his family, arousing the just indignation of the *sans-culottes* and demands for my early death. All that fits in well with the hallucinations of those women who claim to have infiltrated, in disguise, my receptions for aged countesses at the Ministry of the Interior and with the articles in the *Journal de la Montagne* which quote letters addressed to me by refractory priests.

Vile Danton! Sharpen the knife for your victims! Strike! One more murder will hardly add to your crimes. You cannot escape eternal infamy for what you have done. Cruel as Marius, more frightful than Catiline, you surpass their crimes without having their greatness. History will spew up your name with horror when it records the butcheries of September and the savagery of 2 June.

I was not daunted by the new calamity that had befallen me, but I was outraged by their particular cruelty in letting me taste freedom and then binding me with new chains, their barbarous device for cloaking my detention with legality. I found myself in that state of mind in which all external sensations bite cruelly into one's being and actually endanger one's health. I could not sleep at night, I could only dream. But extreme agitation never lasts very long with me. I am hardened in self-control. Why pay my persecutors the compliment of being upset? All they had done, after all, was to add to their own crimes; they had not substantially altered the conditions which I had already learned to endure. Had I not books here, as at the Abbaye? Had I not leisure? Was I not still myself? I began almost to be annoyed at having been disturbed, and resolved to make use of my time and my faculties with the detachment worthy of a strong character under duress. That is the way to defy one's enemies.

But I did think that some change of occupation was necessary. I bought some pencils and took up drawing again, which I had so long ago abandoned.

Fortitude does not consist simply in rising above adverse circumstances by an effort of will; one must sustain it with a suitable regime and way of life. True wisdom is the sum of all the individual steps one takes to act wisely and to preserve one's sanity. When things go badly wrong I do not rely exclusively on philosophy to support my courage: I arrange suitable distractions and observe carefully the precepts of hygiene so as to maintain a balanced outlook. So I now ordered my days in accordance with a regular pattern. In the morning I studied English in Shaftesbury's excellent *Inquiry Concerning Virtue* and construed the verses of Thomson. The sane metaphysics of the one and the enchanting descriptive passages of the other carried me alternately into the realms of the intellect and of nature. Shaftesbury's Reason fortified my own and his thoughts led me into meditation, while the sensibility of Thomson, his joyous and sublime descriptions, warmed my heart and charmed my imagination. I then drew until supper-time. It was so long since I had handled a pencil that I cannot say that I was at all good at it, but it is always a pleasure to try out a skill which one enjoyed as a child. Thus I think that the study of the fine arts, considered as part of a girl's education, should not be directed so much towards developing a special talent as towards inspiring a taste for hard work, inculcating habits of application and enlarging the range of her interests. That is the way to escape boredom, the cruellest scourge of anyone in society. That is the way to preserve oneself from the perils of sin and – worse still – of temptation.

I certainly do not want my daughter to be a virtuoso. I shall always remember that my mother was afraid of my becoming a great musician or devoting myself exclusively to painting because of her overriding concern that I should perform the duties of my sex, that is to say, that I should be a good housewife and a good mother. I want my Eudora to accompny herself gracefully on the harp, or play lightly upon the forte piano. I want her to know enough about drawing to be able to appreciate the works of the great masters, to trace or copy a flower at will and to apply simple good taste and elegance in her attire. I should not like to see her talents excite undue admiration in others or undue vanity in herself. I want her to create a generally agreeable impression but not to make too striking an impact at first sight, and I should rather see her attract friends with her character than impress people with her accomplishments. But, heavens above, I am a prisoner and she lives far away. I dare not even let her come here, to take her in my arms. These tyrants hate even the children of their victims, and my poor girl, eleven years old, with her virginal looks and her lovely blonde hair, can scarcely appear in the street without despicable creatures pointing her out as the offspring of a conspirator! Cruel brutes! You tear a mother's heart in shreds.

Should I have brought her here with me? I have not yet described what conditions are like in Sainte-Pélagie prison.

The building alloted to women is divided into long, very narrow corridors with cells all down one side similar to the one I have described in which I was lodged. Here, under the same roof, in the same row, separated by thin plaster boards, I live with fallen women and murderers. Next door to me is one of those creatures who seduce the young and sell the innocent. Above is a woman forger of *assignats* who tore another woman to pieces on the King's highway with a gang of her accomplices. Each cell is locked with a huge key and opened every morning by a man who leers in to see whether you are asleep or awake. The inmates crowd together for the rest of the day in the corridor, on the stairs, in the small court or in a damp, stinking hall, fit receptacle for these dregs of humanity. I stayed the whole time in my cell, but it was at such close quarters that it was impossible not to hear the conversation of these women, which was indescribable.

And that is not all. The building which houses the men has windows opposite and is very close to the women's section. Conversations take place between depraved men and women such as no decent person can imagine. There is no restraint, no fear. Gesture supplies the want of contact and these windows become theatres for the enaction of the most lewd and shameful debauchery.

This is where the respectable wife of a distinguished public figure is made to lodge! Such is my reward for a virtuous life! It is not surprising that I am ready for death....

I must say that my gaolers soon became more concerned about my situation than I was myself, and wanted to improve it if they could. In July it became so hot that my cell was uninhabitable. I had put paper over the grilles to try and keep out the sun but it beat so strongly on the confined walls that, although the windows were open all night, the air never cooled. The keeper's wife invited me to spend the daytime in her apartment and I accepted for the afternoons. I had the idea of installing a forte piano there, which I sometimes play.

But what fluctuations of hope and fear I experienced at this time! It looked as if some of the departments were ready to avenge the injuries done to their deputies and to restore democratic representation throughout the country. I knew that Roland was in quiet and safe asylum amongst friends and that my daughter, adopted by good people, was continuing her education with their children and under their watchful eye. My friends, who had taken refuge in Caen, were supported by a respectable force. Above all, the man who was most dear to me had succeeded in sending me news of himself; I was able to write back and believed that my letters were reaching him. I thought that the Republic was on the point of being saved and, quite resigned to my own fate, I was still happy. Happiness depends less on external conditions than on one's state of mind and feeling. I employed my time usefully and agreeably. I sometimes saw the four people who used to visit me at the Abbaye: Grandpré, whose duties allowed him to come and go and who often brought with him my dear friend Sophie; Bosc, who faithfully brought flowers from the Jardin des Plantes, cheering my sombre retreat with their sweet forms, colour and scent; and Champagneux, who warmly encouraged me to continue my Historical Notes – which I did, abandoning for a while my Tacitus and Plutarch.

Madame Bouchaud was not content with offering me the freedom of her apartment. She realised that I used it with great discretion and she had the idea of moving me from my gloomy cell and putting me in a nice little room with a chimney on the ground floor, below her own room. So now after three weeks I am delivered from the appalling company which so distressed me. No longer do I have to fight my way twice a day through the crowds of my disgusting neighbours; no longer am I awakened in the morning and locked in again at night like a criminal by the sinister, leering turnkey. Madame Bouchaud' sweet face greets me every day. I am conscious all the time of her delicate attentions. Everything she does for me, even to the planting of jasmine outside my window, so that its delicate tendrils embrace the iron grilles, shows her kindness and respect. She treats me as a guest, and I forget my captivity. Everything I need for study or entertainment is arranged around me; my piano stands by my bed, neat cupboards enable me to enjoy the tidiness and cleanliness which mean so much to me.

But, alas, bribery, lies, intrigue and force of arms have been employed against the departments which stood out for freedom. Deluded or mercenary soldiers have betrayed the brave men of Normandy. Évreux is abandoned and Caen has driven out the deputies whom it had welcomed. The arrogant brigands, still daring to call themselves the Convention, have declared them all traitors to the country, outlawed them, confiscated their property, seized their wives and children and razed their houses to the ground....

All my friends are proscribed, fled or under arrest. My husband has escaped his enemies only by going into hiding and his life is little better than solitary confinement. Now the small number of friends who have been helping to console me are being persecuted in their turn. Grandpré, having dined with a man whom he did not know was a Justice of the Peace and a member of the local tribunal, complained about the negligence of prison officers in allowing too many people to suffer in prison. The man disclosed his identity and expressed great concern to know more about the abuses so that he could help to reform them. He asked Grandpré for his name and address so that he might go with him on his next round of prison visits. It was a ruse. The Justice of the Peace went straight round to the Committee of General Security and denounced Grandpré for complicity in the death of Marat. One might be back in the time of Tiberius and his informers. Grandpré was arrested by an officer and five fusiliers who knocked him up at five o'clock in the morning, seized his papers and put seals on his apartment. He had in his possession a letter which I had addressed to poor Brissot. He realised at once how dangerous it would be, both for himself and for me, if this were found and he managed to conceal it. Only after the most painful argument was he able to persuade the men to let him remain under guard in his own office rather than be sent to the Abbaye, and it took four days to prove the falsity of the accusation against him....

Since Grandpré was released he has come much less often to see me and only with great precaution. He will be done for if they suspect that his work in the prisons is in any way influenced by wanting to visit me. Champagneux is under arrest; he laments that he can no longer alleviate the long hours of *my* captivity, while I suffer from *his* captivity because I know that he owes it to his association with Roland and me. I have begged Bosc, who has already put in his resignation [from a position in the Post Office] not to risk detention by coming to visit me. I see him about once a week, on the quiet.

In the midst of all these troubles it is restful to find myself in the pleasant little room where dear Mme Bouchaud has managed to isolate me from the foul atmosphere of prison life. There are, admittedly, one or two small irritations: a sentry post immediately opposite my window, against which I have to keep the curtains drawn all day (and the man sometimes creeps close enough to hear what is being said when I am not alone); the terrible barking of three large dogs in a kennel not ten paces away; and the fact that I am next door to a large room known grandly as the 'council chamber', in which the police officers assemble when they come to conduct an interrogation. By being so close to this assembly room I have witnessed some strange scenes. Two men whose names I knew at the time but have forgotten (or refrain from mentioning because such scoundrels do not deserve to be remembered) had been arrested for misconduct in the clothing-supply administration of the army, where they were employed. They used to be visited by friends or accomplices who were in fact also police officers. These men had the duty, in their official capacity, of maintaining order in the prisons, supervising the keepers, etc. They used to come to Sainte-Pélagie once or twice a week with other friends like themselves, to the number of ten or twelve and sometimes more. They would summon the two favoured prisoners into the 'council chamber' and hold orgies there for four or five hours at a time. The keeper was made to supply chickens, eggs, wine, coffee, etc., at his own expense. It is impossible to imagine – and I shall certainly not try to describe – the brutish humour, the vulgarity and the indecency of these entertainments: the stupid and sarcastic repetition of the word 'patriot', always in association with that of the scaffold, the bloodthirsty call for the execution of all 'suspected persons', a title now applied freely to anyone who has received an education or who possesses a fortune that has not been recently stolen, the disgusting kisses sloshed by wine-sodden lips on to the cheeks of each new arrival and repeated on their departure, the filthy jokes of men without morals and without shame, the mad conceit of atrocious imbeciles who live by denouncing honest men and filling the prisons with innocent people.

Plato was right to describe democracy as an auction, a sort of fair in which all types of government are to be found on show. But how would he describe the system under which men of this type dispose of the liberty of their fellow citizens? When these parties arrived, Bouchaud or his wife would be careful to remove the key from my room and warn me. I decided simply to close my ears to the racket, and sat down to continue my Notes. I rather enjoyed composing vigorous tirades under the very noses of the brutes who would have murdered me if they had heard a single phrase. When the anniversary of 10 August came round it was feared that there might be a recurrence of the events of 2 September. The administrators managed to drive out the known troublemakers and there were no more civic banquets. If I could bring myself to fork over this dung-hill I would give some astonishing – and very sad – details about abuses in the prisons. I could show every menial servant and tradesman in the place compounding and abetting the crimes of the unfortunate prisoners. I could show prostitutes guilty of some awful offence released without trial in return for sleeping with the administrator on their last day; murderers rich enough to bribe the officials with their ill-gotten gains, to suppress evidence and secure immunity; professional thieves freely planning their operations, communicating with one another both inside and outside the prison and finally escaping with the connivance of the prison staff or the police officers supposed to be guarding them. Everything becomes venal and corrupt in this stinking hole, under a vicious administration whose sole passion is to keep people in, with no thought of correction.

Sympathetic and generous Howard,[8] you who have travelled all over Europe visiting these sombre habitations where enlightened governments can still distinguish humanity from crime and avoid the persecution of innocence; what would you think if you saw the conditions in the prisons in France, once held to be the most

[8] John Howard (1726–90): English philanthropist, author of works on the state of prisons in England and abroad. The Howard League for Penal Reform is named after him.

civilised country on earth? No distinction is made here between the thoughtless youth and the hardened criminal: I have seen a student of botany, accused of having spoken ill of Marat, locked in the same room with highway robbers. There is no respect for morality: I have seen a girl of fourteen, whom her parents were trying to bring home, having to share a cell with the woman who had abducted her and who had been arrested on that account. There is no provision made for decency or hygiene in the construction or use of the premises. At Sainte-Pélagie they are in the process of building a large extension. A small-minded, soulless architect is making totally unsuitable arrangements and nobody in the higher administration has the intelligence or the will to rectify his plans.

The present keeper does what he can, but nothing can overcome the evils of a bad system. What is needed is either two different buildings, one for criminals and the other for political detainees and suspects, or entirely separate sections with no communication whatsoever between the sexes. But this is not the place for a treatise on such matters; I confine myself to expressing my despair for the freedom of a people sunk so deep in corruption.

When I first arrived at Sainte-Pélagie they gave me the services of a woman imprisoned for a minor offence, to help me out in return for some alleviation of her poverty. It was not that I could not easily have looked after myself. 'Nothing is beneath the dignity of a brave and generous man,' as they said of Favonius when he rendered menial services to the disgraced Pompey. This applies equally to the poor devil without means who is trying to meet his barest needs and to the austere philosopher who disdains all superfluous worldly goods. Quintius cooked his own turnips when he received the ambassadors of the Samnites and I would have gladly made my own bed in my cell at Sainte-Pélagie. But it was rather a different matter having to walk long distances and run the gauntlet of the other inmates whenever I wanted a glass of water, and I was grateful to have someone whom I could oblige by giving her such commissions. She continued to do me this service after I had moved to my new room, and one morning she happened to come in just at the moment when an administrator arrived in the 'council chamber'. He asked who was lodged here and insisted on being shown the room. He did not like what he saw and complained to the keeper's wife of the comforts she had provided for me. 'Madame Roland was unwell', she said (it was true), 'and I put her where she could more easily receive attention. Besides, she likes to play the forte piano and there was no room for it in her cell.' 'She can do without it. Send her back to the corridor at once. You must maintain equality.'

Unfeeling brute! Do you throw me in with fallen women for equality's sake? Madame Bouchaud came to tell me of the orders she had received; she was desolate. I consoled her as best I could. It was agreed that during the course of each day I should come down for a change of air and to study; my books and papers stayed where they were. So now I am condemned to see that turnkey again, to hear the great iron bolts screech in their sockets, to breathe the fetid air in the dim corridor, to be choked and blackened with the thick fumes that pour out of the single lamp at night.

Such are the humane dispositions of these dreadful men. Such is the liberty promised by the idealist who, on the Champ de Mars, launched flights of pigeons to carry to the ends of the earth a message of freedom and happiness. Insolent fools! The Governor of the Bastille stamping on Lauzun's spider was not more heartless, more obtuse than you. Your end is nigh; the enemy is at the gate. By your own conduct you have assured your ruin. Mine is assured too, no doubt; I have earned the hatred of all tyrants. My only regret is for France....

For the rest I may say that the continuing persecution has now filled the squalid corridor where I live with women whom I am not ashamed to know and with whom, indeed, it is a pleasure to be associated. I find there, for example, the wife of a Justice of the Peace, denounced by her neighbour for 'unpatriotic talk'; also the wife of a president of a revolutionary tribunal. And I also find Mme Pétion. 'I little thought', I said to her, 'when I was at the Town Hall on 10 August last year, sharing your anxieties, that we should celebrate the anniversary together in Sainte-Pélagie prison, and that the fall of the monarchy would lead to our own undoing.' ...

—II—

PRIVATE MEMOIRS

— 8 —

CHILDHOOD

◆

I AM THE DAUGHTER OF A CRAFTSMAN and the wife of a man of principle, a scholar who became a government minister. I am now in prison and may at any moment suffer a violent death. I have known happiness and adversity. I have seen history in the making and have endured injustice.

My parents were plain, undistinguished people and I spent my youth practising the fine arts and studying. Competence and integrity were our only standards. The education I received should have ensured me an advantageous marriage, but when the time came for that my fortune had disappeared. I married a worthy man and seemed to have overcome this setback. But others followed.

I have an active mind, a determined character and a very affectionate heart. These qualities have endeared me to those who know me. I have made enemies in public but not in private life. Those who abuse me most have never seen me.

Things are rarely what they seem, and the happiest times in my life – and the most unhappy – would often not have appeared such to other people. The truth is that happiness depends more on our friendships than on events.

I intend to make use of my captivity to retrace my personal life from infancy up to the present. What can you do better in prison than re-live the past and imagine yourself back in happier days? You can certainly enrich your experience by reflecting on the past and I hope that it may make the present easier to bear.

During the first two months of my detention I thought and wrote continuously about public events and my immediate reactions to them; I had no time to look further back into my life. The first five weeks were devoted to writing the Historical Notes and they made a very considerable collection. They have now been destroyed.[1] I shall never be able to repair this terrible loss. But I refuse to let anything of that sort depress me. I have always found, when misfortune has struck, that my immediate grief is soon swallowed up in determination to oppose and overcome the forces arrayed against me. I screw up my courage and try to do good in return for evil. I shall not allow events to overwhelm me. Tyrants may persecute me but they shall never get me down. Never!

My Historical Notes are lost; I shall now write my memoirs. I think it will help to distract me, at a time when I am particularly distressed, if I talk a little about myself. I shall do myself strict justice, painting the good and the bad with equal freedom. A man who dares not say a good word about himself is almost always a coward who knows that he has great faults and is afraid that others may see them first; and the man who will not confess his own sins will not have the strength or the means to reform them. With this frankness about myself, I shall not spare others. Father, mother, friends, husband – I shall describe them all as they are or as I have seen them.

So long as I was living a quiet life, wrapped up in myself, my various other qualities were obscured by my natural sensibility. My chief ambition was to please people and to do good. I was rather like the good M. de Gourville, of whom Mme de Sévigné said that love of his neighbour cut his conversation down by fifty per cent; and one of my friends was justified in remarking that I was capable of penning fine epigrams but never allowed any of them to see the light of day.

But now that my character has been hardened by political adversity and other troubles I aspire above all to be frank. I pay little attention to the minor scratches which one is bound to suffer on the road. I no longer compose epigrams: I get no pleasure from pricking bubbles or killing flies. But I do believe in upholding justice with plain truths and I am capable of enunciating such truths with terrible intensity in the presence of those involved, regardless of the effect on them, while remaining entirely detached myself.

Gatien Phlipon, my father, was an engraver by profession. He also dabbled in painting. At one time he wanted to take up enamel

---

[1] Madame Roland described her Historical Notes as containing 'details on all the facts and personalities with which I have been acquainted in public life'. She hoped that they would constitute her 'moral and political testament'.

work, mainly as a speculation, but the heat necessary for working the enamel was damaging to his eyesight and constitution and he had to abandon the idea. In his own line he was only moderately talented, but he was hard-working and there was a demand for his products. He had plenty of work and employed a considerable number of men. Unfortunately, the hope of making a fortune led him into commerce. He bought diamonds and other jewels, or accepted them as payment from the dealers with whom he was trading in order to sell them again at a profit. I mention this because I have noticed that, in all classes, that sort of ambition is usually disastrous. A few are lucky but the majority fail. My father's case was doubly unfortunate; his art would have enabled him to live comfortably, but he wanted to be rich and ended up by ruining himself.

He was a robust and healthy man, energetic and vain. He loved his wife and he loved fine attire. He had no learning but he had the good taste and the surface knowledge which the arts, at whatever level, so often give a man. Despite his veneration for money and what it could buy and the fact that his business dealings were with merchants, his friends were all artists, painters and sculptors. He led a well-regulated life so long as his ambition was held in check and things went smoothly for him. I cannot say that he was a virtuous man, but he had a great sense of honour. He might have made you pay more for something than it was worth, but he would have died rather than fail to pay the proper price for what he had bought.

Marguerite Bimont, his wife, had brought him a very small dowry but she had a saintly nature and a sweet face. She was the eldest of six children and had been a mother to the others until she married at the age of twenty-six. With her gentle disposition and lively mind she should have married someone educated and refined, but when her parents offered her a plain man whose talents were capable of supporting her she accepted him in a practical spirit. She did not expect happiness but felt that she could lead a peaceful life, which is the next best thing. It is very wise to be able to lower one's expectations. Happiness is rarer than one thinks, but the consolations of virtue never fail.

I was their second child. They had seven but all the others died either in childbirth or shortly after as a result of various accidents. My mother used to tell me that I was the only one who gave her no trouble: the delivery was as easy as the pregnancy. Indeed, it seems that I was beneficial to her health.

An aunt of my father found a healthy and respectable nurse for me in the neighbourhood of Arpajon, where she often went in the summer. The woman was highly regarded in the district, largely because she had maintained her good character and behaviour despite a brutal husband who bullied her. Madame Besnard, my great-aunt, had no children; her husband was my godfather. Between them they treated me as if I had been their daughter and they have never ceased to care for me. They are still alive and in their declining years they are deeply distressed at the fate of their great-niece, in whom they had vested such hope and pride. Dear friends, take comfort! Few people are privileged to pass their lives in the peace and quiet which surround you. I am a match for the misfortunes which have assailed me and I shall always honour your memory.

The devotion of my nurse was supplemented and rewarded by my dear parents. She became closely attached to the family; right up to her death she never let two years go by without coming to Paris to see me. She hastened to my side when she heard the cruel news of my mother's death. I remember it well; I was already prostrate with grief and her sudden appearance reminded me too abruptly of my loss. I fell into a convulsion; she was scared and withdrew and I never saw her again. I had been to visit her in the cottage where she had nursed me; she had shown me all my favourite spots, reminded me of my childish mischief and told me a hundred stories of our past together.

At the age of two I was brought back home. I have often been told of the surprise I showed at seeing the lamps lit in the street at night – bottles, I called them – and of my reluctance to use what is primly called a *pot de chambre*, because the corner of the garden had been the only place I knew of for this purpose. They say that I pointed my finger at salad bowls and soup tureens, asking mischievously whether they were for the same thing. But I had better pass over these intimate details, which are of interest only to nurses and can be repeated only to grandparents. I will not be expected to describe here that little brunette of two, bright-eyed, healthy and happy. There will be a better time to paint my portrait and I shall not make the mistake of anticipating it.

My mother's good sense and kindness gave her an ascendancy over me which she never exploited except for my good. In all my childhood she never had to impose any graver discipline than calling me 'Mademoiselle' coldly or looking at me severely. I can still feel the power of that look, normally so loving and caressing, and hear with a tremble the solemn, formidable 'Mademoiselle' instead of her usual gentle 'my child' or the affectionate 'Manon'. Yes, she called me Manon. I am sorry to disappoint the romantic reader, for this is not a noble name and hardly fits a heroine in the grand style. But after all it is what I was called and I am writing history. And in any case, anyone who had heard my mother pronounce the name and observed its effect on me would at once have become reconciled to it. Any name my mother used for me with affection touched me and made me want to deserve it.

I was a lively child without being obstreperous, and naturally thoughtful. I wanted always to be busy and quickly absorbed any ideas that were presented to me: so much so, that I can never remember having actually learned to read. I have been told that it was all done by the time I was four, and that after that all they had to do was to see that I had plenty of books. Whatever reading-matter they gave me or whatever I might procure for myself, absorbed me completely. The only things that could distract me from a book were flowers. The sight of a flower sweetens my imagination and soothes my feelings to a degree I can hardly express; it awakens in me a truly voluptuous sense of being. From earliest childhood, under my father's tranquil roof, I was always happy with flowers and books; and now in the narrow confines of a prison, shackled under a most revolting tyranny, I can forget the injustices of men, their follies and my own wrongs, so long as I have books and flowers.

Needless to say, they took advantage of all this to make me absorb the Old Testament, the New Testament and the greater and lesser catechisms. I learned whatever they wished. I would have recited the Koran by heart if they had taught me the script. I remember a painter called Guibal, since settled in Stuttgart, who often came to my father's house. He had painted a picture called *In praise of Poussin* which I saw some years ago. He was a queer fellow, who told me children's stories which amused me greatly and which I have never forgotten. He enjoyed making me show off my knowledge. I can see him to this day, with his rather grotesque face, sitting in an armchair, with me crouching on the floor, my elbows on his knees, making me recite the Athanasian Creed and then rewarding me with the story of Tangu whose nose was so long that he had to wind it around his arm when he wanted to walk.

From the age of seven I was sent every Sunday to a parish school class, known as 'catechism', to prepare me for Confirmation. The way things are going nowadays I dare say anyone who reads this passage will need to be told what that means. I shall tell them. In the far corner of a church, chapel or similar building they arrange some rows of chairs or benches, facing one another. A wide passage is left between them and at the top end of this is placed a somewhat higher chair, the curule chair, for the young priest who is to instruct the children. The children are made to recite by heart the Gospel of the day, the Epistle, the Lord's Prayer and the chapter from the catechism appropriate to the week. When the numbers are great the teaching priest has a young clerk to hear the children's lines, reserving himself for questions of substance. In some parishes the children of both sexes go to the same catechism; in others they are entirely separate. Some mothers and other good women ever-hungry for the Bread of the Word attend these sessions, seated according to age and readiness to receive Confirmation or to take their First Communion. A zealous curé appears from time to time in the midst of this young flock; they rise respectfully at his approach and he addresses a few questions to the best-looking ones, to test their instruction. The mothers of those being questioned glow with pride and the pastor then withdraws amidst their curtsies.

Monsieur Garat, curé of St Bartholomew, my parish in what was then called Paris la Cité, was reputed to be very learned but could not string two words together when he was in the pulpit where he loved to be (rather as Minister of Justice Garat is considered so clever today although he does not know his job). Monsieur Garat, my curé, came one day to my catechism. Wishing to test me and at the same time display his own knowledge, he asked me how many Orders of Spirits there were in the celestial hierarchy. I could see from the triumphant, sly look in his eye that he expected to embarrass me. I replied with a sweet smile that although several such Orders were indicated in the preface to the Mass, I had read elsewhere that there were nine in all, and I proceeded to pass in review the Angels, Archangels, Thrones, Dominations and Powers etc. Never was a curé more satisfied with the accomplishments of his neophyte. It made my reputation amongst the sainted ladies. I became one of the elect, as will shortly be seen.

It may well be asked why, with a such a sensible and loving mother, I should have been sent to catechism at all. There is a reason for everything. My mother's younger brother was in the Church and in our parish. He was in charge of the catechism for Confirmation, as it was technically called. The presence of his niece in the class set an edifying example which could persuade other ambitious parents to send their children too, which would please the curé. Besides that, I had an exceptionally good memory and was usually top of the class. My parents were proud of me and liked to show me off in a modest way. It happened one year that, without any special favouritism, I won first prize in the great annual prize-giving. All the church wardens and clergy thought my young uncle a very lucky man; it brought him attention, which was all he needed to make him appreciated. He was good-looking, very kind, easy-going, open and jolly – qualities which remained with him all his life. He died quite recently as a canon in Vincennes, just before the Revolution put an end to all these religious offices. He was the last of my relatives on my mother's side and I remember him with tenderness. Seeing that I had such an aptitude and taste for study he had the idea of teaching me Latin. I was delighted to take up any new subject. I was already having lessons at home in writing, geography, dancing and music and my father had just made me start drawing; but nothing was too much for me. I would get up at five o'clock in the morning when everyone was still asleep, slip on a dressing-gown and creep down in bare feet to my mother's room, where my work stood ready on a little table in the corner. I would read, copy out, memorise, and of course I made rapid progress.

My teachers began to be fond of me. They gave me long lessons and their obvious interest encouraged me still more. There was not one who did not seem as pleased to teach me as I was to be taught; not one who, having followed my progress for a few years, did not volunteer that I no longer needed him, that he could not accept payment any more but would like to be invited in from time to time to talk to me. I shall honour the memory of good M. Marchand, who taught me to write at the age of five and then introduced me to geography and to history. He was a wise, patient, clear-headed and methodical man, and I called him 'Mr Sobersides'. He married a good woman related to the de Nesles family. I went to visit him during his last illness: he died of consumption at the age of fifty. I was then eighteen.

Nor have I forgotten the lively and talkative little musician, Cajon, born in Mâcon where he had been a choirboy and then, successively, soldier, deserter, Methodist, odd-job man and refugee. He had arrived in Paris with wife and children, without a penny but with the advantage of an extremely pleasant counter-tenor voice, rare in men who have not undergone a certain operation and just right for teaching singing to young people. Someone introduced him to my father and I was his first pupil. He was very attentive. He frequently borrowed money from my parents and spent it immediately and never gave me back a book of exercises by Bordier which he pillaged with some skill in order to compose *Éléments de musique*, published under his name. He became rather fashionable, but without making any money, and after fifteen years he quit Paris, leaving a lot of debts behind and went to Russia where I do not know what became of him.

Then there was Mozon, the dancing teacher, a good Savoyard of incredible ugliness. He had a wen on his right cheek which showed up when he twisted his pockmarked face to the left over the violin. I could make fun of him, and also of poor Mignard, the guitar teacher, a Spanish giant with hairy hands like Esau, the gravest, most polite, most blustering of his compatriots. The timid Watrin was not with me very long. He was over fifty, wore a pince-nez and had a red face; the general effect seemed to me altogether chaotic as he arranged my fingers on the treble viol and showed me how to hold the bow. The Reverend Father Collomb, a Barnabite and former missionary, head of his House and my mother's confessor, sent her his bass viol to console me for the loss of the treble viol and used to accompany me himself when he visited our house and asked me to get out my guitar. I once astonished him by taking hold of his bass and playing, quite well, one or two tunes on it which I had practised in secret. If there had been a double bass I would have climbed on a chair and made something of it.

But I anticipate; just now I was seven years old, and I must go back to that. I have not yet spoken of my father's influence on my education. It was not great because he took little part in it, but I must describe an event which made him determined to take even less. I was very opinionated: that is to say, I did not readily accept anything that I could not see the reason for, and when I sensed an attempt to impose an opinion on me, or thought I detected caprice, I never gave way. My mother was clever and tactful; she knew perfectly well that I must be governed by reason or persuaded by sentiment, so she never met with resistance. But my father was brusque; he was the master and he gave the orders. The result was that I obeyed him very reluctantly if at all. If he tried to punish me injustly, his dear little daughter became a lioness. He whipped me two or three times and I once bit him on the thigh when he had bent me over for that purpose.

One day I was a little unwell, and there was a talk of medicine. They brought the mixture and I put it to my lips, but the smell disgusted me and I pushed it away. My mother tried to overcome my repugnance and I wanted to obey her; I really tried, but every time the stuff was put under my nose my senses revolted and I turned away my head. She became exhausted; I started to cry, both on her account and on my own, but I was still unable to swallow the medicine. At this point my father came in. He became angry and whipped me, attributing my refusal to obstinacy. From that moment all wish to obey was gone. Howls, more threats, a second whipping. I raged, screamed terribly, raised my eyes to heaven and prepared to throw the mixture in their faces. My father, furious, threatened to beat me a third time. All of a sudden – and I can feel it as I write, all these years later – a change of attitude took place inside me, a new strength flowed through my veins. My tears stopped abruptly and in a sudden calm all my senses seemed to coalesce into a single resolution. I sat up in bed, turned away my head and leaned it against the wall, tucked up my shirt and offered myself silently to the blows. He could have killed me, I would not have uttered a sound.

My mother was devastated by this scene. She needed all her wits not to increase my father's rage, but eventually got him out of the room. She put me back to bed without a word. Two hours later she came back in tears, begging me not to upset her any more and to take the medicine. I looked straight at her, took the glass and swallowed it in one gulp. But I threw it all up fifteen minutes later. I then had a violent attack of fever which called for subtler treatment than foul drugs and whipping. I was little more than six years old.

All the details of that scene are as vivid to me today as if they had taken place yesterday and the feelings I had then are just as real. I have experienced the same stiffening at other dramatic moments in my life and I know that if I have to mount the scaffold I shall submit myself to barbarous treatment with the same pride as I did then. They can kill me but they shall not conquer me!

From that moment, my father never laid hands on me again. He did not even scold me for anything. He caressed me a lot, taught me to draw, took me for walks and treated me with so much kindness that I began to respect him again and show him deference. They told me on my seventh birthday that I had reached the age of reason and that rational behaviour would now be expected of me. This was a clever way of encouraging me without arousing my vanity. My life slipped gently by in domestic peace and great activity of mind. My mother stayed at home and hardly received anyone. We went out twice a week: once to visit my father's grandparents and once, on Sunday, to see Mama's mother, attend divine service and take a walk. We always began by going to see Grandmama Bimont after vespers. She was a tall, fine-looking woman but she had had a stroke early on in life and was mentally affected. She had sunk back into childishness and spent her days in a chair near the window or in front of the fire according to the season. An old spinster, Marie, who had seen forty years of service in the family, looked after her.

As soon as I arrived Marie always gave me tea. It was a very good tea but when that was over I was terribly bored. I looked for books, but there was nothing in the house but a Psalter. I had read and sung its contents to myself twenty times. If I was cheerful, my grandmother moaned; if I hurt myself or fell down, she burst out laughing. This upset me. It was no use their telling me that it was the result of her illness, I still found it depressing. I could have borne it if she had mocked me, but her tears came bursting out with a mixture of gloom and madness which froze my spirits and frightened me. Old Marie jabbered away endlessly with my mother, who felt morally bound to stay for at least two hours each time listening to her. It was a painful trial of my patience, but I had to go through with it because one day, when my boredom was such that I cried and asked to go home, my mother stayed the whole evening. She never lost an opportunity to impress on me that these visits to her mother were a sacred duty in which I was honoured to have a part and somehow, though I do not know quite how, she managed to convince me. The only time I enjoyed the visits was when my dear little uncle, the Abbé Bimont, was there too. He made me laugh and sing. But he could not come often; he was the master of a choir school and fully occupied. I particularly remember one of his pupils, a cheerful-looking boy whom he was always praising because he gave him so little trouble. This boy showed great promise; he got a scholarship a few years later at some college whose name I have forgotten and became the Abbé Noël, known first for his minor writings and subsequently called into the diplomatic service by Minister Le Brun: he was sent to London last year and is now serving in Italy....

My father was kind enough to give me a present of books from time to time, knowing that I preferred them to anything else. But since he prided himself on encouraging my serious tastes he made some rather curious choices. For example, he gave me Fénelon's treatise on the education of young women and the works of Locke on the upbringing of children. It appeared to be a case of giving to the pupil what had been intended as guidance for the teacher. But on the whole this was quite successful; more so, perhaps, than a more conventional selection might have been. I was very mature and I liked to think. I really felt that I was educating myself; that is to say, I studied the movements of my mind and tried to know myself. I had already begun to feel that I had a destiny to fulfil for which I ought to be preparing. Religious thoughts began to ferment in my head and were soon to produce a moral and emotional crisis.

Before describing that we must know what happened to our Latin. The basic rules of grammar were already well ordered in my head. I could decline and I could conjugate, though they both seemed to me rather sorry exercises. The hope of being able one day to read the fine works that other people spoke of, or which were hinted at in my present reading, encouraged me to persevere. But no such thoughts inspired my little uncle (the one I called the Abbé Bimont). He was young, a bit of a child, idle and cheery, taking not the least trouble over anyone else and very little over himself. He was bored by his duties as a pedagogue with choirboys and much preferred going for a walk to giving me a lesson or hearing me recite my rudiments. He was extremely unreliable and my lessons became rarer and rarer. Yet I wanted to learn and did not like giving up what I had begun. It was arranged that I should go to him three times a week in the morning. But that was not a success either: I always found him occupied with parish affairs, distracted by the children or having breakfast with a friend. I was wasting my time. The bad weather came and Latin was abandoned. All I retained from this attempt was a sort of instinct, or preliminary understanding, which allowed me in the days of my devotion to repeat or sing the psalms without being totally ignorant of what they meant, and a great facility for the learning of languages in general and particularly for Italian, which I taught myself without difficulty some years later.

[135]

My father did not press me at all hard over drawing. He was quite amused by my aptitude but did not try to develop in me any great talent. From a snatch of conversation I gathered that my mother, prudently, did not wish me to go too far in that direction. 'I do not want her to become a painter,' she said. 'She would have to take part in communal studies and make connections of which we would not approve.' They made me take up engraving. This went very well. I learned how to hold the engraving tool and soon overcame the initial difficulties. On the birthday of any of our grandparents, which we always, religiously, went round to celebrate, I used to take as my tribute either a little head which I had specially designed for the occasion or a small copper plaque on which I had engraved a bunch of flowers and a carefully inscribed encomium composed by Mr Sobersides. In return I was given illustrated catalogues, which greatly amused me, or something pretty to wear. My mother enjoyed dressing me up. She herself was simple and sometimes negligent in her attire, but her daughter was her little doll, so I was always elegantly and even quite expensively dressed; rather above my years, in fact. Young people in those days wore what were known as *corps-de-robes*. They were along the lines of a court dress, very close fitting at the bust, full in the skirt and with a long train decorated with various chiffons according to fashion. Mine were usually of fine silk, with a light pattern and modest colours but similar to my mother's in price and quality. I always had some trouble over my toilet because they curled my hair with curl-papers, hot tongs and all the ridiculous and barbaric gear they used in those days. I had a very sensitive scalp and was reduced to tears by the pulling and twisting when they dressed my hair. But I never complained.

The reader may ask for whose benefit all this dressing-up was intended, considering the quiet life I was leading. But remember that I went out twice a week. Anyone familiar with the habits of the Parisian bourgeoisie in my day will know that there were thousands of people who dressed themselves up at great expense simply to spend a few hours walking in the Tuileries every Sunday. Their wives had the additional pleasure of walking sedately to church under the critical eyes of their neighbours. Add to that family visits, saints' days and New Year's Day, weddings, baptisms and so on, and it will be seen that there were plenty of occasions for showing off. And in any case, there was more than one contrast in my upbringing. The young lady who appeared in church and in the

parades on Sunday dressed as if she had just stepped down from a
carriage, and whose bearing and language fully supported her
distinguished appearance, was quite capable of going to market
with her mother on a weekday in a little linen frock or even going
out by herself, not too far from home, to fetch parsley or lettuce
which the housekeeper had forgotten. It must be admitted that I
did not enjoy this very much, but I never showed it and found ways
of making the task a pleasant one. So polite was I, with a touch of
dignity too, that the greengrocer or whoever it was would take
pleasure in serving me first, and the people in front of me did not
seem to mind. I had a kind word for anyone who greeted me in the
street and I was much admired. This child, who read serious books,
could explain the orbits of the heavens, handled pencil and graving
tool and at eight years old was the best dancer of all the children in
the family, even those twice her age, was also the child who was
constantly called into the kitchen to make an omelette, shell the
peas or skim the broth. The mixture of serious study, enjoyable
play and orderly domestic chores seasoned with my mother's good
sense made me fit for anything. It seemed to foreshadow the
vicissitudes of my life and help me to bear them. I was never out of
my depth; I could make my own supper as easily as Philopoemen
could chop wood and yet no one who looked at me would have
thought of burdening me with such a menial task.

It can be imagined from what I have said that my mother did not
neglect her religious duties. She was pious though not devout. She
had – or tried to have – Christian faith and conformed her conduct
with the rules of the Church with the modesty and regularity of one
who feels a need for the broad consolations of religion and is not
going to quibble over the details. My own first introduction to
religious notions had made a respectful impression on me. My
lively imagination was fired and although I had some trouble to
begin with over the transformation of the devil into a serpent,
which my reason told me was a cruel thing for God to have done,
I ended by believing and worshipping.

I took Confirmation very seriously, pondering deeply on the
importance of my action and on the duties I was undertaking.
There was talk of preparing me for my first Communion: I was
filled with holy terror. I read works of devotion and meditated
unceasingly on the prospects of eternal bliss or eternal damnation.
At this sensitive moment in my development an event took place

which, because of its influence on my mind and on my conduct, I cannot pass over. I am a little embarrassed in recounting it; I want my memoirs to be chaste, as I am chaste myself, and this incident cannot be so described.

The layout of the apartment gave me easy access to my father's workshop. I seldom went there and my mother did not encourage it, but there were occasions when I needed to do so. I used to go to show my father my work, to fetch or return drawing models which I shared with his pupils, or to have my gravers sharpened (a small operation which demands strength of wrist and which I disliked because it made me dirty). The youngest of the pupils, a boy of about fifteen, who had more time on his hands than the others, used to be very attentive to me, doing me small services for which I thanked him politely. His parents were not in Paris and this, together with his age, made my mother specially kind to him. On long Sunday evenings in the winter she used to invite him to sit with us so that he could be persuaded to go to bed early and avoid keeping bad company. As a result I regarded him as less of a stranger than the others and had the sort of easy relationship with him that is appropriate, but at the same time very dangerous, for an innocent girl. So I was not in the least afraid to go into the workshop, if I needed to, even when he was alone there – something I would not have dared to do with any of the others when my father was absent. My mother was busy in her apartment, often supervising the cooking in the kitchen, and she did not always notice when I went to the workshop. One evening I went in to look for something. The young man seemed to be working alone under a lamp. I went up to him to collect the thing I had asked for, and he suddenly caught hold of my hand. He seemed to be playing with it and then, putting it under the workbench at which he was sitting, made me touch something most extraordinary. I cried out and tried to take my hand away, but without letting go he laughed and said in a very quiet voice: 'Hush! what are you afraid of? Don't be stupid. Don't you know me? I won't do you any harm. Hush! your mother will come. She will scold me for giving you a fright. But let me tell you, I won't have taught you anything *she* doesn't know well enough.' I was paralysed with horror, drew my hand away and wanted to get out of the room. But he still held my hand in his and then, half turning in his seat, he uncovered the thing that had so frightened me. I turned my head away. 'Really, that's horrible!' I cried, struggling to get away. 'I'm sorry to upset you,' he said.

'Forgive me. Don't say anything. I didn't mean to make you angry. And anyway, what's wrong with letting you see something which life-drawings uncover every day? But please yourself, you can get me into trouble if you like.' I was horrified. 'All right, all right, I won't say anything. But let me go.' He released my hand and I escaped. I fled to my room, but had hardly closed the door when I heard my mother calling me. I was trembling and wanted time to think but I had to go. I ran choking to my mother's room. 'What's the matter child?' she said, 'You look so pale.' 'Nothing,' I stammered, 'a little faintness. May I have some water?' My legs were shaking. I drank the water, did whatever it was my mother had wanted and pulled myself together.

I had great difficulty in sorting out in my head what impression this scene had made on me. Every time I tried to think about it some distraction interrupted my thoughts. After all, what harm had he done? None. Should I give him away? The very thought of having to describe what had happened made that impossible. Should I hold it against him? Even that seemed doubtful. Then, too, the comparison with the life-drawings seemed false, and that surprised me. Curiosity began to play a part and the boy's obvious anxiety drove out my angry feelings. For several days I did not go to the workshop. Of course I saw him at dinner, where he and two others ate with us, but nothing of a personal nature was ever allowed to disturb the gravity which reigned at my father's table. The young man eventually caught me alone in the kitchen. 'Are you cross with me?', he asked. 'Of course.' 'But I did you no harm.' 'You did something horrible.' 'Not at all; your mama plays like that with your father and is not afraid.' 'Shame on you! That's a wicked thing to say.' 'But I swear to you that I am sure of it; only they do it differently. I will show you if you like.' 'I don't want to know. Leave me alone.' 'All right, I won't show you; but then you must not be angry. You never come to the workshop any more, but you will, won't you?' 'All right', I promised. And I fled.

I often thought about this rôle which he had attributed to my mother. There was something so imposing about her that I could never imagine her behaving other than the way she would behave in public. But he had said it with such assurance. It made me remember certain pleasantries, incomprehensible to me, which my father sometimes addressed to my mother with a loud laugh and for which she always rebuked him crossly, saying 'Hold your tongue, M. Phlipon.' I would like to have known what it was that the young man wanted to teach me; I would have liked to hear about it without being myself the person to whom he said it. In short, the world began to seem a strange place. I sometimes went back to the workshop in the usual way to talk to my father when he was there and to look for things I needed whether he was there or not. Eventually my fear evaporated entirely. The young man took various opportunities to make funny remarks to me and make me laugh and the net result was that we became a little bit more familiar, with the sort of familiarity which always establishes itself between two people who have said something to one another which they have not said to anyone else.

One day, when my father had made me work for a few minutes with him and had then been suddenly called outside, I was about to leave the workshop after him when some sort of fanfare sounded from the Pont-Neuf quite close to where we lived. I stepped up on to a stool by the window because I could not see properly. 'Climb on to the edge of the bench,' said the young man, helping me to do so. The others went out to see what was happening. He stood behind me and when I started to get down he put his hands under my arms and lifted me up, pressing me against himself in such a way that my skirts were pushed up and I found myself sitting on his knees, as he himself sat back on a chair at the same moment. I then felt this extraordinary thing behind me. 'Let me go, sir,' I cried. 'What?' he said, 'Are you still afraid? I'm not doing you any harm.' 'But I want to go. My dress –'. 'Never mind your dress, I'll see to that.' He then put his hand where nothing else had reached and started to caress me. I struggled, trying to push his arms away and change my position, and managed to slip my feet to the ground. Then I caught sight of his face. I was horrified. His eyes were starting from his head and he was breathing hard. I nearly fainted. He noticed my condition and suddenly, his crisis over no doubt, began to be very gentle and conciliatory. He did all he could to pacify me and would not let me go until he had calmed me down. But far from having increased my curiosity he had disgusted me by taking these liberties. I could no longer bear to see him. I became nervous and unhappy, felt offended, wanted to tell my mother but did not dare. She soon saw that something was wrong and at her first question I poured it all out.

My mother's emotion and her air of panic deeply distressed me. She was evidently horrified to find how narrowly she had escaped losing the fruit of all her care. She may have thought I was hiding something from her; she asked me a thousand tortuous questions, torn between not wanting to teach me more than I already knew and wishing to assure herself that my knowledge was limited. I had nothing more to tell her than what I have just described. She very skilfully exploited the repugnance which my youth and bashfulness had already made me feel; she painted in such terrible colours my sin in having failed to inform her and having taken so lightly a young man's first excesses that I thought myself lost. Religion, virtue, honour, reputation – my mother in her concern invoked them all. She wanted to transform the dangers I had run into an impenetrable defence against future temptation. I do not know whether she meant to push things so far or whether my sensitivity drove me further than she intended, but I ended by convincing myself that I was the greatest sinner in the universe. I had no rest until my mother had taken me to confession – as she had already done two or three times a year since I was seven. It was terrible to have to recount this kind of thing to my confessor, but it was a form of expiation and I derived some consolation from finding the courage to go through with it.

So there I was, a penitent before having been a sinner. From that moment I became steeped in religion. I spent the first years of my adolescence in a sort of divine frenzy, my already precocious character entirely permeated with love of God. Later these same emotional impulses carried me into philosophy and seem to have provided me for the rest of my life with some protection against the tides of passion. Even in middle age I am just able, with their help, to hold my own like a swimmer breasting a great swell.

This devotion to God had a strange effect upon me. I became profoundly humble and timid. I looked upon men with a sort of terror, especially if they seemed in any way friendly to me. I watched my own thoughts with excessive scruple and any image at all attractive which presented itself to my mind seemed to me a temptation of the devil. Such was my reserve that when at the age of sixteen I read Buffon's *Histoire naturelle*, though I was no longer a believer I skipped any passage which dealt with the generation of man and if there were plates illustrating these matters I averted my eyes as if I were on the edge of a precipice. I did not get married until I was twenty-five. It will not surprise the reader, knowing my mentality and my inflammable feelings, to hear that my first night of marriage gave me some disagreeable surprises. I had received so much instruction on so many other subjects and none at all on this.

When she had heard my sad tale my mother asked me whether I was in love with the young man and craved his company. 'On the contrary,' I said, 'I hate coming into meals now and finding him there. I wish I need never see him again.' At once she found a pretext for changing the arrangements, and in future we ate alone in her room. It was a great relief to me and I loved her the more dearly for it. This arrangement continued until my father's contract with that boy came to an end. It had been thought advisable to avoid the fuss that his dismissal would have caused.

I met him only once again, seven or eight years later. He had just married and had found himself a good position and he asked my mother if he might introduce his wife. She agreed and I was present at the visit, which was a short one. He paid me a sort of respectful compliment which showed that he hoped that I would not think ill of him. He is still alive today, no doubt the father of a family, and that is why I do not mention his name. The impression left on me by the whole affair was so strong that even today, in an age of enlightenment and reason, I cannot recall it without pain. I have never opened my mouth on the subject either to my most intimate woman friend or to my husband, from whom I conceal very little.

It is frightening to think what constant, all-round vigilance a mother must exercise over her daughter. Everything conspires against the precious treasure in her care and only the greatest prudence will preserve it. The giddiness of youth, precocious natural instincts, ignorance or inclination and the ingenuity of innocence itself conspire to expose our timid sex, even before adolescence, to the thoughtless advances, dangerous seductions and audacious assaults of men, most of whom are impetuous and brutal unless tamed by education into strict morality or delicacy of feeling. The danger can be countered only by complete trust between the young girl and the person whose duty it is to protect her; but the art of inspiring such confidence is very rare, for the simple reason that it is difficult and that perhaps not all girls are susceptible to it. The essential rules are threefold; example, which encourages respect for the precepts taught; real concern for the young person's happiness; and, most important of all, kindness, with no caprice and no harshness.

My life was now even more retired, but I soon began to think it too worldly for my First Communion preparations. This great affair, which must so powerfully influence our eternal salvation, occupied all my thoughts. I acquired a taste for divine service, impressed by its solemnity. I avidly read up the origins and purposes of the Church's ceremonies and steeped myself in their mystical significance. Every day I consulted my folio copy of the *Lives of the Saints* and sighed for the days when the fury of paganism offered a martyr's crown to the gallant Christian. I thought seriously of taking up a new mode of life and after profound meditation I made my plans. Up until then, the very thought of being separated from my mother had made me burst into tears, and I had ignored the playful suggestions of my family, when they saw me in a self-pitying mood, to the effect that convents were places in which young people might do well to reside from time to time.

But what must one not sacrifice to Christ! My vivid imagination had formed a grand, romantic image of the cloister, its solitude and its silence. The more solemn the life there the better it matched the yearnings of my soul. One day after supper when I was alone with my parents I threw myself on my knees before them and burst into tears. I could not speak. They were greatly surprised and alarmed and asked me the reason for this strange behaviour. 'I beg you', I said between sobs, 'to do something for me which tears at my heart; for the love of God, put me in a convent!' They lifted me up. My dear mother was deeply moved. She would no doubt have been even more troubled but for the fact that, not having let me out of her sight for many months, she had no cause for fear. They asked me why I wanted to take this step, pointing out that they had never denied me any reasonable request. I said that I must take my First Communion in all proper tranquillity. My father applauded my zeal and said that he agreed. We discussed suitable houses. My family had no connections of that sort but we remembered that my music teacher had spoken of a convent where they taught young ladies and we decided to make enquiries. It was found to be a reputable establishment of a not too austere Order. The nuns were said to be moderate in their principles and not over-addicted to the usual mummery. They specialised in teaching the young. They held external classes where poor children from outside were taught free to complete their vows, in a hall set aside for that purpose. But there was a separate boarding house for children committed to their charge to be educated. My mother took the necessary steps. I was taken round to see all the grandparents, who applauded my decision, and was finally brought to the Convent of the Congréga-tion, rue Neuve-St-Étienne, in the faubourg St-Marcel, quite close to where I am now incarcerated. There I was separated from my darling Mama for the first time in my life. I pressed her to my bosom, choking back my tears, deeply affected. But I was obeying the voice of God. I crossed the sacred portals in tears, offering to my Maker the greatest sacrifice in my power. That was on 7 May 1765 – I was eleven years and two months old.

How shall I describe, from the depths of this prison and in the thick of the turmoil ravaging my country and destroying everything I hold most dear, the deep calm and rapture of those days? What fresh pen can describe the tangled feelings of a young, sensitive heart, hungry for bliss, feeling the first stirrings of maturity but seeing only the divine in all things? My first night in the convent was restless; I thought of home and of my dear mother who was surely thinking lovingly of me. There was a faint glimmer of light in the room where I had been put to bed with four other children of my age. I got up quietly and went to the window. I could just make out the garden in the moonlight. Complete silence reigned over the long shadows of the great trees, over my own awe-struck fancies, over the sure promise of peaceful prayer and meditation which I could see ahead. I raised my eyes to the night sky; it was pure and serene. I felt the divine presence smiling at my sacrifice and offering me already the rewards of a peaceful and saintly sojourn in this house of prayer. Blissful tears coursed down my cheeks; I renewed my vows with holy fervour and retired to the sleep of the elect.

I had arrived in the evening and had not yet met all my future companions. There were thirty-four of us, ranging in age from six to seventeen or eighteen, all in a single class but divided into two tables for meals and into two groups for the exercises of the day. My serious demeanour made it quite obvious that, despite my small size, I must be placed amongst the older girls. I became number twelve at their table and was the youngest there. My polite way of talking, learned from my mother, my sedate manner and the quiet, correct way in which I expressed myself were in striking contrast to the noisy abandon of these giddy girls. The younger ones developed a sort of confidence in me because I never rebuffed them, while the older ones treated me with some respect because I was obliging, despite my reserve, and because the mistresses showed me favour. Considering my upbringing it is not surprising that I turned out to be better educated than most of my companions, even the oldest among them.

The nuns found that they could take pride in my education, since I was one of their pupils, without having to go to much trouble to expand it. I already knew, or could easily learn, what they gave me to study and soon became their favourite. They all fussed over me and paid me compliments. The one who taught writing was a woman of about seventy who had become a nun twenty years before after some personal tragedy. She was educated and knew something of the world. She took a pride in teaching, had an excellent hand, did fine embroidery, gave good spelling lessons and knew some history. But because of her small size, her age and her slightly pedantic manner, she was not respected as much as she deserved by the youngsters. Even the dear Sisters, if I remember right, were jealous of her talents and encouraged the girls to make fun of her. This good woman soon allied herself with me on account of my taste for study. After taking her class she gave me private tuition, hearing me my grammar, checking my geography and going over passages of history. She even got permission to take me to her cell, where I read aloud to her. I still had one of my previous masters, the music teacher, coming to teach me and two other girls in the parlour under the supervision of a nun. For drawing, I had a mistress who came especially to the Convent from outside. Altogether it was a busy and regular life which suited me very well. I was usually top of the class and I still had free time because I worked so hard.

When we had walks or recreation I did not run around with the others but preferred to sit and read or dream under a tree. I was acutely sensitive to the beauty of foliage, the breath of the wind in the trees, the scent of flowers. Everywhere I saw the hand of Providence, felt its kindly influence and admired its handiwork. Glowing with gratitude for all this I would enter the church to worship and there I would be enraptured by the great organ's majestic tones and the sweet young voices of the Sisters singing motets. Apart from Mass, which all the boarders attended in the morning, half an hour was set aside each afternoon for meditation or pious reading, restricted to those who were thought capable of benefiting from it. I did not even have to ask to be included in this. But I did have one request, which was that I might take my First Communion on the next saint's day, which was the Feast of the Assumption. Although this was very soon after my arrival the request was granted by the teachers and by the Director.

The Director was a man of good sense. He was a member of the Order of St Victor and was a curé. He had agreed to take confession from the pupils of the Congrégation and he was very suited to this by his age, which was over fifty, and his moderation, wise opinions and austerity. My curé, M. Garat, took the trouble to come to the convent to hand over his little lamb to his colleague. They met in the parlour in my presence and talked Latin. I did not understand it very well, but well enough to hear some complimentary remarks about myself. However young and whatever the language, a girl can always understand that kind of thing. I profited greatly from this exchange; Garat was simply a pedant, though I respected his spiritual guidance, but the other was a just, knowledgeable father-figure who gave direction to my pious inclinations and made religion come alive for me without resort to mysticism. I loved him like a father and during the last three years of his life, after I had left the convent, I used to go regularly to St-Victor on the eve of Church festivals to be confessed by him.

It must be admitted that the Catholic faith, though not acceptable to an enlightened and strictly rational mind, exerts a strong appeal over the imagination. It arouses consciousness of the sublime and provokes feelings of terror, while at the same time satisfying the senses with mystical ceremonies, some elevating and some melancholy. Its votaries are kept perpetually conscious of eternity: that is what induces them to meditate and gives them such strong opinions about right and wrong, while the solemn daily rites and practices of the Church attract their attention and offer easy methods for obtaining salvation. Women are particularly adept at exploiting these practices and endowing the ceremonial with irresistible glamour, and none more so than the Sisterhood. Shortly after my arrival at the Convent a young novice took the veil. Flowers, bright lights, silken curtains and fancy ornaments decorated church and altar. A huge crowd of people in festive mood, as for a family wedding, filled the place. The young victim, proudly dressed up and exulting in her moment of glory, appeared for a short while at the Convent grating. She then retired, removed her splendid robes and reappeared covered in a white veil and crowned with roses. I can still remember the wave of emotion that came over me when I heard her rather trembling voice melodiously chanting the appointed antiphon:

Haec requies mea in saeculum saeculi: hic habitabo quoniam elegi eam.
(Here shall I reside, for I have chosen it for my home.)

I remember every note of this little affirmation; would that I could sing it myself in America!² What passion I should put into it!

But when she had pronounced her vows and prostrated herself before the altar, they covered her with a winding sheet as if she were dead and buried. I was horrified; it seemed to symbolise total severance of mortal ties, renunciation of all that she held most dear. I was no longer myself; I was that child. I felt that I was being torn from my mother's arms and I was in floods of tears. All my life I have suffered from this sensitivity. Things which ordinary people take in their stride and hardly notice can strike me to the heart, so that my life is never placid. I have thought about my existence from my earliest days and never found it burdensome, even when under the severest trials. I am not yet forty, but if I reckon by the depth of my feelings I must say that mine has been a prodigiously full life.

A thousand similar scenes from the days of my piety have left indelible impressions on my mind. Philosophy may since have swept away some of my religious illusions, but it has not stopped particular objects from having deep effect on my senses and arousing associations and ideas and feelings from the past. I still take a serious interest in divine service when it is conducted seriously; I overlook the charlatanism of the priests, their ridiculous fairy tales and their mumbo-jumbo and all I see is a gathering of pathetic men and women imploring the help of a Supreme Being. My mind fills with thoughts of Man's unhappiness and of his perennial hope for consolation and justice at the hands of a powerful avenger. Alien images fade to the background, passions cool, the sense of common duties lights up my mind. If there is music too, I am transported into another world; and from a scene where feeble-minded people have come to worship a piece of bread I emerge a nobler woman.

Like so many other human institutions, religion does not change a man's nature; it becomes assimilated in him and rises and falls with him. The common man thinks little, but believes what he is told and acts by instinct, and there is a perpetual contradiction between the precepts that he receives and the action he takes. Strong minds are very different; they need harmony, and their conduct mirrors their faith. I held to the faith which I was given in childhood until I was sufficiently clear-headed to dispute it. Until

² Madame Roland hoped at that time that Buzot and the other Girondins, who were in hiding in the neighbourhood of Quimper, might be able to take ship for the United States.

then, all my actions were the direct consequence of that faith. I am astonished at the frivolity of people who profess a faith yet behave otherwise, just as I despise today the cowardice of those men who would have a republic but will not risk their lives for it.

I do not want to repeat myself, but I must mention very briefly the occasion of my own First Communion. I had been prepared for it by all the usual convent methods: pious retreats, long prayers, silence, meditation. I regarded it as a solemn engagement and an assurance of eternal felicity, and when the time came I was so worked up emotionally and spiritually that I was in floods of tears and could not walk to the altar without assistance. A nun had to take my arm and guide me. These displays of religious fervour, which were entirely spontaneous, earned me much credit and many good ladies asked to be remembered in my prayers.

I can imagine the reader asking at this point why such a loving heart, such an affectionate nature could not have applied itself to more real issues; why, in fact, after dreaming such dreams of my own happiness, I could not have thought of others. Wait a moment, would be my reply. I will not linger much longer on these peaceful days of saintly illusion. In such a corrupt age as this, in such a badly organised society, it is impossible to be content for long with the goodness and innocence of nature. Common spirits may find satisfaction there, but for the others such simple pleasures are not enough. Nobler ambitions, more demanding duties beckon, leading them on to glorious achievement or to cruel failure. For the moment, I ask the reader to bear with me while I describe a dear friendship vouchsafed to me at that time, to which I owe many hours of happiness.

Several months had gone by since my arrival in the Convent. I passed my days as I have described. Every Sunday my father and mother took me out after divine service for a walk in the Jardin du Roi, now known as the Jardin des Plantes. I always shed a tear on leaving them, but it was for their sake and not because I regretted my situation. I was always glad to re-enter those silent cloisters, stepping slowly along the paths in order to savour the solitude. I would pause before the tomb of some saintly departed Sister, read the praises engraved upon the stone and murmur to myself 'She is in Heaven.' Then a sweet melancholy would take hold of me and I would imagine a state of perfect bliss in the bosom of the Lord, hoping to be received there one day.

Great excitement had been caused in our little group by the

announcement that two young ladies from Amiens were about to
join us. It was towards evening on a summer's day and we were
walking under the lime trees. 'Here they come!' was the cry. 'Here
they come!' The senior mistress led the new arrivals forward and
handed them over to the Sister in charge. We crowded around,
chattering, staring, whispering and finally settled down to a close
examination of the two Cannet girls. They were sisters. The elder
was about eighteen, with a fine figure, lively air and graceful step.
There was something sensitive, proud and discontented in her
look. The other was not more than fourteen; she had a silk veil over
her face which did not conceal the fact that she was crying. I noticed
her at once, stopped to look at her and went to ask the gossips what
they could tell me about her.

They said she was very attached to her mother and was her
favourite child, and that because she had been so upset at being
parted from home they had sent the sister along to help her bear it.
Both girls were put at my table for supper that night. Sophie, the
younger one, sat sad and silent and ate little. The other sister
seemed less concerned to console her than to lament her own lot –
with some justification. An eighteen-year-old girl, torn from a
social life which she enjoyed and made to go back to a convent in
order to keep her younger sister company, might well think herself
ill-used. The truth seems to have been that Mme Cannet's real
purpose was to tame an impetuous girl whom she could not control
herself. This was evident from Henriette's behaviour. She was
frank to the point of rudeness, impatient and over-excitable ...
Poor Sophie suffered a good deal from the character of her sister
and clearly was sometimes envious of her qualities and made to feel
inferior. She was essentially a rational, unemotional girl who liked
to think things out. Although she did not inspire passionate
feelings she was quietly friendly to everyone and was generally
liked. She enjoyed working and reading. I was touched by her sad
manner and we became inseparable friends. ...

Sophie was a firm believer like myself and our friendship
developed under the wing of Providence, as it were. We supported
one another in our search for perfection. Sophie was a relentless
reasoner. She analysed everything, wanted to know and discuss
everything. I talked much less and was really only interested in the
outcome. She liked being with me because I was a good listener and
when I did not agree I expressed my opinion so gently and with
such care not to offend that we never quarrelled. Her company was

infinitely precious to me because I needed someone to confide in and to share the strong feelings which seemed to have increased since I left home. She was about three years older than I and was a little less humble. Outwardly she had a sort of advantage over me which I did not envy; she was a good talker, whereas I was more adept at answering questions put to me. People greatly enjoyed asking me questions; not everyone, of course, has the skill to answer them. Sophie was really the only one with whom I could communicate properly; only she was able to lift the veil under which, unconsciously but naturally, I was hiding.

Henriette sometimes came with us, but not very often. She formed a more suitable friendship with Mlle Cornillon, a girl of eighteen, ugly as sin, sparkling with wit and malice, a real goblin to frighten the children. She would have been quite out of her element with us.

I cannot refrain from recording the friendly interest shown in me from the moment I arrived by another nice girl who comforted me on many occasions. Angélique Boufflers came of a penniless family and had taken her vows at the age of seventeen. She had not yet found herself in any sense. Nature had moulded her, as it were, in sulphur and saltpetre and her repressed energies drove her into extremes of liveliness and sensibility. Owing to her poverty she had been put amongst the lay sisters, with whom she had little in common apart from their simple religious practices. There are some types of people who have no need of culture; Sister Agatha (that was her religious name) had received little help in the way of education but she was superior to all her companions and to most of the ladies of the choir. Her merits were known and although, as usually happens in a society where there is no such thing as gratitude, they overwhelmed her with duties, she did enjoy a deserved reputation. She was responsible at that time for looking after the schoolgirls and she did this, on top of all her other tasks, with diligence and cheerfulness.

I hardly noticed at first that she had singled me out, but her kind behaviour soon attracted my attention. At table, without my knowing, she watched to see what I liked and helped me to it; in the dormitory she willingly made my bed and whenever we met she said something nice to me and kissed me tenderly. Sometimes she took me to her cell, where she had a nice little parrot which she had taught to speak. She secretly gave me a second key to this cell, so that I could enter in her absence, and there I read her small collection of books, the poems of Father Cerceau and works of mysticism. When her duties prevented her from spending a few minutes with me, or seemed likely to do so, I would find a charming note to which of course I replied. She kept these replies like precious stones and showed them to me afterwards neatly folded in her prayerbook.

Agatha's attachment to me soon became common knowledge in the Convent. But it was regarded as quite natural. My friends never seemed to resent her favouring me and when the other nuns taxed her with it she asked them with her natural frankness whether they would not do the same thing in her place. And if some crabbed octogenarian like Mother Gertrude told her that she liked me too much Agatha replied that she said that only because she herself was incapable of loving. 'And anyway,' she added, 'don't you stop and talk to the child yourself whenever you meet her?'; old Mother Gertrude would then toddle off, muttering. But if she met me an hour later she would not fail to give me sweets. When the Cannet girls arrived and I formed an attachment with Sophie, Agatha seemed a bit jealous. The other nuns laughed at her for this, but her kindness to me did not change. She seemed quite happy that Sophie was so fond of me and in fact enjoyed the thought of my having a friend of my own age with whom I could spend the whole day.

Agatha was then twenty-four. I have always felt the truest respect for her character and her affections and am honoured to have been able to express it at all times. During the last years of the existence of convents she was the only person I ever visited in hers. Today, when age and ill health make that asylum more than ever necessary for her, she is deprived of it and lives, or vegetates, on her wretched pension not far from where I am now in prison. Yet in all the misfortunes and hardships of her old age her only complaint is of the imprisonment of her daughter, as she still calls me. Dear friends, you may spare yourselves from pitying me, considering the consolations that Heaven has granted me. And you, my persecutors, with all your power, none of you can boast of such a loyal friend as Agatha, whose love only grows when times are bad.

The winter was now over; I had seen rather less of my mother during these months, but my father never let a Sunday go by without coming to see me and taking me for a walk in the Jardin du Roi if the weather permitted. We would brave the cold and run gaily over the snow – delightful afternoons of which I am reminded twenty years later as I read these favourite lines of Thomson:

> Pleas'd have I, in my chearful morn of life
> When nurs'd by careless solitude I liv'd,
> And sung of nature with unceasing joy,
> Pleas'd have I wander'd thro' your rough domain,
> Trod the pure virgin snows, myself as pure.

It had been agreed when I entered the Convent that I should stay only one year. I wanted this myself because it set a term to my separation from my mother. The nuns on their side, when they agreed to let me take my First Communion within four months of my arrival, had been careful to stipulate that I should not leave them any sooner on that account but should complete my year. The year was now over and it was time for me to go. My mother told me that Grandmama Phlipon, who was very fond of me, wanted me to go and live with her for a while to keep her company. Mama said that she had agreed to this knowing that I would have no objection, since she would be able to see much more of me there than when I had been at the Convent. It was a perfect arrangement. My father had taken on community duties which meant that he was frequently called out, and I understood very well that my mother, who in the past had never concerned herself with the young apprentices, would now have to keep a closer watch on their work; she therefore no longer had the time she would need for devoting herself to me.

It was a gentle transition from our total separation to my eventual return home. I accepted it the more readily as I was very fond of my grandmama. She was a graceful and good-humoured little old lady, pleasant and well spoken with a nice laugh and a look in her eye that suggested she had once been attractive. She was about sixty-five or sixty-six and took a lot of trouble with her dress, which was always appropriate to her age. Her great pride was to observe the proprieties in thought and deed. She was plump, light on her feet and upright in her bearing and made full use of her small, expressive hands. She did not seem old because she talked so gaily and with such feeling. She liked the company of young people and they liked her. She was always proud to be sought out by the younger generation.

She had been widowed within a year of her marriage and my father had been her only child, born after her husband died. The small business on which she had depended failed and she was obliged to earn her living looking after the children of some rich distant relations. That is how she came to reside with Mme de Boismorel as tutor to her son Roberge, of whom I shall have more to say, and her daughter, later Mme de Favières. A small legacy had subsequently assured her independence and she was now living on the Île St-Louis in a neat little apartment with her sister, Mme Rotisset, whom she called Angélique. This old girl, racked with piety and asthma, pure as an angel and simple as a child, was entirely devoted to her elder sister. The cares of the little household devolved exclusively on Angélique. The menial tasks were performed by a daily woman who came in morning and afternoon, but Angélique did everything else and dutifully dressed her sister. When I arrived, Angélique automatically became my nurse, while Mme Phlipon undertook my education. So here I am in their hands, having left the house of our Lord and Saviour under a shower of endearments, kisses from the nuns, tears from Agatha and Sophie, choked with my own emotion and swearing to soften the bitterness of the separation by frequent visits in the future.

I did not fail to keep this promise. Our walks turned often towards the Congrégation. My aunt Angélique and my father were always glad to take me there. The news of my arrival in the parlour would spread quickly and I would see twenty friends within an hour. But of course these visits were no substitute for the daily contact of the past; they became rarer, and I supplemented them with letters, chiefly to Sophie. This was the origin of my taste for letter-writing and of my facility in it.

— 9 —

GROWING UP

◆

I CAN FEEL MY RESOLVE WEAKENING. I am agonised by the suffering of my country and the loss of my friends. It saps my courage. My senses are dulled, my imagination clouded and my very heart broken by the deep depression stealing over me. France is nothing but a field of carnage, a bloody arena where her children tear one another to pieces.

The enemy advances on every side, aided by our internal divisions. The towns of the north are fallen; Flanders and Alsace are under threat. The Spaniards are ravaging Roussillon; the Piedmontese, rejecting an alliance which our state of anarchy has made odious to them, return to their old master, whose troops now invade our frontiers. The rebels in the Vendée are still ravaging a vast extent of territory and the Lyonnais, foolishly provoked, are preparing to resist. Marseilles is rushing to their assistance;[1] the neighbouring departments are wavering. In all this universal agitation, these innumerable broils and feuds, there is only one steady factor – the relentless advance of foreign armies. Our government is a monster whose form and behaviour are equally disgusting. It destroys everything it touches and devours itself.

The armies, ill equipped and badly led, fight and run away alternately like desperadoes. Competent generals are accused of treason by political commissars who know nothing of war and who brand as an aristocrat anyone better instructed than themselves. The legislative body, the Convention, which was feeble from the very start, did at least debate the nation's problems so long as it had on its benches some brave and intelligent members. But all such men, all upright and patriotic men devoted to their country's interest, have long since been driven out with abuse and

---

[1] Madame Roland was not aware that a few days earlier, on 23 August, Marseilles had opened its gates to the troops of the Convention.

calumny, and their places taken by ignorant intriguers and brigands. They were the élite, and they leave behind them a wild rabble of mediocre fools, criminal and corrupt artificers of the nation's ruin. The nation itself, cowardly and ill-informed (being too idle and egotistic to look at the facts), has now accepted a scandalous new Constitution which, even if it had been a better one, should have been rejected with indignation coming from such wicked hands.[2] The nation lays claim to a rule of law and liberty, yet it allows its representatives to be oppressed. The people are already under an iron yoke and any change seems to them an improvement, but the truth is that France, incapable of her own reform, is simply waiting for the first master who will come along and subdue her.

O Brutus, whose bold right arm freed the corrupt Romans in vain from tyranny, we have been mistaken, as you were! We, too, thought that the overthrow of tyranny would usher in a reign of justice and of peace, whereas it has merely been the signal for the outbreak of hateful passions and vice. After the proscription of the triumvirs you said that you were more ashamed of what had caused the death of Cicero than distressed by the act itself. You told your friends in Rome that they had become slaves more through their own weakness than through the wickedness of the tyrants, and that they were *cowards* to tolerate the abuses from which they were suffering. That is exactly how I feel here in my prison. But, alas, the time for indignation is over. One can no longer hope for any good or be surprised at any evil.

How will history ever describe the horrors of these dreadful days and the abominable men who defile France with their crimes? Their wickednesses far exceed the cruelties of Marius or the bloody expeditions of Sulla. When Sulla rounded up 6,000 men who had surrendered to him and slaughtered them under the noses of the Senate, forcing the senators to continue their debate to the sound of his victims' screams, he was only behaving as a typical tyrant, coldly abusing an usurped authority. But to whom may we compare our hypocrites here in Paris who, in the guise of legality and employing the language of the law, have set up a tribunal[3] to serve their own vengeance, and who regularly send to the scaffold, with insulting legal formality, those whose virtue offends them,

---

[2] The Constitution of 24 June 1793, which was in fact never applied.
[3] The revolutionary tribunal, set up on 10 March 1793.

whose talents put them to shame or whose property they covet?...

But the fugitive deputies, have they been able at last to escape this inhospitable land which devours its noblest sons and drinks the blood of the virtuous? My friends, I pray Heaven that you reach the United States, sole asylum of liberty. My prayers speed you thither; I have hopes that you are on your way. But I myself, alas, am done for; I shall never see you again. I am well aware that your departure and your safety, for which I pray so fervently, mean our final separation. And you, my venerable husband, wasted and weak, prematurely aged in flight from your assassins, shall I ever see you again? Shall I ever have a chance to offer some amends to your pride, which I have so bitterly wounded? How many days are left to me to watch the desolation of my country and the degradation of my fellow citizens? These sad thoughts overpower me; I cannot escape from my sorrow. Tears pour from my weary eyes and I have laid down the pen with which I have so lightly traced the story of my childhood.

But I will try again to think back to those times and to follow them through, and perhaps one day these artless pages may lighten the darkness of some other unfortunate captive, helping him to forget his own misery in thinking of mine. Possibly, too, those who seek to understand the human heart through a novel or a play may find something worth studying in my story....

Let us leave this unhappy age, savage as the reign of Tiberius. Come back to me now, tranquil memories of my happy youth!

I spent my thirteenth year with my grandmother. The quiet of her home and the piety of my aunt Angélique well suited the reserved, serious disposition with which I left the Convent. Every morning my aunt took me to Mass, where I was very soon noticed by those fishers of souls who seek to please God by filling the cloisters. Father Géry, with stooping and obsequious look, came up to what he supposed was my governess and congratulated her on the edifying example set by her pupil. He ventured to express the hope that he might be chosen as the guide to conduct the young lady in the paths of Christ; and he learned with regret that I had already completed the main ceremonies and had confided my spiritual welfare to another. He then desired to know whether I had no plans for my future and for renouncing this wicked world, to which I replied that I was too young as yet to know my vocation.

Father Géry sighed, paid me saintly compliments and took care to meet us on our way out to offer further devoted salutations. My youthful piety did not extend so far as to incline me to Jesuitical affectations; I wanted no dealings with ridiculous bigotry and Father Géry's subservient posture gave me no pleasure.

But I did, all the same, have the secret intention of devoting myself to a religious life. I had been completely seduced by St Francis of Sales, one of the most amiable of the saints in paradise, and I was already an adopted sister of the Order of the Visitation, which he founded. But I realised that as an only child my parents would never allow me to take my vows before I was of age and I had no wish to upset them ahead of time. Besides, if my faith were to falter during the period of preparation I should merely be giving a handle to the unbelievers. So I decided to keep quiet about my decision and to pursue the objective in secret. I made use of my grandmother's little library. The *Philotée* of St Francis of Sales and the Manual of St Augustine were the sources of my favourite meditations, delicious nourishment of love and devotion for an innocent, ardent nature steeped in celestial illusions! The controversial works of Bossuet introduced a very different note. However favourable they might be to the cause which they set out to defend, these works drew attention to some of the opposing arguments and this encouraged me to test my beliefs by applying reason. It was the first step, still a long way from the scepticism at which I arrived some years later, having been successively a Jansenist, a Cartesian, a Stoic and a deist. What a journey! And finally to end up in irons for having become a patriot!

As well as all that, I fed my imagination with old travel books and stories of mythology, and my literary tastes with the letters of Mme de Sévigné. I found her free and amiable style, her liveliness and her tender feelings entirely to my taste and became so familiar with her circle that I might have been living with her. My grandmother saw little of society and rarely went out, but I was always happy in her company, talking or learning how to make something with my hands, because her conversation was so full of life and good humour. Madame Besnard, the great-aunt who had kept an eye on me when I was out to nurse, came every day to spend a couple of hours with her sister after dinner. My grandmother sometimes teased her for her austere character and the solemn formality of her behaviour, but gently, careful not to offend her; and in any case the old lady was quite able to hold her own, coming out with many a plain home truth, and was forgiven for any rudeness on account of her goodness of heart. My grandmother attached great importance to the courtesies of social intercourse and was always touched when I gave her evidence of my very genuine affection. She would say nice things to me, and when I responded suitably she would bridle with pleasure and cast a proud look at Mme Besnard. The latter would shrug her shoulders, wait until I was a little further away and then say in a low voice which I could hear perfectly well, 'Really! you are insufferable. You will spoil her. Such a pity!' At which my grandmother would straighten herself up and assure her sister, with a superior look, that she knew what she was doing. Then dear Angélique, with her pale face, her chin stuck out, her glasses on her nose and her knitting in her hands, would assure them both very quietly that there was no danger and that it did not make the slightest difference what they said because I had enough sense to educate myself without anybody's help. Yet Mme Besnard, who was so strict and so well aware of the dangers of flattery, would be deeply worried if she saw me lying on an uncomfortable bed, and if I cut my finger she would come round twice a day to see how it was getting on. A touching old lady.

I truly believed that Heaven had placed me in the company of these good souls in order to make me as loving as possible. One day my grandmother had the idea of going to call on Mme de Boismorel, partly no doubt for the pleasure of seeing her and partly in order to show off her granddaughter. Great preparations ensued, elaborate toilet from dawn onwards; and here we are, together with Aunt Angélique, arriving in the rue St-Louis in the Marais around noon. As soon as we entered the building all the servants, beginning with the porter, greeted Mme Phlipon with great affection and respect, vying with one another in their polite attentions. She replied to them all in a gentle voice and with dignity. That was all right. But then they saw the child. My grandmother had not drawn any special attention to me, but the *servants* started straight away paying me compliments. I began to feel uncomfortable; it is difficult to explain why, but I think I felt that, though the servants were entitled to look at me, it was not their place to pay me compliments. We moved forward into the house; a large footman announced us and we entered the drawing-room in which we found Mme de Boismorel seated with her dog on what in those days was called not an ottoman but a sofa, solemnly embroidering a tapestry.

Madame de Boismorel was a woman of about the same age, shape and corpulence as my grandmother. But her clothes had evidently been chosen to display opulence and superior quality rather than good taste, while the expression on her face, far from indicating a wish to please, suggested that she meant to be esteemed and was quite sure she deserved it. She had a little bonnet of rich pleated lace perched on the top of her head, decorated with two spikes like the ears of a rabbit; and her hair, probably a wig, was arranged around this construction with that discreet artifice so important for women over sixty. Her cheeks were thickly rouged, giving her insignificant eyes more hardness than they really needed to make me lower mine. 'Ah! Good morning, Mlle Rotisset!' cried Mme de Boismorel in a loud, cold voice, rising at our approach. (What! my grandmother is addressed by her maiden name in this place?) 'Indeed, I am charmed to see you. And this child? Your grand-daughter? She will do well. Come, sweetheart, come and sit beside me. She is shy. How old is she, Mlle Rotisset, your granddaughter? She is a little on the dark side but basically her skin is excellent; it will soon freshen up. She has a good figure already. You must bring luck, child. Have you ever bought a ticket in the lottery?' 'Never, Madame. I do not like games of chance.' 'I believe it. At your age one thinks one is bound to win. And what a charming voice, how sweet and full ... but she is very serious! Are you not a little inclined to religion?' 'I know my duties, Madame, and try to perform them.' 'Very good. You want to take the veil I believe?' 'I do not know my destiny or try to foretell it.' 'How sententious she is! Does she read, your little granddaughter, Mlle Rotisset?' 'Reading is her greatest pleasure. She spends some time reading every day.' 'Oh! I can see that; but take care that she does not become a scholar. That would be a thousand pities.'

Then the two ladies started talking about the family and about Mme de Boismorel's social circle. My grandmother asked news of the uncle and the cousin, the daughter-in-law and the friend, of Father Langlois and the marquise de Lévi, of counsellor Brion and of the curé Parent. They talked about the health, the connections and the eccentricities of these people; of Mme Roudé, for example, who despite her age still liked to show off her figure and always went around with her bosom uncovered except when entering or descending from her carriage when she covered it with a large handkerchief kept specially in her pocket for that purpose because, she said, it was not made to be seen by lackeys. During this dialogue Mme de Boismorel put a few stitches into her canvas, stroked her dog once and stared at me a great deal. I disliked her look and did my best to avoid it by glancing around the apartment; I thought it looked much more agreeable than the woman who lived in it. My heart was beating faster than usual; I felt flushed and oppressed. I did not quite get to the point of asking myself why my grandmother was not on the sofa and Mme de Boismorel playing the part of Mlle Rotisset, but I was beginning to think along those lines and when the visit came to an end I felt like someone rescued in the nick of time. 'Ah! Now, don't forget to get me the lottery ticket. Your granddaughter must choose the number, do you understand, Mlle Rotisset, and I must receive it from her hand. Kiss me then. And you, my heart, don't lower your eyes so; they are good to look at, those eyes of yours, and the confessor will not want you to keep them hidden. Mlle Rotisset, you will receive some compliments on your granddaughter before long I can assure you'; and at that Mme de Boismorel rang her bell, ordered Lafleur to collect the lottery ticket in two days' time, silenced her dog and was back on the sofa before we had reached the antechamber.

We walked home in silence and I went straight to my books so as to forget Mme de Boismorel, whose compliments were no more welcome to me than those of her servants. My grandmother, not entirely pleased, talked occasionally about the woman and her eccentricities. She had noticed her egotism; when my grandmother mentioned her children's needs as a reason for avoiding great expense, Mme de Boismorel observed that children were only a secondary consideration. She had also heard of her free and easy manners: Mme de Boismorel would change her clothes while her confessor and others were in the room, though admittedly, according to my grandmother, this was common practice among society women. I found such behaviour very strange. Out of curiosity I let my grandmother talk about it but I kept my own opinions to myself.

A fortnight later we received a visit from M. de Boismorel, the son, who had not been present when we called on his mother. He was a man of about thirty-seven or thirty-eight, serious-looking and quiet, with a respectable and distinguished manner and large, rather prominent eyes which looked out upon the world with openness and understanding. His deep, strong voice, which he appeared to be keeping under control out of deference to others, suggested genuine feeling and good manners. He approached my grandmother with respect, calling her his dear friend, and greeted me with that kind of bland civility which men of feeling like to show towards young ladies. The conversation became easy, though somewhat restrained. He acknowledged very gracefully how much he owed to my grandmother's care and I understood him to say, in a roundabout but delicate manner, that Providence had evidently rewarded her for her generous attentions to other people's children by bestowing a blessing upon her in the form of her own grandchild.

I found M. de Boismorel much more agreeable than his mother and I was always delighted to see him come again, which he did every two or three months. He had married, very young, a charming wife and had one son whose education greatly preoccupied him. He had decided to undertake it himself, following philosophical precepts which brought him into sharp conflict with his mother's prejudices and his wife's religious feelings. They accused him of eccentricity. He had suffered some sort of nervous attack following a serious inflammatory illness, and all the old countesses, fat lawyers and little priests in his family and amongst his mother's friends attributed his opinions and his ideas for the education of his son to an affection of the brain caused by his illness. When I got to hear all the circumstances I became very interested and concerned. I found the arguments of this singular man most convincing and I began to suspect that there must be two different realities, one of the world (practical); and the other of the study (theoretical); in other words, that morality might not be quite the same thing in practice as in principle. And I wondered whether the conflict between these two realities might explain some of the strange contradictions which I had always observed in life. Society, perhaps, called any man mad who was not suffering from the general madness. These kind of thoughts piled up insensibly in my mind.

My grandmother sometimes contrasted M. de Boismorel's behaviour with that of his sister, Mme de Favières, of whose conduct she had real reason to complain. The brother himself found it necessary to remind Mme de Favières that Mlle Rotisset was, after all, a relation of theirs, a fact which their mother seemed to forget or wished to ignore. To my great relief I was not asked to call on Mme de Favières and there was never any question of repeating the call on her mother.

My father's stint of community duty was now over, my year with my grandmother completed; I was now going home to my dear

[161]

mama. It was sad to be leaving the Île St-Louis, that lovely *quartier* with its quaysides where I walked every evening with my aunt Angélique, following the graceful curve of the river and admiring the distant outline of the countryside. How often I had passed those riverside gardens, my head full of pious thoughts on the way to church! And how happy I had been for so many a day with Grandmama in the cheerful atmosphere that she created. I cried when I left her, despite my deep love for my mother, whose qualities were after all far deeper and more imposing. I was confused to find myself at that moment making comparisons to her disadvantage for the first time in my life.

I was a child of the Seine and still dwelling on its banks. My father's apartment did not have the quiet solitude of my grandmama's. It looked out over the busy, ever-changing traffic of the Pont-Neuf, so that in going home I was brought back into the world, both physically and figuratively. But it had a fine view and gave plenty of scope to my wandering, romantic imagination. How often I have sat at my window there, gazing northwards into the great deserts of the sky, the azure, sharply delineated vault of heaven, from the smoky eastern horizons beyond the Pont-au-Change round to the flaming, golden sunsets behind the trees of the promenade and the mansions of Chaillot! At the end of a fine day I would almost always spend some moments there. Soft tears would drop silently from my eyes and my heart would fill with inexpressible feelings, happy to be alive and thankful to the Supreme Being for my existence. I do not know whether it is the sensibility of the heart which gives all objects a livelier colour, or whether material conditions, commonplace in themselves, have the power to create these emotions; or whether perhaps each is both cause and effect. But when I look back over my life, I cannot decide whether circumstances or my own character are more responsible for the great variety and depth of the feelings which have marked every stage of it and which have left me with such vivid memories of every place where I have lived.

I still had music lessons from Cajon. He liked to make me argue the theory, or rather the mechanics of music, for though he composed a little he was not strong on mathematics, still less on metaphysics and he liked to show off his technical knowledge. He admired my ability to follow a line of reasoning but was distressed at the coldness of my singing. 'Do put some feeling into it,' he constantly implored me. 'You sing a light air as if you were a nun chanting the Magnificat.' The poor man could not see that my soul was too great to be confined in a song. The fact is that I would have found it embarrassing to put feeling into a tender passage of music, just as I had always been shy of reading aloud to anyone an episode from Eucharis or Herminie. I always found myself transformed into the person who was supposed to be speaking. I could not *imitate*; I actually *felt* the sensations which were to be depicted. The result was that my breathing became agitated, my voice trembled and I could control myself only by adopting a flat and serious tone of voice. I did not dare to be passionate.

Mignard, whose courteous Spanish manners greatly appealed to my grandmother, had begun teaching me the guitar while I was living with her and continued to give me lessons after I returned home. It did not take me long to learn the usual accompaniments; Mignard wanted to make me play really well, and in the end I became more skilful than he. The poor man lost his head over that, as I shall describe in due course. Mozon was brought back to perfect my dancing and Mr Sobersides for arithmetic, geography, writing and history.

My father started me engraving again. He confined me to a very narrow range of work in which he thought he could interest me by introducing the profit motive; as soon as I was good enough to be useful to him he gave me small jobs to do, for which he shared the price with me, adding up the amounts owed to me at the end of the week in a little book which I was instructed to keep. This bored me. Nothing seemed more insipid than engraving the edges of a watchcase or crosshatching a little snuff box. I would much rather read a good book than be able to buy myself a ribbon. I made my feelings clear and he did not insist. So I put away the graving tool and the thimbles and have not touched them since.

I went out every morning with my mother to Mass, after which we sometimes went shopping. When this was done, and when lessons and meals were over, I used to retire into my room to read, write and think. In the long evenings I revived the habit of doing something with my hands and my mother used to read aloud to me for hours at a time. I enjoyed those readings very much but as I could not take it all in thoroughly enough I took to writing extracts. Each morning, first thing, I put down on paper what had most struck me from last night's reading and then took up the book itself to check references or to copy out a passage if I wanted to preserve it intact. This became a habit, a need and a passion. As I had already read everything in my father's small library, I began to borrow or hire books and I could never give them back until I had mastered what was best in them. . . .

Father Jay was a good old man, generous in both body and soul, a terrible preacher, a pitiless confessor, a casuist, I know not what. But he knew his business. He had set up his two brothers as notaries in Paris, where they were doing well. He had invited one of his relations to keep house for him, a Mlle d'Hannaches, a great horse of a woman, frazzled and faded, with a rough voice and an obsession with her noble origins, who bored everyone to death with her ingenious economies and her titles. But at least she was a woman, which always livens up a priest's house. Besides, she kept her cousin's table well stocked and respectable, which meant a lot to him. Father Jay had my great-uncle Bimont as a boarder (my grandmother Bimont having departed this life) and greatly enjoyed it. It made his table jollier and his cousin better tempered, and it assured him his game of backgammon. My mother and the cousin made up the four. I, left out in the cold, had the free run of his large library which suited me admirably. I made full use of it so long as he lived, but that was only three years. One of his brothers got into trouble; he became depressed, languished for six weeks, threw himself out of the window and died of the fall. Mademoiselle d'Hannaches, who was engaged at the time in a law-suit over the succession of her uncle, 'the captain', was taken pity on by my mother and spent eighteen months with us. During that time I acted as her secretary. I wrote her business letters, copied out her beloved family tree, drew up the petitions which she addressed to the First President of the Court and to the Procurator-General of the Paris Parliament (trustees of the pension established by a certain M. de Saint-Vallier for the benefit of distressed noblewomen) and sometimes accompanied her when she went to solicit the support of various persons. I observed that despite her ignorance and uncouth language, her unwieldy figure and old-fashioned dress and all the other absurdities about her, she was respected on account of her birth. They listened solemnly to the names of her ancestors, which she constantly repeated, and did what they could to meet her demands. I compared the respectful attention given to her with the treatment my grandmother and I had received from Mme de Boismorel, which still rankled with me. I knew that I was worth more than Mlle d'Hannaches, whose forty years and blue blood had not equipped her to write a letter which made any sense or was even readable; and I concluded that the world was an unfair place and the social order most unreasonable. ...

Sophie had gone back to her family in Amiens. Before she left, we had arranged that our mothers should meet and in this way they gave our friendship a kind of official status. Each congratulated the other on the choice which her daughter had made and they smiled fondly at the promises we exchanged in their presence never to forget one another. These turned out to be more lasting than we thought at the time, despite the changes of fortune that were to come. I began a very regular correspondence with my dear friend, writing to her at least once a week and more often twice. 'And what did you write about?', I hear the reader ask. About everything; about what I had seen, about what I had thought and felt, what I had learnt; there was plenty to write about. A correspondence of this kind feeds itself. I learned to reflect, the better to convey my reflections, studied more keenly because I enjoyed sharing what I had learned and observed things more closely because it was such a joy to describe what I had seen. Sophie wrote less often. Hers was a large family and the house was always full of people. She had all the social duties of provincial life and was constantly engaged in frivolities or in good works and in exchanging meaningless visits; there was little time left for writing descriptions of all this to me. This made her perhaps all the more grateful for what I wrote to her and it encouraged me to continue writing.

The death of Father Jay deprived me of access to his books ... and I was obliged to have recourse to the bookshops. My father would obtain anything I asked for, and I usually chose books which I had read about or heard quoted. Thus I noted translations of the ancient historians, Diodorus Siculus and others. Then I wanted to read the history of my own country by an author other than Mézeray and chose Father Velly and his much less talented followers. I read Pascal, Montesquieu, Locke, Burlamaqui and our principal dramatists. I had no special purpose other than to develop my faculties and to improve myself. I do not know what I might have become if I had been in the hands of a skilful teacher; and I dare say that if I had concentrated on one particular subject I might have acquired a very extensive knowledge or developed great talent. But would I have been any the better for it, or more useful? I cannot tell. I certainly would not have been happier. Nothing can compare with the fullness, the peace, the contentment of those days of innocent study. And yet, there were things to worry me too. Is there ever a time when this is not so?

I usually had several books on hand at the same time, some for study, others for relaxation. Long-term historical works were read aloud, as I have said, in the evenings after dinner. That was almost the only time I spent with my mother; during the rest of the day I was alone, making notes, amusing myself, thinking. On rest days in fine weather we used to go out and join the public promenades. My father took me to all the picture exhibitions and art collections to be seen in Paris in those prosperous days. He enjoyed these occasions very much; he was able to show his superiority by drawing my attention to things he knew better than I did and when he saw that I had good taste he took it as a credit to himself. That was our real point of contact; we were entirely at one about it. He was given to exhibitionism in all its forms. It was clear that he liked showing himself off in public with a well-dressed young person on his arm, especially when nice things were whispered in his ear about her freshness and charm; and if anyone approached who showed any hesitation or doubt about the status of his companion he would say 'This is my daughter' with modest triumph. I always noticed this and it touched me; it did not make me proud, because all I saw in it was his affection. If I said anything, I could see him glance at the other person to watch the effect upon them of my voice or my comments, as if to say 'Have I not the right to be proud?' I was conscious of all that and it sometimes made me shy. I felt that I had to compensate for my father's pride by being extra modest myself.

But meanwhile, how was I to reconcile this world, the arts, the images they evoked, my feminine desire to please, my religious devotion, my studies, my reason and my faith – all these conflicting aims and impulses? That was the problem: that was the worry that I mentioned just now. It was growing every day and I must try to describe it, difficult though this may be.

With most people, naturally disposed to feel rather than to think, the first assault upon their faith comes from the passions; and it is the passions that set up conflict between their acquired principles and their innate desires. A faith based on education and experience is then found to be an inadequate reconciling force. But in the case of a young person who thinks, and who is brought up far removed from the pitfalls of social life, it is Reason that first rebels. Reason causes such a person to examine her faith even before she has any interest in doubting it. However, even though my doubts were not caused by personal considerations, that does not mean they were independent of my feelings; I thought with my heart, and my reason though remaining impartial was never indifferent.

The first thing I found repugnant in the religion which I was professing so seriously and so steadfastly was the eternal damnation of all who disowned it or who had never heard of it. I had, after all, studied history and when I thought of the size of the world, the succession of the centuries, the march of empires, the public virtues and errors of so many nations, I found it paltry, ridiculous, atrocious to think of a Creator who would consign to eternal torment those innumerable individuals, feeble creatures of his own hands, whom he himself had cast into this perilous world and into the darkness of ignorance. I must be mistaken about this proposition, surely. But are there others? Let us look and see! The moment a Catholic starts thinking like that, the Church may consider him a lost soul. I can understand perfectly well why the priests want blind submission and are so assiduous in preaching a religious faith which demands unquestioning acceptance of what they say. It is the only basis for their power. The moment people start reasoning, the priests lose control over them.

After the cruelty of damnation, the doctrine of infallibility struck me as the greatest absurdity. I rejected them both. What then is left that is valid? That became the object of my most intense and anxious search for the next few years. It is hard to describe my passionate enquiry. Critics, philosophers, moralists, metaphysicians became my favourite reading. I hunted them out, compared them with one another and tore them apart. I had lost my confessor, good Father Lallement, whose wise guidance had meant so much to me, and in looking for a successor I thought of Father Morel of my own parish, whom I had met at my uncle's. He was quite a bright little man, professing very austere principles, which is what I wanted. He was the first to be told when my faith began to waver (for I was never one for concealing the truth) and he urged on me the great apologists and defenders of the Christian religion. The irony is that it was through these works that I heard of the critics whom they were trying to refute, and I noted down the titles so as to get hold of them....

10

ADOLESCENCE

•◠•

I T IS NOT ONLY THE MIND that develops new powers; the body, too, has its processes. On May Day, when I was fourteen, my puberty burst upon me, effortlessly, like a rosebud opening under the rays of the spring sun. Although my mother had never told me exactly what I should expect she had dropped hints now and then and my grandmother had rather enjoyed making veiled prophesies on the subject. So I was not wholly unprepared.

I noticed it with a kind of pride, as though I were being initiated into the company of grown-ups. When I told my dear Mama she kissed me tenderly and was delighted to see me pass so successfully through a period which she had feared might be damaging to my health. Before that time I had once or twice been woken in a rather surprising manner from a deep sleep. It had not been due to any imaginings on my part; I kept my imagination too firmly concentrated on serious matters, and my conscience was too strict a guardian over my curiosity for any unruly images to intrude. But in the warmth of sleep I experienced an extraordinary surge of physical sensations, which, through the agency of a healthy constitution and without any conscious participation by me, was like a sort of purification all on its own. My first reaction was a kind of fear. I had read in my *Philotée* that we are not permitted to derive any sort of pleasure from our bodies except in legitimate marriage. Recalling this precept I felt that I must be gravely at fault since the sensations I had experienced must certainly be described as pleasurable. Furthermore, the pleasure in question was undoubtedly one which would be most displeasing to the Spotless Lamb. So I fell into an agony of heart-searching, prayer and mortification. How was I to avoid such things happening again? For although I had not foreseen it, when it happened I had not done anything to check it. I began to watch myself very closely. If I noticed that any particular situation exposed me to temptation more than another, I avoided it. My anxiety was such that I sometimes woke up before the catastrophe; but if this did not happen I would leap to the foot of the bed, my cold, bare feet on the tiled floor, my arms stretched out to Heaven, and would pray to Our Lord and Saviour to protect me against the wiles of the devil. I also imposed penances upon myself and occasionally put into practice the advice handed down to us by the Prophet King, probably merely as an oriental figure of speech, to mix ashes with our bread and to water it with our tears. Several times I poured cinders instead of salt on to my roast beef in penitence. This did me no more harm than the nocturnal accidents for which it was intended to atone.

In the end I understood that these could be trials imposed upon us by Heaven in order to keep us humbly on guard against ourselves. I remembered St Paul's laments and how he prayed to be delivered from the importunate pricks of the fiend; and I imagined that it was perhaps for *this* that St Bernard kept throwing himself into the snow, that St Jerome wore a hair shirt and that fasting was so strongly recommended to those aspiring to perfection. How humble, how fervent was my spirit when *that* happened! I am almost happy to be in prison now, so as to be able to recall these absurd emotional conflicts and distractions. I have not had time to think of them before now; it really makes me laugh.

But what was I to say in confession? That really was an embarrassment. However thoroughly I might reassure my conscience as to *intention*, I kept coming back to the precept of *Philotée* and to the sequent argument. In any case, if it was a trial of the devil, I must surely inform my spiritual mentor. But how? What should I call it? How should I describe it? 'Father, I confess ...' Well, what? What? My heart beat, I blushed crimson, I was sweating. 'I confess having had physical sensations contrary to Christian chastity.' Ah! excellent phrase, 'Sensations contrary to Christian chastity'; I felt like a poet who has found an elusive rhyme or Archimedes when he had solved his problem. But supposing he asked questions? I decided that that was his business, and that I should not say another word. I was shaking like a leaf that morning, as I kneeled before the holy oratory, and I was veiled from head to foot. I hastened to acquit my soul of the grievous charge: 'But did you contribute to it?' he asked. 'I do not know; certainly not willingly.' 'Have you been reading wicked books?' 'Never!' 'Or having wicked thoughts?' 'Certainly not; I am afraid of them.' 'I see – and what else?' I do not know whether good Father Morel may have had to defend himself at that moment from some wicked thoughts, but as he wisely said no more I took his 'I see – and what else?' as a signal to move to the next item on the agenda, and concluded that I was perhaps not so sinful as I had feared. But in his final exhortation he was at pains to urge me to keep a watch on myself, to remember that angelic purity is the virtue most acceptable to the Lord and other banalities of that kind. I came to the conclusion that I had been right to regard this as a trial, and took comfort from the example of St Paul and the others. My conscience was relieved of a very tiresome scruple and from then on I was watchful but no longer distressed.

It is remarkable what benefit one can derive for the rest of one's life from a habit of restraint in matters of this kind, no matter how one has acquired it. It took such a hold on me that I have been able to conserve on ethical and fastidious grounds a strict morality which I originally owed to my faith. I remained mistress of my imagination by constantly curbing it. I acquired a sort of aversion to any solitary or animal pleasure and when I found myself in a dangerous situation where surrender would have offended my reason or my principles I was able to find a voluptuous charm in remaining virtuous. For me pleasure, like happiness, must satisfy the heart as well as the senses and must not be such as to give rise to regrets. With such a philosophy it is hard to slip up and impossible to disgrace oneself. But of course that does not protect one from the agony of a real passion; in fact, it may simply store up fuel for it. We shall see!

Alongside these new physical sensations I developed a strong wish to please in every sort of way. I wanted to be thought good, enjoyed being told so and sought every opportunity to earn praise. This is perhaps as appropriate a place as any to draw my portrait. At fourteen, as today, I was about five feet tall, fully developed, with a good leg, very prominent hips, broad-chested and with a full bust, small shoulders, an erect and graceful posture and quick, light step. So much for first appearances. There was nothing special about my face apart from its fresh softness and lively expression. If one simply added together the individual features one might wonder whether there was any beauty there; none of them was exactly regular and yet the whole was pleasing. The mouth is rather large; one may see hundreds prettier but none with a sweeter or more winning smile. The eyes, on the other hand, are smallish and prominent. The irises are tinged with chestnut and grey. The impression they convey is of openness, vivacity and sympathy, reflecting the various changes of mood of an affectionate nature. Well-moulded eyebrows of auburn, the same colour as the hair, complete the picture. It is on the whole a proud and serious face which sometimes causes surprise but more often inspires confidence and interest. I was always a bit worried about my nose; it seemed to me too big at the tip. On the other hand, seen in its setting, and especially in profile, it did not damage the general effect. The broad forehead, issuing from a high brow and covered by a fringe, was unusually expressive of the most fleeting emotions and the firm, rounded chin suggested a natural sensuality. No one so obviously made for voluptuous pleasure has enjoyed so little of it. Nature had endowed me with high and vivid colouring, often enhanced by blushing, a soft skin, rounded arms and practical hands, good teeth and a healthy, well-covered body. I have lost a lot of these blessings now, particularly so far as freshness and plumpness go, but those which I still possess are sufficient, without any artificial assistance, to conceal five or six of my years. Even people who see me every day have difficulty in believing that I am more than thirty-two or thirty-three. I did not really appreciate my attractions until I had lost most of them. That may have enhanced their value; at any rate I have the comfort of knowing that I did not abuse them. If my conscience would allow me today to make fuller use of the attractions which I still possess I should not be sorry.

My portrait has been done several times, both in oils and in engravings, but none of them gives a real idea of my personality (Langlois's cameo is the least bad). I am a difficult subject because I have more feeling than figure, more expression than good features. An ordinary artist cannot reproduce this and probably does not even see it. My face lights up when I am interested and not otherwise, just as my wit corresponds to the wit of whoever is addressing me. I am so stupid in the company of stupid people that for a long time, whenever I found myself shining in the presence of really clever men I generously assumed that it was they who were responsible. People usually like me because I avoid giving offence, but not everybody finds me pretty or appreciates my worth. Camille was right to be surprised that at my age and with so little beauty I should have had what he called admirers.[1] I have never met

---

[1] Camille Desmoulins, who was a friend and ally of Danton, had written, in January 1793: 'It is not to be supposed that the deputies who dined with Roland were interested in the food alone, or that the local Circe was not capable of turning Barbaroux's companions into swine; she has recourse to other enchantments which, considering her age and her lack of beauty, argue her a great magician.'

him, but it is a safe bet that I should be cold and silent, if not positively hostile, towards a person of that sort. But he guessed quite wrong in attributing a 'court' to me. I hate courtiers as much as I despise slaves and I know exactly how to get rid of flatterers. What I demand above all is respect and goodwill; admiration may come later if it will. With people who know me well and who have sound sense and good hearts it usually does.

This desire to please, and the obvious delight I took in hearing nice things said about me, consorted oddly with my timid modesty and with the strictness of my principles and lent my person – and my general appearance – a rather unusual charm. Nothing could have been more respectable than my dress, more modest than my deportment; I took care to ensure that the overall impression was one of neatness and reserve, and this was found attractive. But this sort of restraint and renunciation of worldly values, though constantly recommended by Christian morality, does not accord with the impulses of nature. The contradiction worried me for a long time. But I found that I could apply reason to my code of behaviour just as I had applied reason to the mysteries of my faith. I devoted as much attention to considering how I should act as I did to deciding what I should believe. Philosophy, as the science of behaviour and the foundation of happiness, became the sole object of my reading and observation.

In studying metaphysics and the systems of philosophy exactly the same thing happened to me as when I read poetry; I found myself tranformed into whatever character in the drama I could identify with or admire. If I was struck by the novelty or brilliance of an opinion I adopted it as my own and clung to it until some new, more profound discussion supervened. Thus, in debate I ranged myself on the side of the authors of the Port-Royal;[2] I liked their austerity and their logic, whereas I had a natural distaste for Jesuitical subterfuge and smoothness. Among the ancient thinkers I most admired the Stoics and tried to pretend as they did that pain was not an evil. When this absurd idea did not hold, I fell back on the determination never to allow myself to be conquered by pain. My various experiences had proved to me that I could endure very

---

[2] The Port-Royal was an educational establishment near Paris. Started in 1683, it continued for nearly seventy years until it was suppressed by a papal Bull in 1704 on the grounds that it had become a centre for Jansenism. Its academic fame was due to its work in linguistics.

great suffering without crying out. My first night of marriage upset this pretension, though it must be said that surprise played a large part in that. The stoical novice is more likely to be strong in the face of an evil she has foreseen than when confronted with the unexpected.

For two months, reading Descartes and Malebranche, I had considered my cat when he mewed to be no more than a mechanism performing its natural function. But I soon came to the conclusion that by denying that the cat's action resulted from feeling I was, as it were, splitting nature in two and discounting the more attractive half. I found it much more satisfactory to believe that everything had a soul, and I would have adopted the soul as defined by Spinoza rather than none at all.

Helvétius was positively painful to me; he destroyed all my most cherished illusions and depicted a world dominated by the most unattractive self-interest. But what acute thinking – what logic! I persuaded myself that Helvétius had been describing men *as they had become* through the corruption of society, and that to study him was a means of equipping myself for survival in the social world. But for judging Man in his natural condition, or in assessing my own true character, I could never have adopted his principles. I knew that I should have found myself undervalued by these standards, for I was conscious of having generous instincts of which Helvetius denied the existence. In refutation of his bleak doctrine I recalled the great sweep of history and the virtues of all the heroes who have adorned it. Whenever I read of some noble action I would say to myself 'That is what I would have done!' I was passionate for the republics of the ancient world, adorned by men and deeds I could admire, and I persuaded myself that this was the only acceptable type of régime. I felt fully up to the level of these men and lamented that I had not been born amongst them.

We visited Versailles, my mother, my little uncle, Mlle d'Hannaches and I. The sole purpose of the trip was to show me the Court and to enjoy the spectacle. We had rooms in the château. Madame Legrand, a lady-in-waiting to the Dauphine, known to Father Bimont through her son who had been a fellow student of his, lent us her apartment. It was in a garret, in the same corridor as the apartment of the Archbishop of Paris and so close to it that the good prelate had to be careful not to let us hear everything he was saying. We were under a similar constraint. The apartment consisted of two rooms, very inadequately furnished, in one of which there was an arrangement enabling a valet to sleep on a sort of shelf. It had a disgusting approach through a dark corridor stinking with the privies. Such was the accommodation which a duke and peer of France was proud to be allotted so that he could go crawling every morning to the levée of their Majesties. And this was the puritanical Beaumont himself.[3] We spent eight days there, gaping at the Greater and the Lesser collations of the entire family, both severally and united, attending the Masses, the promenades, the play, the presentations. Madame Legrand's connections procured us certain facilities. Mademoiselle d'Hannaches penetrated proudly into every corner of the building, ready to throw her name at any person who might offer opposition and believing that they should be able to recognise six hundred years of proven *noblesse* in her grotesque visage. She recognised two or three royal guards whose genealogy she recounted to us in detail, and found herself to be related to the one who bore the most ancient name, but who so far as I could see was very small beer at Court. The fine figure of a little Abbé such as Father Bimont and the stupid pride of the hideous Mlle d'Hannaches were not out of place in these surroundings; but the unpowdered cheeks of my respectable Mama and my own decent outfit pronounced us to be bourgeois. If my looks or my youth attracted any comment it always seemed to be patronising and caused me as much discomfort as the compliments of Mme de Boismorel. Philosophy, imagination, sentiment and calculation were all exercising my mind. I was by no means blind to the effects of a splendid pageant, but I resented seeing it used to elevate a few individuals who were already too powerful and whose personal qualities were so unmemorable. I preferred looking at the statues in the garden to the grandees in the château. When my mother asked me whether I was enjoying the visit I replied 'Yes, so long as it is over soon. In another few days I shall detest these people so much that I shall not know what to do with my hatred.' 'But what harm do they do you?' 'It is all so unfair and so absurd.'

I sighed for Athens, where I could have admired the arts without being confronted with despotism. I imagined myself a stranger in Greece, attending the Olympic games, and was ashamed to find myself French. In my infatuation with the great days of the republics I glossed over their storms and stresses, forgot the death of Socrates, the exile of Aristides, the condemnation of Phocion. I

[3] Christophe de Beaumont, Archbishop of Paris since 1746.

did not know then that I was myself destined to witness similar atrocities and to partake in similar persecution. God is witness that my personal sufferings never drew from me a sigh or a regret; I weep only for those of my country. At the time of the conflicts between Court and Parliament in 1771 my nature and my opinions inclined me to support the latter. I got hold of all their written protests and always preferred the most boldly expressed. My ideas expanded. I thought of my own duty and the part I could play in the future. I began to read history and to cast a critical eye on all around me. I was already deeply preoccupied by the relations of the human species with the divine, which puzzled and confused me. I now began to think of the interests of men in the mass and of the organisation of society.

Although full of doubt and uncertainty on the general questions, I had little difficulty in perceiving that personal well-being depends on being able to preserve what I might call the unity of one's nature; that is to say, the greatest possible consistency between one's beliefs and one's actions. The first thing is to decide what is right; after that, one must act rigorously in accordance with the decision. One has a duty to oneself, quite independently of anyone else in the world, to control one's affections and one's habits so as not to become the slave of any of them. An individual is *good* in himself when all the elements in his make-up are contributing harmoniously to his conservation, to his effectiveness and to his fulfilment. This is just as true in morals as it is in physics. Physical health consists in a steady constitution, a proper balance of the life forces, which healthy feeding and moderate exercise help to preserve. Moral health, by the same token, entails disciplining the passions and harmonising the desires, and only self-control can ensure this. The interest of the individual himself is involved here, and it could be argued that virtue is no more than a tribute which a man pays to his own well-being.

But virtue in the true sense of the word comes into effect only in a man's relations with his fellow men. One can be wise for one's own sake but one is virtuous for the sake of others. In society everything is relative; there is no such thing as independent happiness for the individual. One is always obliged to sacrifice some part of what one might hope to enjoy in order not to risk losing it all. Here again, reason is the best guide. However burdensome may be the life of a just man, it is not so bad as the life of a scoundrel. Nobody can feel at ease who has set himself up against the interests of the great majority and a man who is surrounded by enemies or potential enemies can never forget the fact, however favourable his immediate situation may seem. To these considerations we may add a more fundamental point. No amount of corruption and false doctrine can drive from Man's conscience that sublime instinct which impels him to admire wisdom and generosity in deeds, just as he admires symmetry and grandeur in nature and in the arts.[4] Here we find the true source of the human virtues, quite independent of any religious system, any metaphysical nonsense or any priestly imposture.

Once I had convinced myself of these truths I was delighted. They offered me a port in the storm and I could now consider with less anxiety what was wrong with the faith of nations and with our social institutions. Could it be that the sublime ideas of a God, Creator and Protector of the Universe, and of the spirituality and immortality of the soul, ideas which offered the sole hope of comfort to the oppressed, were nothing but amiable, glittering illusions? No! Cloudy and obscure these questions may be; countless may be the objections and the difficulties thrown up by the mathematical approach; but the human mind is not called upon to judge its own predicament by strict rules of evidence. What does it matter to a sensitive person if he cannot prove these truths? It is sufficient that he can feel them.

In concentrated study or in abstract argument I would be prepared to agree with the atheist or the materialist that certain questions are unanswerable. But when I am in the country contemplating nature different rules apply. My understanding is overwhelmed by the life-principle that motivates nature and by the intelligence and goodness which so obviously control it. Vast oceans separate me from the one I love and society unloads all its troubles upon our heads, as if to punish us for having desired its good. Where can I expect to see the reward for our sacrifices, where can I hope for the joy of our reunion, if not beyond the grave? How?

---

[4] In a footnote, Mme Roland wrote 'I write these words at eleven o'clock at night on 4 September to the sound of laughter from the next room. The actresses of the Théâtre-Français were arrested yesterday and brought to Sainte-Pélagie, where the officer in charge is now entertaining them. A riotous party is in progress, with lewd talk and foreign wines. I am struck by these contrasts – the place, the times, the people and my own condition.' Members of the cast had been arrested following outbreaks of disorder during the performance of Paméla by François de Neufchâteau.

In what form? I cannot tell; I only know that it must be so.

I do not consider the atheist necessarily mistaken; I can live with him more easily than with a believer, because he makes better use of his reason. But he has one sense missing and I cannot entirely accept his position. The most ravishing spectacle leaves him cold and he will always be looking for a syllogism where I am simply giving facts. It was some while before I settled on this relaxed position which enables me to enjoy the truths which have been demonstrated to me, accept happiness confidently when it is offered and be content to overlook what I cannot know, quite independently of other people's opinions. These, in a very few words, are conclusions which I have reached after many years of meditation and study during the course of which I have toyed with deism, atheism and scepticism. My experiments have always been made in good faith, because I have never been tempted to change my beliefs in order to relax my moral principles, these having been firmly fixed by me quite independently of my faith. Thus my religious waverings have not been motivated by fear or by self-indulgence. I conformed to the established religion because my age, sex and situation made this a duty. I said frankly to Father Morel, 'I come to confession to edify my neighbours and in order not to distress my mother, but I really do not know what I have to confess. I live so quietly and my tastes are so simple that my conscience does not reproach me for anything, though I admit that there is no great merit in my good works. However, I am sometimes too keen to please and I am inclined to be impatient with my maid and others when anything goes wrong. I am also perhaps too severe in my judgements and form a dislike too easily – though of course without showing it – for people who seem to me stupid or disagreeable. I must watch myself about that. And as to my religious devotions, I certainly perform them too coldly and superficially. I agree that one ought to pay proper attention to anything one thinks worth doing for whatever reason.'

Good Father Morel, having exhausted his library and his rhetoric in trying to keep me in the faith, sensibly reconciled himself to the fact that I was a reasoner. He urged me to be on guard against pride, demonstrated the sweetness of religious faith to the best of his ability, wisely gave me absolution and was reasonably content to see me take Communion two or three times a year out of philosophical tolerance, not faith. I took the Holy Bread thinking of the words of Cicero, who said that after all the foolishness of men in regard to God it only remained for them to turn Him into food and eat Him. My mother's increasing piety made it more difficult for me every day to escape the conventional religious practices, and I would have done anything to avoid upsetting her. But she allowed me to read whatever I liked.

Father Legrand, who was a friend of Father Bimont, sometimes called on us. He was a very intelligent man with not much religiosity about him apart from his habit. His family had put him into the Church because they thought it only right that one of their three sons should be a priest. He had been chaplain to the prince de Lamballe, from whose family he received a pension, and he had settled in our parish to be near his friend. He had very bad eyesight and became blind at an early age, which made him contemplative. He liked talking to me and often brought me books of philosophy and discoursed upon them with great eloquence. My mother never joined in these discussions and I had to be careful, but she did not try to control my reading....

For a while I became interested in physics, then in mathematics. ... I enjoyed geometry so long as I was not expected to study algebra; once I had finished with first-degree equations, algebra seemed to me to be horribly dry. Multiple fractions and square roots had little attraction compared with reading good poetry. Some years later M. Roland, when he was courting me, tried to revive these old tastes; we wrote down a lot of signs and figures together. But I never found the logic of x a sufficiently congenial system to stay with it for long.

5 SEPTEMBER

I am dividing this notebook in half in order to send out these sheets in the little box; for when I read that a revolutionary army has been formed, bloodthirsty new tribunals set up, starvation threatened and the tyrants are standing with their backs to the wall I realise that they will look for new victims and nobody is assured of living another twenty-four hours.[5]

[5] On 5 Sept. 1793 the Convention decreed the formation of a revolutionary army in Paris and the reorganisation of the revolutionary tribunal so that sentences should be passed more rapidly. The 'little box' was the cover under which Mme Roland's visitors smuggled the fragments of her memoirs out of the prison as and when she wrote them.

My correspondence with Sophie continued to be one of my greatest joys, and our friendship was strengthened by several visits that she paid to Paris. My sensibility was such that I really needed, I will not say an imaginary recipient, but a principal target for my confidences. My friendship with Sophie provided this and I made the fullest use of it. My intimacy with my mother, close though it was, would not have met this need: there was always a sort of formality about it, as befits a relationship of respect on the one side and authority on the other. My mother could *know* everything; I had nothing to hide from her. But I could not *tell* her everything. One confesses to one's mother, but confides in one's contemporaries and equals.

Thus, although my mother never asked to read the letters I wrote to Sophie, she was very happy that I should let her see them. We had a nice arrangement, thoroughly understood between us though never referred to. When news arrived from my friend, as it did regularly each week, I would read out a few passages from the letter but did not show it to my mother. When I had written to Sophie I left my letter for a whole day on my desk, folded and addressed but not sealed up. My mother would almost always find a moment to have a look at it, though rarely in my presence. If I happened to be in the room when she picked it up, I would find an excuse to go out. Then, after leaving enough time for her to have read the letter, I would come back and seal it whether she had done so or not – occasionally having added a postscript. My mother never once alluded to anything she had read in this way, but the point was that I was able by this means to convey to her whatever I wanted her to know about my feelings, my tastes or my opinions, and to do so with a freedom which I should never have dared to employ directly with her. I lost nothing by this frankness, for I had a perfect right to be candid and yet could not be criticised for anything I wrote.

I have often thought since that if I had been in my mother's place I should have wanted to become my daughter's closest friend. If I have any regrets today it is that I have not been closer to my own daughter. If she had been more like me we could have been intimate partners and friends, which I should have enjoyed. But my mother, though very kind, was also a little cold; she was wise rather than feeling, more sensible than loving. Perhaps she also saw that there was something in me which would carry me beyond her; she gave me complete freedom but withheld familiarity. She would observe me tenderly but never caress me. I knew that she loved me but her reserve created a similar reserve in me and we became if anything less intimate as I emerged from childhood. My mother was proud, touchingly proud I must say, but proud nonetheless. My burning enthusiasms were checked by her and it was not until I lost her that I fully understood in agony and despair the depth of my attachment to her.

Our days went by in a delightful calm. I spent a large part of my time by myself, studying the history and arts of antiquity and steeping myself in its opinions and precepts. The only times I spent with my mother were at Mass in the morning, a few hours of reading aloud, at mealtimes and on walks. We did not go out often and when visitors came, if I did not like them, I stayed closeted in my little room. My mother knew better than to disturb me. Every Sunday and feast day we went out for a walk, sometimes a long one, and I always preferred going out into the country rather than into the public gardens of the capital. ...

My favourite expedition was to Meudon, and we went there often. I greatly preferred the wild woods and isolated pools, the long rides of spruce and forest trees to the familiar paths and clipped copses of the Bois de Boulogne, the decorative scenery of Bellevue or the well-kept gardens of St-Cloud. 'Where shall we go tomorrow if it's fine?' asked my father on Saturday evenings in the summer. He would look at me with a smile. 'St-Cloud? The fountains should be playing and there will be plenty of people.' 'Oh, Papa, I should much rather we went to Meudon.' And so at five o'clock on Sunday morning everybody would be up and about. Clean, light clothes, very plain, a few flowers and a gauze veil, and we were ready for the day's outing. The odes of Rousseau, a volume of Corneille or something similar was all I carried. The three of us went on board a small boat at the Pont-Royal, which I could see from my window. This conveyed us silently and rapidly to the riverbank of Bellevue, not far from the glassworks whose thick black smoke could be seen in the distance. From there we climbed by a steep path to the avenue de Meudon and about two-thirds of the way along we could see, high up on the right-hand side, a little cottage which became one of our regular stopping places. It belonged to a widowed dairywoman, who lived there with two cows and some hens. In order to make the best use of the daylight we decided to stop there on our way back and asked the woman to have a bowl of fresh milk ready for us. This arrangement became a habit; each time we came up to the avenue we went in to warn the dairywoman that she would be seeing us again in the evening or the next day, and that she should not forget the milk. The good woman always received us most kindly and these rustic meals, eked out with a little brown bread and a great deal of good humour, became regular events which, of course, my father made worth her while. We usually ate our lunch with one of the park-keepers. But my desire to avoid crowds soon led us to discover a still more secluded retreat.

One day, after we had been walking for a long time in an unfamiliar part of the forest, we came upon an open space, very isolated, at the end of an avenue of large trees. Other trees, standing on the green-sward, half hid from view a small two-storey house, neatly and elegantly constructed. What have we here?, we wondered. Two children were playing before the open door. They looked neither like townspeople nor poverty-stricken country folk. We went closer and saw on our left an old man working in the kitchen garden. We were soon in conversation with him and learnt that this place was called Ville-Bonne and that the man who lived there was a turncock to the Red Mill, responsible for maintaining the canals and conduits that carried water to all parts of the park. The old man was his father and the children we had seen were his. With the small emoluments of the job and by selling the vegetables which his father grew in the garden he was able to maintain his little family there in modest comfort. The garden was a rectangle divided into four parts, each surrounded by a wide path. There was a fountain in the centre from which the whole enclosure was watered and at the far end an arbour of yew with a great stone seat provided rest and shade. Flowers planted among the vegetables lent the garden a bright, pleasant atmosphere and the old man himself, healthy and happy, reminded me of Virgil's description of rustic contentment on the banks of the Galesus. I found the whole scene delightful. We asked whether they ever received strangers. 'Very seldom,' said the old man, 'for the place is not well known; but if any do come we are happy to serve them with the produce of the farmyard and the garden.' We asked them to give us dinner; they gave us fresh eggs, vegetables and salad under a honeysuckle bower behind the house. I have never enjoyed a meal more; I was overwhelmed by the innocence and the happiness of this charming set-up. I played with the children and showed my respect for the old man. The wife (who managed the whole little household) seemed very pleased to receive us. There was talk of two rooms being available for anyone who wished to rent them for three months and we made a plan to do this, but alas! this plan never came off and I never went back to Ville-Bonne. We had been visiting Meudon for many years when we made this discovery and had already arranged to sleep in one of the village inns whenever two close public holidays enabled us to get away for more than a day or two. An amusing incident occurred in this inn which was called, I think, the 'Queen of France'. We had a room with two beds. I slept in the larger one with my mother, and my father in the other, over in the corner of the room. One night, having got into bed, he tried to close the curtains more tightly; he gave them such a hard pull that the whole canopy collapsed and entirely covered him up. After a few moments of panic we all laughed and thought how clever it had been of the gods to envelop him so neatly without hurting him. We called for help to get him out. The landlady arrived, gazed with astonishment at the dilapidated bed and cried out ingenuously 'My God! how is that possible? It has been there seventeen years and has never fallen down before!' This reasoning made me laugh more than the accident itself and I have often compared it with similar arguments I have heard people use. I used to say to my mother, in a low voice: 'That (whatever it was) cannot break: it has been there seventeen years.'

Dear Meudon, how often under your shadowy bowers I have sighed and dreamed, blessing the Author of my existence, gilding the image of the coming years with bright rays of hope and patient expectation! How often in your fresh meadows I have gathered fronds of the speckled fern, the bright blossoms of the orchid; how often rested under those great trees and seen perchance a timid deer pass across the clearing. Your dark places too I loved, where we took cover from the heat of the day. I see my father lying there stretched out upon the green-sward and my mother reclining on the pile of leaves which I have gathered for her. They both surrender to after-dinner sleep while I sit wondering at the silent majesty of the forest. I loved Nature, and Providence which had created it. It was like paradise on earth.

These walks, and the happiness they gave me, were ever the subject of my letters to Sophie. Sometimes my prose would break into verse, irregular, simple, occasionally well turned, the outpouring of a mind inspired by life and intoxicated by imagery.

Sophie, as I have already written, was caught up in a social whirl in which she could enjoy none of the pleasures of my solitary life.

I knew one or two members of her family and when I had to talk to them I appreciated all the more my own estrangement from the world.

When she came to Paris with her mother they always stayed with the two Mlles de La Motte. They were two old spinsters. One of them was a pious crosspatch who never left her room and spent the day praying, scolding the servants, knitting socks and talking quite pertinently about the stock market. The other, a good person, stayed in the salon, ran the household, read the psalms and played patience. They both attached enormous importance to having been born ladies and would hardly conceive of accepting the society of anyone whose father had not been a member of the nobility. They preserved as a sort of family title-deed, though they never dared to use it, the workbag which their mother used to have carried before her into church. They had taken up and had living with them a young cousin whose small fortune they intended to increase provided that she found herself a gentleman for a husband. Her name was Mlle d'Hangard. She was a large brunette, alarmingly healthy and robust, whose provincial bearing in no way concealed a rather blunt character and a very common mind. But the most curious phenomenon in the house was a retired lawyer named Perdu, a widower, who had dissipated his fortune doing nothing. His sister (Sophie's mother) had pensioned him off to live with these two cousins so that he might get through the remaining years of his useless life in decency. Monsieur Perdu, fat and baby-faced, spent most of the morning attending to his toilet, ate a large lunch complaining all the time about the food, went to the Luxembourg to chatter for several hours every afternoon and ended the evening playing cards. He attached more importance than did even the two old cousins to gentility. He prided himself on his aristocratic airs and laid down the law on the subject of manners. When writing to Sophie I always referred to him as the Commander because he reminded me of the Commander in Diderot's *Père de famille*. Towards his nieces he adopted a tone of superiority covered over with politenesses but towards Mlle d'Hangard his behaviour was a little bizarre. Her vivacity and her habitual presence in the house seemed to have aroused his imagination and stimulated some thoughts which he would never have dared to avow. This sometimes put him out of humour with his nephew.

The nephew, whom they called Selincourt, was a tall young man, gentle in voice and in appearance, who looked rather like his sister

Sophie. He talked well and had good manners, not marred in my opinion by a certain timidity which was particularly marked, I noticed, when talking to me. He seemed to be generally considered in the family to be a pretender to the hand of Mlle d'Hangard. ...

As Sophie's good friend I was rather curiously placed in this company. They commented behind my back that it was a pity that such a well-brought-up girl had not been born a lady. I expect the Commander gave serious thought to the question whether it was proper for his niece to cultivate such a friendship. But as I had good manners and an air of respectability, by which the old cousins set much store, the Commander could not refrain from paying me a few compliments, though he complained to his niece that some of my turns of phrase 'savoured of the intellectual'. He even undertook sometimes to deliver his niece's letters when she was away and bring them personally to my mother's house. Selincourt would gladly have done that even more often if his sister had consented to give him such a commission.

The insignificance and absurdity of these people, no worse I suppose than many other fashionable men and women, made me think how empty society people were and how lucky I was not to have to consort with them. Sophie's descriptions of all the people she met in Amiens showed how few of them were of any interest and I came to the conclusion that in the course of a year I saw more worthwhile people in my life of solitude than she did in her social whirl. Nor is this surprising, considering that my father's friends were all artists who came to see him when they felt like it. People who live in a capital, even if they are not of high rank, have a breadth of knowledge and experience and a modicum of civilised manners which one cannot expect to find in the provincial squirearchy or amongst tradesmen, whose sole concern is to make money to buy themselves a title. ...

11

SOCIAL LIFE
AND COURTSHIP

◆

The girlhood romance with M. Pahin de la Blancherie, of which Mme Roland gives some account in this chapter and the next, was much more fully treated in her letters to Sophie Cannet, written twenty years before. La Blancherie was the only one of her early admirers who lived up to her intellectual requirements. She met him at one of Mme l'Épine's concerts and although she described him to Sophie as 'rather ugly' she developed a violent – albeit purely cerebral – passion for him. Unfortunately he was penniless and M. Phlipon refused to let him marry his daughter until he was in a position to support her. This episode in Mme Roland's life attracted the interest of Sainte-Beuve. 'She speaks a lot in her memoirs', he wrote, 'about la Blancherie, a second-rate writer and would-be philosopher whose suit she describes somewhat patronisingly and then, after speaking of other things, dismisses with the remark "We must now put an end to this personage." Before being put an end to, the young man succeeded in making himself loved by her, and there could be no better proof, if proof were needed, that love is an entirely subjective matter and that the object of a passion counts for practically nothing. Here was this strong, sensible young woman, with the clearest and severest possible intelligence, picking out for her favour a creature who was a combination of all the silliness and insipidities then in vogue and taking him to be the ideal of her dreams. The truth is that this la Blancherie, this young sage, this friend of Greuze, with his verses, his schemes, his moral precepts for parents, represented at its most extreme the shallow romanticism and sentimentality of those times; and it has to be admitted that romanticism, initially at least and when presented in a certain form, has a good chance of making a hit in the heart of a young woman even when she is destined to become Mme Roland.'

THERE IS NO DOUBT that our character and our opinions are greatly influenced by the situation in which we find ourselves. In my case the education I had received and the ideas I had acquired by study and example combined to make me a keen republican, by drawing my attention to the absurdity and injustice of so many social pretensions and distinctions. In my reading I always identified with the reformers: I was Agis and Cleomenes in Sparta, Gracchus in Rome and like Cornelia I would have reproached my sons for treating me merely as the mother-in-law of Scipio. I would have gone up into the Aventine Hill with the people and voted for the tribunes. Today, now that experience has taught me to judge matters more impartially, I can see harm and mischief which I had not sufficiently noted before in the actions of the Gracchi and in the conduct of the tribunes.

When I used to witness in Paris the kind of spectacle which attended the *entrées* of the Queen or the princes, or the thanksgivings on the occasion of a royal birth etc., I compared this oriental luxury and insolent pageantry with the abject misery of the crowds lining the route, waving their flags and stupidly applauding the brilliant display all paid for at their expense. I was amazed and indignant at the dissolute conduct of the Court in the last years of Louis XV's reign and by the collapse of moral values which had spread to all classes and was the constant topic of private conversation. I did not see that it carried in it the seeds of revolution and could not imagine how things would work out – all I knew was that they could not go on in that way. In my history books I had seen all those empires crumble and fall which had reached such a degree of corruption, and yet I heard the French laughing and singing at the spectacle of their own decay. I thought their English neighbours were right to regard them as children. I became deeply interested in these neighbours; Delolme's books[1] had already familiarised me with their constitution and I now tried to get to know their writers. I studied their literature but unfortunately only in translation.

Despite Ballexserd's urging my parents had never allowed me to be vaccinated when I was a child, so that I went down with smallpox at the age of eighteen. I have the most vivid memories of that time – not through fear of the disease, for I had enough philosophy to bear that trial with constancy, but because of my mother's incredible, touching solicitude. What gentleness, what tireless attention, what loving, anxious concern! At any hour of the night, when I thought my nurse was about to tend me, it was my mother's hand, my mother's voice that comforted me. When the doctor came I could see her watching his every gesture, hanging on his every word and I observed the furtive tear that escaped her eye

---

[1] Jean-Louis Delolme's *La Constitution de l'Angleterre* was published in 1771.

whenever she looked at me. I would try to ease her anxiety with a smile. Neither she nor my father had ever had smallpox, and yet they both kissed my sick cheeks every day, ignoring my effort to spare them this risk.

Dear Agatha, who to her great regret could not come to see me because of the rules of her convent, sent along instead a friend of hers, a mother of four children, to whom she seemed to have imparted some of her own affection for me. This good woman insisted on seeing me and kissing me without any thought for herself. Sophie was in town, but they managed to conceal my condition from her until I had ceased being infectious by saying that I had left suddenly for the country. But Selincourt came every day to enquire after my health and I could hear from my bedroom his woeful exclamations when he was told that complications were feared of typhus fever and smallpox. I had miliary fever, and because the eruption specific to this disease counteracted that of the other, my smallpox pustules were very large and very few in number, and they soon went down without bursting, leaving dry skin which fell off easily. Doctor Missa told me that this was the type of smallpox known to the Italians as *ravaglioni*, which produces non-suppurating blains and leaves hardly a trace. And indeed my complexion was not affected in any way by this illness. But when the danger was over I was left very depressed and tired and took four or five months to recover.

When I am in good health I am very reserved, too shy to show much gaiety and content to take pain patiently. But when I am ill my only thought is how to distract myself from my own suffering and to render more agreeable the pains which others are obliged to take over me. I then let my imagination run free and talk nonsense and I am the one that makes the others laugh. Doctor Missa was an intelligent man whom I liked very much. He was old enough for me not to feel the sort of constraint that I usually feel with the opposite sex. We had the most agreeable discussions during his visits; he willingly prolonged them and we became close friends. 'One or the other of us', he said one day, 'has made a grave mistake. Either I came into the world too soon or you too late.' Although I was greatly interested in Missa's mind, his advanced age had prevented me from thinking that I missed anything by having been born later than him; so I merely gave him a nice smile. He had two nieces for whom he was responsible and wanted us to be friends. We did meet once or twice but as they never walked out without their governess nor I without my mother, and since he was a busy man, the friendship never took hold. Missa scolded me one day when he found *La Recherche de la Vérité* by Malebranche on my bed. I countered: 'For goodness sake, if your other patients were to read this sort of thing, instead of lying there complaining about their ill health and about you, you would not be so overworked.' There were several people in the room and they were talking about some loan which had just been floated and to which all Paris was subscribing. 'The French,' said Missa, 'will pay anything for security.' 'Say rather, for appearances,' I replied. 'That is very true,' he said. 'Then do not scold me for reading Malebranche,' I exclaimed with feeling. 'You can see that I'm not wasting my time.'

Missa used to be accompanied on his visits by a young, newly qualified doctor whom he occasionally sent on in advance to await his arrival. This young man had certainly not committed the error of being born too soon and he had quite an agreeable appearance. But there was something pompous about him which I did not like. I have such an aversion to affectation and conceited airs that I always assume them to be signs of mediocrity and even stupidity, although it is true that under the *ancien régime* they were often nothing more than youthful eccentricity. They certainly never impressed me; in fact they put me off anyone who displays them. And so it was with M. Macquart, the young doctor. I never saw him again and I probably never will, for I have heard that a Paris doctor of that name emigrated after the Revolution.

I needed country air for my convalescence, so we went to stay with M. and Mme Besnard. My mother and I had spent the month of September with them for the past two years and it was an ideal place in which to nourish my philosophy and confirm my thoughts about the iniquities of the social order.

Madame Besnard, when she and her sisters had fallen on hard times, had entered the employment of a farmer-general called Haudry as his housekeeper. There she had married one of the stewards, M. Besnard, long since retired, and they now lived modestly and happily together on the estate.

My grandmother sometimes recalled in my presence that she had always disapproved of this marriage. She was quite wrong, so far as I could judge. Monsieur Besnard was an honest and thoroughly respectable man with unusual delicacy of feeling for one of his station. His behaviour towards his wife was impeccable; he was respectful, gentle and devoted and between them they presented an ideal picture of virtuous, harmonious domesticity. I was honoured to know them and should have felt the same even if he had been a lackey.

Old Haudry, a self-made man, was dead. He had left a considerable fortune to his son, who, having been brought up in opulence, was destined to squander it. The son, who had already lost a charming wife, had expensive tastes. Like many other rich people he spent part of the year in the country in his château at Soucy, where he led a life more suited to the town than to the country. His estate consisted of several properties joined together. The nearest to Soucy (Fontenay) had an ancient castle which he liked to see inhabited; he had installed there a notary and a bailiff and he invited M. and Mme Besnard to take an apartment and spend part of the summer there. It was a good arrangement from the point of view of the upkeep of the property and it gave the place an air of prosperity which pleased him. Monsieur and Mme Besnard were well lodged and they were permitted to walk about in the park whose unkempt woodlands made a pleasant contrast to the formal gardens of Soucy and which gave me personally much more pleasure than the luxury of the farmer-general's residence. When we came to stay with Mme Besnard she asked up to pay a call at Soucy, where Haudry's mother-in-law and sister-in-law lived with him and did the honours of the house. The visit took place quietly after dinner. I did not enjoy entering that drawing-room, where Mme Pénault and her daughter received us with great politeness, admittedly, but with a certain air of superiority. My mother's dignity and my own composure beneath my outer shyness (I knew my own worth but was not sure of being appreciated) did not allow them much scope for condescension. I received compliments that did not much please me and these were taken up by certain hangers-on with decorations in their lapels, such as always hover around the rich like the spectres on the banks of the Acheron. I managed to turn them aside with some finesse.

These ladies duly returned our call a few days later. They had made their visit to Fontenay the object of a walk and were accompanied by the same parasites as we had met up at the château. This time I was more amiable and managed to inject into my welcome enough dignified politeness to restore the equilibrium. In due course Mme Pénault invited us to dinner, but I was more than astonished to discover that it was not with her, but *below stairs* that we were expected to eat. I realised at once that since that was where

M. Besnard had formerly carried out his duties, I must be careful out of regard to him not to seem dismayed to find myself there. But I took the view that Mme Pénault should have arranged things differently or spared us altogether this double-edged courtesy. My great-aunt shared this opinion, but in order not to make trouble we accepted the invitation. I must admit that it was a new experience for me to see these second-degree deities. I had never before seen housemaids playing the lady. They had prepared themselves to receive us like veritable understudies in the theatre: dress, deportment, little airs and graces, nothing was omitted. Recent cast-offs from their mistresses' wardrobes gave their dress a richness which honest bourgeois taste would not have allowed, while their idea of fashion lent them a sort of elegance quite as alien to bourgeois modesty as to the artistic taste. But the chattering and the dressing-up would have appealed to provincial tastes. It was worse with the men. The sword of M. le maître d'hôtel, the lordly bearing of M. le chef, the elegant gentility and gorgeous apparel of the valets did not redeem their awkward manners, the inadequacy of their language when they wanted it to sound distinguished or the triviality of their conversation when they forgot for a moment the part they were playing. The talk was all of marquesses, counts and big financiers whose titles, fortunes and alliances you would have thought the personal concern of these upstarts. The left-overs from the first table were passed on to the second table, having been cleaned up and re-arranged so as to look like new, and there was still enough left over for the third table where the 'true domestics' ate (for the occupants of the second table called themselves 'officers').

After the meal there was gambling, for quite high stakes, and it appeared that these 'ladies' were accustomed to playing cards every day. I realised that I was looking at a new world which reflected all the prejudices, vice and stupidity of the one I already knew and was neither more nor less worthless. I had heard many times about old Haudry's origins; how he came up to Paris from his village, amassed a fortune at public expense, married his daughter to Montulé and his granddaughters to the marquis Duchillau and comte Turpin and left all his treasures to his son. I thought of Montesquieu's remark that financiers support the state as the rope supports the hanged man. I came to the conclusion that public functionaries who enrich themselves to this extent and buy their way into titled families which are supposed to adorn and defend the kingdom could only be the product of a detestable régime and a corrupted nation. I did not know then that there could be even more terrible régimes and even more hideous corruption. But who would have thought that possible? All the philosophers were mistaken like me.

On Sunday there was dancing at Soucy, in the open air under the trees. On those occasions social distinctions were more or less forgotten and as soon as I realised that I would be taken on my merits I had no fear of not being given my proper place. New arrivals asked one another who I was, but I did not force myself upon anybody and after an hour's relaxation I made my escape and went for a walk with my parents – an infinitely preferable pastime, in my opinion, to the noisy and empty round of social life. I sometimes saw Haudry, who was still young, playing the squire, fancying himself a generous and noble host. His family were beginning to be worried about him; his follies with the courtesan Laguerre were beginning to prepare his ruin. But they were more inclined to pity him as a ne'er-do-well than to find fault with him. He was a spoilt child of fortune who would have been worth much more if he had been born in mediocrity. He was dark and proud, with a politely protective manner and I daresay he was quite amiable to people he considered his equals. But I hated meeting him and I always stood on my dignity when he was present.

Last year, as I was coming out of the elegant dining-room which Calonne had designed in the comptroller-general's building, then occupied by the Minister of the Interior, I ran into a tall, white-haired, respectable-looking man who approached me with deference. 'Madame, I was hoping to have a word with the minister when he rises from table; I have some business to discuss.' 'Sir, you will see him in a moment; he has been detained in the next room but he will come through shortly.' I bowed and went on to my apartment. Sometime later Roland came in and I asked him who the man had been who seemed so anxious to meet him. 'Oh, that was M. Haudry.' 'What? The former farmer-general who has swallowed up so much wealth?', I said. 'Yes', he replied. 'But what does he want with the Minister of the Interior?' 'He has dealings with us as head of the Sèvres china factory.'

What a turn of fortune; what fresh food for thought! I had had a similar feeling when I first entered those official apartments, then occupied by Mme Necker at the height of her glory. Now here was I, installed in these rooms myself for the second time and all too conscious of the mutability of human affairs. At least I shall never be taken unawares by misfortune. That was in October. Danton was focusing attention on me as part of his plan to discredit my husband; he was quietly preparing a pack of lies with which to destroy us both. I did not know what he was up to, but I had seen the way things go in a revolution and my only ambition was to keep my conscience clear and preserve my husband's good name.[2] I knew very well that this was not a recipe for success in all respects, but my wish has been granted. Roland may be persecuted and proscribed, but posterity will remember him. I am a prisoner and will probably perish on the scaffold, but my clear conscience sustains me. Solomon asked only for wisdom, and other advantages were vouchsafed to him. I have asked only for the peace of the just and I too will have some enduring place in the minds of future generations.

Meanwhile let us return to Fontenay, where my parents' small library still supplied me with new reading.... I must record that in all the mass of literature which had passed through my hands up to this point there had been no Rousseau. I think my mother must have been at pains to keep him away from me, for although I had heard his name and looked out for his works the only one I had read up to the time of her death was his *Lettres de la montagne* and some other letters, though I had already by then read all Voltaire... and a host of other philosphers and critics. I have no doubt that my dear mother, realising that I must be allowed to exercise my mind, was quite glad to see me study philosophy at the risk of losing my faith, but thought that my heart was too easily moved and needed protection from too much emotion. But oh dear me; what useless efforts to escape destiny! The same motive must have lain behind her refusal to let me take up painting and her opposition to my learning the harpsichord despite the golden opportunity I had for that.

We had met in our neighbourhood Father Jeauket, a great musician, ugly as sin and a good table companion. He had been born near Prague, spent several years in Vienna, attaching himself to the high-ups at court there, and at one stage had given lessons to Marie Antoinette. Circumstances had then taken him to Lisbon for some years, but he had finally chosen Paris in which to enjoy his pension for his remaining days. He was extremely keen that my mother should allow him to teach me the harpsichord. He claimed

[2] This is thought to be a reference to her relationship with Buzot.

Jean-Marie Roland, Minister of the
Interior, 1792.

A late portrait of Roland by
Gabriel, done from life.

The 'oath of the tennis court', 20 June 1789.

The women of Paris on their way to Versailles, 5 October 1789.

The arrest of Louis XVI at Varennes, June 1791.

The execution of Louis XVI, 21 January 1793; an engraving by Helman.

The miniature portrait of Mme Roland carried by Buzot when a fugitive.

Buzot and the miniature, by Le Guay.

The portrait of Buzot which Mme Roland had with her in prison.

'The estimable Bosc'.

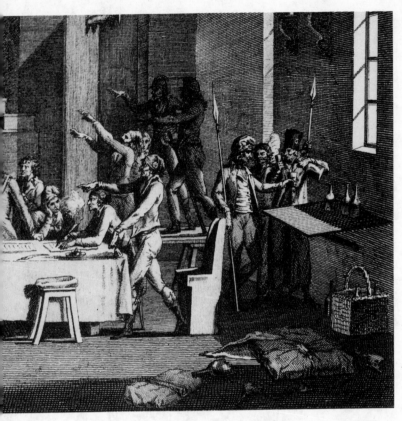

A revolutionary tribunal during the Terror, 1793. An engraving by Berthault after E. Fragonard.

The Abbaye prison; an engraving by Berthault after Prieur.

Mme Roland at the revolutionary tribunal; an engraving by Lips after a sketch from life by Bréa.

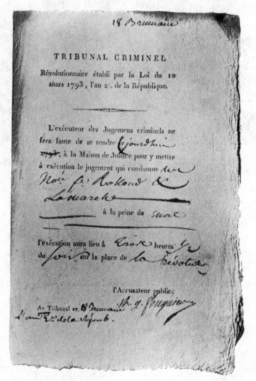

The order for Mme Roland's execution.

that my fingers and my head, between them, should ensure great progress and that I might very well take up composition. 'What a shame to spend time humming to a guitar when one is capable of writing and performing good music on the king of instruments!' But my mother was unmoved by his pleas and I myself, although always ready to take advantage of whatever I was allowed to learn, was accustomed to accepting my mother's decision. I never asked for anything. Moreover, my general studies offered me such a wide field that there was no risk of my having time on my hands. I said to myself that when I became a mother in my turn I should have to make use of whatever I had learned; there would be no time then for further study. So I applied myself to working hard and not wasting a single minute.

Father Jeauket met genteel society from time to time and when he gave a party for these people he always asked us too. Most of the individuals I met in that way are not worth recalling, but I must mention the learned musicologist Father Roussier and the saintly M. d'Odimont; and I particularly remember Paradelle. This Paradelle was a great big impertinent fellow, habited like a priest, and the most conceited braggart I have ever met. He claimed to have kept his own carriage with the best society in Lyons for twenty years, but in Paris he was obliged to give classes in Italian (which he hardly knew) in order to avoid starvation. There was also Madame de Puisieux,[3] who was supposed to be the author of the volume entitled *Caractères* which bore her name; at the age of sixty she still preserved, along with a bent back and toothless gums, all those childish airs and pretensions which are hard to forgive even in the young. I had always supposed that an authoress must be a respectable person, particularly if she had written on the subject of morality. But the absurdity of Mme de Puisieux made me think again. There was no more wit in her conversation than there was good sense in her eccentricities and she made me realise that it is possible to talk big about Reason without applying any rational standards to one's own behaviour. I began to think that the men who make mock of female authors might not be so far wrong, except in applying exclusively to women faults which many of their own sex share.

Thus while leading a very full life myself I was able to add to my stock of impressions. I was situated in my own cocoon on the fringe

[3] Madeleine d'Arsant de Puisieux, who had been Diderot's mistress.

of social life and was able to observe many interesting things without becoming obsessed by any of them.

Madame l'Épine's concerts offered me another point of view. Monsieur l'Épine was a pupil of Pigalle and his right-hand man. He had married in Rome a woman who I suppose must have been a singer, whom his family here had not looked upon very favourably to begin with. But she proved by her exemplary behaviour that their doubts were unfounded. She had formed a small choir consisting of talented amateurs who met in her apartment and gave concerts, to which she invited only what she called good company. It took place every Thursday and my mother often took me along. ... There was a wonderful magic lantern. Madame l'Épine's apartment in the rue Neuve-St-Eustache was not particularly fine and the music-room was rather restricted; but it opened out into another room through wide doors which were fixed open, and there, sitting in a circle, one had the double advantage of hearing the music, seeing the performers and being able to talk during the intervals. I always sat with my mother, all eyes, all ears, but in silence as is thought proper for young ladies. But whenever we found ourselves alone with Mme l'Épine I asked her questions and learned a lot from her.

One day she suggested to my mother that we should attend a *charming* reception given by *such* a talented man whom we had sometimes met at her apartment. We would meet really enlightened people there, she said, and women of taste, and there would be interesting literary and political readings. It would be *delightful*. The invitation had to be renewed before it was accepted. 'Let's go and see,' I said to Mama. 'I'm beginning to understand enough about the world to know that it will be either great fun or utterly absurd and even if it is the latter there is bound to be something which will amuse us, just once.' So we agreed to go. Wednesday was the day of M. Vâse's literary gathering. We went with Mme l'Épine to his apartment near the gate of the Temple. We climbed to the third floor and there we found quite a large room, furnished with several rows of straw-covered chairs which the spectators were beginning to fill. The remarkably plain chamber was lit with candles and very dirty brass chandeliers and seemed quite appropriate to the spartan austerity and poverty of an intellectual and a wit. Elegant women, young girls, a few dowagers, a great many minor poets, one or two busybodies and the odd adventurer: that was the sum of the society.

The master of the house sat down at a table and opened the proceedings by reading a piece of verse of his own composition. It was all about a dear little monkey which the aged marquise de Préville always carried around in her muff. The old lady was present in person and she thought it only proper that the hero of the poem should be displayed to the ecstatic admiration of everyone present. Monsieur Vâse was loudly applauded; he was delighted with his success and seemed to want to hand over his seat at the table to M. Delpêches, who wrote little comic dramas for the d'Audinot theatre and was in the habit of 'consulting society' about them before he sent them in, that is to say, of seeking the encouragement of his friends' applause. But this time he missed his cue, whether because he had a sore throat or because some verses were missing from a number of scenes in his drama, I do not know. The chair was immediately seized by Imbert, author of *Jugement de Pâris*, who read a pleasant trifle and was applauded to the skies. He had his reward; Mlle de la Cossonnière followed him by reading some not very skilful but quite touching verses called 'Farewell to Colin' which everyone knew was addressed to Imbert, he being about to embark on a journey. Compliments flowed in plenty and Imbert acquitted his debt to his art and to himself by kissing all the ladies. This brisk and cheerful ceremony, though performed with decorum, was not at all to my mother's liking and I myself found it embarrassing. Then, after I do not know how many indifferent quatrains and epigrams, a man with a huge voice read some verses in praise of Mme Benoît. She was present, too, and I must say a word about her for those who have not read her novels, entirely forgotten since long before the Revolution, upon which heaps of dust will have settled by the time anyone reads my memoirs.

I had read in a history of illustrious French women published by some society of literati, that Albine Benoît was born in Lyons. I also found in that history, to my great surprise, the names of various other women whom I saw in society, such as Mme de Puisieux, Mme Champion and others.

Some of them may still be alive or only recently departed. Be that as it may, Albine married the theatrical designer Benoît. She lived with him for a while in Rome and became an associate member of the Académie des Arcades. Recently widowed and still in mourning for her husband, she had now settled in Paris where she wrote verse and composed romances, not all of them on paper, in a lighthearted manner. Ladies of quality were happy to pay her, in cash or in clothes, for the pleasure of having a witty and attractive woman at their table.

Madame Benoît had once been beautiful. The resources of the dressing-table and the desire to please, both of them extended rather beyond the age at which they can be sure of success, still assured her many triumphs. Her eyes sought admiration with such fervour, her bosom, habitually uncovered even to zones beyond the little rosette usually reserved for secret mysteries, heaved so invitingly, the desire was so evident and the facilities offered so blatant, that it would have been churlish to refuse them the tribute which men find it so easy to render when not called upon to show constancy. The openly voluptuous air of Mme Benoît was something quite new to me. I had of course seen on the Esplanade those priestesses of pleasure whose profession is proclaimed by their shocking indecency, but this was something different. I was no less surprised at the poetical compliments showered upon the lady, with expressions like 'modest Benoît' and 'chaste Benoît' repeatedly recurring in these verses. At these flattering allusions she would pass a discreet fan across her eyes, while some of the gentlemen enthusiastically applauded the more explicit eulogies which they doubtless had reason to know well placed. I recalled what my reading had taught me about gallantry and considered what the relaxed morals of this age and the indiscipline of the Court must have added in the way of licentiousness and false values. I saw effeminate men gushing over bad verse and slight talents and over a woman who set out to seduce them all indiscriminately and without love. A wave of disgusted misanthropy swept over me and I returned to my solitary life in quiet melancholy.

We never went again to M. Vâse. Once was enough for me and as for my mother, the embrace of M. Imbert and the apotheosis of Mme Benoît had cured her of any wish to take me there again. Madame l'Épine was also kind enough to send us tickets and invitations to the concerts of the baron de Back, but we seldom went. They were sometimes quite pleasant but more often very boring on account of the baron's musical pretensions. We were also wary of the numerous musical gatherings of what were known as the 'amateurs'. We once went, accompanied by a M. Boyard de Creusy who had amused himself by writing a Method for the guitar and asked my mother's permission to present me with a copy. He was a decent, worthy man and I mention him here because later on, when I was at the ministry, he was complimentary to me about my attitude to old friends. He had called upon me there, in what many people might have thought my elevated station, and I had shown him by my welcome that I still cherished my memories of those earlier days.

As to the theatre, it was worse still. My mother never went. I was taken once only in her lifetime to the opera and to the Théâtre-Français. I must have been about sixteen or seventeen. *L'Union de l'amour et des arts*, by Floquet, did not live up to my expectation in any way, either in the music or in the drama. It was badly constructed and cold and completely lacking in charm. I disliked the inappropriate ballet scenes and was shocked by the costumes of the dancers – they wore hooped petticoats and looked quite ridiculous. Piron's critique of the wonders of the opera seemed very superior to this spectacle. At the Théâtre-Français I saw *l'Écossaise* by Voltaire. This did not thrill me much either, except for the acting of la Dumesnil. My father used to take me to performances at the fairground but I was disgusted by their mediocrity. Thus I was inoculated against the absurdity of the wits, just as the children of Sparta were inoculated against drunkenness by being shown its excesses, and I never experienced the thrill of a really great theatrical performance. What I had seen made me content to read the works of the great masters in the privacy of my study and to savour their beauty at leisure.

One day when we had not been to any of Mme l'Épine's concerts for some time, a young man who attended them regularly turned up at my mother's to enquire whether we were indisposed. His open manner, vivacity and amusing talk, added to the fact that we rarely received such visits, made us easily forgive him for employing this ruse to gain entry into the house. La Blancherie – for that was his name – plucked up his courage and made his declaration. But since I have now come to the history of my suitors I must present them in a *levée en masse* – a charming expression which dates my recital and recalls those famous days when everything was ordered *en masse* despite the greatest possible individuality of tastes and needs.

We have not forgotten the Spanish giant, with hands like Esau whose name, M. Mignard, contrasted so agreeably with his size. After having admitted that there was nothing more he could teach me on the guitar, he had asked permission to come and hear me play from time to time, and he presented himself at fairly long intervals without always finding us at home. He was proud of his young pupil's talent, which he took to be his own achievement, and proceeded from there to attempt to justify his familiarity. He claimed he was a nobleman from Malaga compelled by misfortune to seek his living in music, and he very soon allowed his imagination to run away with him. He did not have the courage to express his feelings in person but asked another man to demand my hand in marriage. This man, having tried to dissuade him, duly carried out the commission and was duly advised to recommend that our friend should not set foot in the house again. All this was done with appropriate courtesy. My father recounted to me with great amusement what had passed; he loved telling me of the prayers and supplications he received on my account and since he was rather proud of them he did not spare any suitor who lent himself to ridicule.

Poor Mozon had lost his wife. He had had the small wen removed from his right cheek and was thinking of purchasing a cabriolet. I was fifteen when he was brought back to give me more tuition. It went to his head. He had a very high opinion of his art and compared himself favourably with Marcel.[4] Artist for artist, why should he not enter the lists? He revealed his hopes and was dismissed like Mignard.

As soon as a girl reaches adolescence, a crowd of pretenders follow her about like bees around a newly opened flower. I had been strictly brought up and lived a secluded life, so there was only one prospect. My mother's respectability, the evident existence of some fortune and the fact that I was an only child made it quite an enticing one for many young men. They presented themselves in large numbers, and since it was not too easy to gain access to our apartment, most of them wrote to my parents. My father always showed me their letters. Quite independently of what the writer said about his state and fortune, I was influenced in the first place by the way he expressed himself. I prepared a draft for the reply, which my father copied down faithfully. I had him dismiss the suitors in a dignified manner, firmly and without offence. Thus the youth of the *quartier* passed in review before me. In the majority of cases I had no difficulty in justifying my refusal. My father had little concern for anything but money. He had pretensions for me and would not look favourably on anyone too recently established or anyone whose present means or future prospects did not guarantee me an easy life. He was upset when I hesitated to accept candidates

[4] A celebrated dancing-master who died in 1759.

who met these requirements. Differences of opinion began to develop between us on this subject and they increased as time went on. He loved and respected commerce because he regarded it as the source of all wealth. I hated it as the source of avarice and fraud.

My father realised that I could not accept anyone engaged in the trades as such, and in any case his own pride would not have allowed it. But he could not understand why I refused a fashionable jeweller who handled nothing but beautiful objects on which he made a huge profit and who had a well-established business most likely to make him a fortune. This jeweller, like the little haberdasher he thought so far beneath him and the rich cloth merchant who considered himself so far above them both, seemed to me entirely wrapped up in covetousness; he thought of nothing but money and how to amass it. The high ideals and delicate sentiments which make life bearable for me had no meaning whatever for him.

Having concerned myself since childhood with the relationships of men in society, having been nourished on the purest morality and steeped in the ideas of Plutarch and the philosophers, how could I possibly marry a merchant who would not think or feel like me about anything?

As I have said, my wise Mama wanted me to be as handy in the kitchen as in the drawing-room and to feel as much at home in a market as on the promenade. From the time when I came back from the Convent I used to go with her when she did the household shopping, and later on she sometimes sent me out with a maid to do it myself. Our butcher, who had just lost his second wife, was a young man with a fortune of 50,000 écus and good prospects of making a lot more. I knew nothing of this; I only thought how nice it was to be so obligingly served, though I was quite surprised to keep seeing this individual on our Sunday promenades, in a fine black suit with lace cuffs, bowing ceremoniously to my mother. This went on for a whole summer. Then I was unwell, and the butcher sent round every morning to enquire what delicacies we might require and offering us special bargains. These unequivocal attentions began to amuse my father. One day, for fun, he brought to my room a demoiselle Michon, a grave, religious lady, who had come to ask for my hand formally on behalf of the butcher. 'You are aware, my dear child,' he said, 'that on principle I never thwart your inclinations' and he repeated the proposal that Mlle Michon had made. I pursed my lips, annoyed that my father's sense of humour should place upon me a decision which he ought to have made for me. 'You are not unaware, my dear father,' I replied, imitating his tone, 'that I find myself well content with my present situation and have no intention of changing it for a number of years. You may draw such conclusions as you wish from this' – and I withdrew.

But later, when we were alone, my father said, 'That excuse which you thought up just now is a fine way of putting everyone off.' 'I was only repaying your little joke, Papa,' I said, 'by coming out with a platitude which sounds well on the lips of a young lady. I left you the responsibility for a formal refusal which it would not have been right to take upon myself.' 'That is all very well,' he replied, 'but what sort of future *do* you want?' 'I want the sort of future for which you have prepared me by teaching me to think and to study seriously. I do not know who I shall marry, but it has got to be a man with whom I can communicate and who knows what I am talking about.' 'There are plenty of people in commerce who are refined and knowledgeable.' 'Yes, but not of the sort I need. Their refinement consists of a few phrases and courtesies and their knowledge has all to do with money; it would hardly help me educate my children.' 'Then you could educate them yourself.' 'I should find that an ungrateful task if it was not shared by their father.' 'But don't you consider the wife of Lempereur a happy woman? They have just left commerce, have bought themselves a good position, keep a fine house and receive distinguished society.' 'I am no judge of other people's happiness but as for my own I do not associate it with wealth. To me, there can be no bliss in marriage without an intimate union of hearts and I would only marry a man who was like me. Besides, my husband must be worth more than me; nature and the laws have given him the primacy and I should be ashamed if he did not truly deserve it.' 'Do you want, then, to marry some lawyer? Women are not happy, I believe, with these desk-men. They have plenty of conceit and very little money.' 'But Good Lord, Papa! I do not judge men by their robes! I am not saying that I want someone from this or that profession. I want a man whom I can love.' 'And you say you cannot find such a man in commerce?' 'Well, I confess that it is very difficult; I have not yet seen anyone to my taste and the way of life is itself repugnant to me.' 'But my dear child, listen to me. It is really not a bad life sitting quietly in your apartment while your husband is out all day doing good business. Look at Mme d'Argens. She knows diamonds as well as he does; she conducts negotiations with courtiers in his absence, concludes deals with private buyers and would carry on the business herself if anything were to happen to him. They have already amassed a considerable fortune; it is their firm which has just bought Bagnolet. You are intelligent, you already know a lot about the business since you read that treatise on precious stones; people would trust you, you could do what you liked. You could have a really agreeable life if you would take Delorme, Dabreuil or L'Obligeois.' 'Look, Father, I have seen only too clearly that one can succeed in commerce only be selling dear what one has bought cheap, by lying a great deal and exploiting the poor worker. I could never lend myself to such things nor respect a man who is engaged in that way from morning until night. I mean to be an honest woman. How could I be faithful to someone for whom I had no respect, even supposing I had married him in the first place? Selling diamonds and selling little pies seem to me much the same thing, except that the latter have a fixed price and there is less scope for swindling, even if one gets one's fingers dirtier. But I do not care for the one any more than the other.' 'Are you saying that there are no honest men in commerce?' 'I cannot say that, but I think there are very few and even those few are not at all what I want in a husband.' 'You are making yourself very hard to please; what if you fail to find your paragon?' 'I shall die a spinster.' 'That might be harder than you suppose. You still have time to think but do not forget the fable; you may wake up one day to find that the audience has departed and that you are left all alone.' 'I am not afraid. I deserve happiness and I defy the fates to deprive me of it.' 'There you are, up in the clouds again! It is all very fine to get up there, but not so easy to stay. Do not forget that I want grandchildren before I am too old.'

And I should like to give them to you, I thought to myself when my father had gone. But I refuse to marry a man who does not suit me. Then I became a little depressed, thinking of what was on offer and not seeing anything there which remotely accorded with my tastes. This mood did not last long; my happiness in the present was sufficiently strong to drive away anxiety about the future. 'Perhaps this time you will be satisfied, Mademoiselle,' said my father one day with the important, self-satisfied air which he always assumed when someone had asked him a favour. 'Read this letter.' It was an extremely well-written letter, both as regards the handwriting and the style, and it made me blush. Monsieur Morizot de Rozain said some very nice things, but he also observed that his name was to be found amongst the nobility of his province. It seemed to me in very bad taste to boast of an advantage which I could not claim and which he had no right to assume I should covet. 'There is hardly sufficient evidence here for a decision,' I said shaking my head. 'We must make the gentleman talk. One or two more letters, and I will know the whole truth. I shall prepare you a reply accordingly.'

Every time we had to write to this aspirant my father was docility itself; he copied down exactly what I wrote. I much enjoyed playing the responsible father, treating my own affairs with all the seriousness they deserved and clothing my own feelings in paternal style and wisdom. We extracted as many as three explanatory letters from M. de Rozain. I kept them for a long time because they were so well done. They proved to me that even intelligence and wit cannot satisfy me unless accompanied by more good judgement than this man showed and by qualities of *soul* which cannot be counterfeited and which are detectable at the first encounter. Besides, de Rozain had no resources but the title of lawyer, and my present fortune was not enough for two. His other qualities were not such as to make one want to overlook this drawback.

When I said that I would present a *levée en masse* of my suitors I did not promise to name them all and I dare say the reader will forgive me for not doing so. I meant only to draw attention to the curious situation in which I was sought after by a lot of men whose faces I had never seen and yet whose looks and character I was apparently entitled to criticise. At church and on the promenade I kept seeing new faces watching or following me and I would say to myself 'I shall soon have to write another letter for my father.' But I never saw one that attracted me.

La Blancherie, as I have said, had got himself introduced into the house and had had the wit to see that before declaring himself he should try to make himself liked. He was still very young. He had travelled a lot, read a lot and even published a book. It was not worth much but it was full of fine morality and sound ideas. He had called it 'Notes from my Travels for the Enlightenment of Parents' – not over-modest, certainly, but one was inclined to forgive him because he based himself on very respectable authorities, quoted them effectively and inveighed with the sincere passion of youth against the coldness or negligence of parents responsible so often for the downfall of the young. La Blancherie was short, dark and plain and he did not appeal to me. But I had no objection to his ideas and I could see that he found me attractive.

One evening, returning with my mother from a visit to my grandparents, we found my father in a meditative mood. 'I have news,' he said smiling. 'La Blancherie has just left. He spent two hours here and opened his heart to me. Since the matter concerns you I am bound to inform you at once.' (My father always drew this conclusion, though it was not absolutely obligatory.) 'He loves you and proposed himself to become my son-in-law. But he has not got a penny and it would be folly, as I told him. He is studying law and his idea is to buy himself some sort of position in a magistrate's court. Unfortunately his own resources would not suffice for that so he thought that, if we approved, his wife's dowry might be used for the purpose. He also thought that since my daughter was an only child, the young couple might live with us for the first few years. He adorned all this with a lot of optimistic ideas typical of a young man. But prudent parents need to be circumspect. Let him open an office or buy himself a position of some sort. In short, let him establish himself and then we shall see. Marriage might come after that. It would be a folly to marry beforehand. Besides, we must look into his background. This should not be difficult. I should prefer him not to be a gentleman and I would like him to have about 40,000 écus. He's not a bad boy. We talked for a long time. I'm afraid he was a little cast down by my reasoning, but he heard me through. He ended by begging me not to close the door on him and he asked this so charmingly that I consented, provided that he does not come here more often than in the past. I told him that I would not say anything to you, but as you are a sensible girl I prefer to hide nothing from you.' A few questions from my mother and some wise reflections about how careful one must be before forming a preference for anyone, saved me from the necessity of saying anything. But it set me thinking.

My father was of course right. But on the other hand the young man's proposal did not seem to me wholly unreasonable. I decided that I should take more interest in him and find out more about him. But there were not many opportunities. Several months went by, La Blancherie left for Orléans and I did not see him again for two years. In the interval I was on the point of marrying a doctor called Gardanne[5] , under pressure from one of our relations, Mme Desportes, née Provençale. This good lady had married a business-

[5] Joseph-Jacques Gardane (born 1739): a specialist in venereal diseases.

man in Paris who died shortly afterwards. She had one daughter and continued to run the business, so strongly approved of by my father, of buying and selling jewellery. She was a clever, correct and efficient woman with a persuasive manner and was generally admired. She managed to give the impression that she did business only to oblige the people who applied to her. She had an elegant apartment where she received respectable society including very often clients on the look-out for treasures or fashionable bargains, and she succeeded in maintaining a comfortable fortune without having to step into the street. She was supported in her old age by her daughter, who had dutifully declined all other offers in order to live in devoted seclusion with her mother.

Gardanne came from Mme Desportes' part of the country. He was a straightforward, virtuous southerner, well educated and extremely ambitious. He had begun well in his profession and was expected to go far. Madame Desportes took a kindly interest in him and with her usual concern for other people's affairs decided that he would make a good husband for her young cousin. She died before this could be accomplished, but her daughter took up the cause. Gardanne both desired and feared to get married. In adding up the pros and cons of joining the great fraternity he did not confine himself, as I did in my romantic fashion, to the question of personal compatibility. He counted everything. I was worth only 20,000 livres on marriage, but my prospects made up to some extent for the meagreness of the dowry. The financial calculations were made before I knew anything about it, and the deal was to all intents and purposes concluded by the time I was told that I might be going to marry a doctor. As far as that went I had no objection, and I gathered that he was an educated man; but I needed to see him in person. It was arranged that we should meet by chance out walking in the Luxembourg gardens. But rain intervened – or was feared – so we took refuge in the apartment of one of Mme Desportes' friends, a Mlle de la Barre. This lady was a great Jansenist. She was delighted with the plot and offered us refreshment, during which by a fortunate chance her doctor and fellow southerner called upon her.

We examined one another closely, without of course appearing to do so. My cousin was triumphant and appeared to be saying 'I did not claim that she was pretty, but what do you make of her?' My dear Mama looked on tenderly; Mlle de la Barre distributed little sweets and dainties with an arch look. The doctor himself prattled away and ate a great many sugar cakes, saying with somewhat studied gallantry that he liked sweet things; to which the young lady replied in a small voice, blushing slightly and smiling, that men were said to have a sweet tooth because they needed to be treated sweetly. The proud doctor seemed to be encouraged by this reply. My father would have given his benediction there and then – in fact he quite angered me with his politenesses. The doctor was the first to leave, to do his evening rounds, and we all went home the way we had come. That was what they called an 'interview'. Madame Desportes, a great stickler for the formalities, had arranged it all because the man who intends marriage may not set foot inside the young lady's house until he has been accepted. And furthermore, once that has happened the contract must be drawn up and the occasion celebrated immediately. Such is the law and the prophets.

A doctor in his professional garb is not an alluring sight for a young person and I have never in all my life fancied love in a periwig. Gardanne with his doctorial air, his southern accent and his close-knit black eyebrows seemed better equipped for curing a fever than for inspiring one. But although that is what I felt, I did not consciously admit it to myself. I took such an austere view of marriage that I saw absolutely nothing laughable in these proceedings. 'Well,' asked my mother gently, 'what do you think of him? Will he suit?' 'Dear Mama, I cannot decide that so quickly.' 'But you can say whether he is repugnant to you.' 'Neither repugnant nor attractive; but he could turn out to be either.' 'Yes, but what are we to say if they come formally to ask for your hand?' 'Will that be a commitment?' 'When one has given one's word to an honest man one must certainly keep it.' 'And what if I don't like him?' 'A reasonable girl like you does not take important decisions of this kind lightly. Once she has weighed up all the arguments and made her decision she does not go back on it.' 'Then I have to decide on the basis of that one interview?' 'That is not quite how it is. Monsieur Gardanne's relations with the family enable us to judge his way of life and his morality, and we can make enquiries which will help us to assess his character. Those are the basic things on which we have to make a decision; the man's looks are not important except at a superficial level.' 'Oh Mama! I'm in no hurry to get married.' 'I know, dear. But you will have to settle down sometime and you are at the right age now. You have turned down many offers from the business world which, after all, is where most of your admirers are likely to come from. You seem determined not to accept anyone from that walk of life. But this man has quite a different background and seems from all accounts to be suited for you; take care not to reject him lightly.' 'Surely I have plenty of time. Monsieur Gardanne himself may not have made up his mind; after all, he has never seen me before today.' 'I agree, but if that is your only excuse it may not last you very long. In any case, I am not asking for a decision now. Think about it and let me know in two days' time.' So saying, my mother kissed me and left me to my own thoughts.

Reason and nature conspire so effectively to persuade a wise, modest young woman that she must get married that the only point left for deliberation is who should it be. On this my mother's arguments seemed to me quite sound. But I also thought that whatever they might say my provisional acceptance could not possibly be binding; it was absurd to regard me as committed just because I had agreed to meet in my father's house a man who wanted to marry me. I was quite determined that nothing on earth would make me go through with it if I did not like him. So I decided not to say no and to keep my options open.

We were on the point of leaving for a fortnight in the country. I thought it would be undignified to postpone this journey while we waited for a suitor to make his move, and my mother agreed with me. However, one fine morning just before our departure Mlle de la Barre arrived, dressed up to the nines, to present what was known as the 'suit' on behalf of the doctor. My parents responded with the generalities usually employed in the case of acceptance, but with the unexpressed reservation that we might still change our minds on reflection. Permission was sought and granted for the 'suitor' to present his case in person. Mademoiselle de la Barre, ever cautious, concluded that she should bring him along herself. Then a ceremonial supper, attended by her and one of my relations, marked his formal admission into my father's house. We left next day for the country, where we were to spend exactly the amount of time laid down for what are called the 'enquiries'. This second interview had hardly made more impression on me than the first, but it did seem to me that Gardanne was an intelligent man with whom a thinking woman could live and I reckoned, in my inexperience, that if a man and woman could communicate properly and understand one another they had all the ingredients for a happy marriage. My mother was afraid that she detected signs of an overbearing character in the doctor, but this did not strike me at all. I was used to examining myself, regulating my affections and controlling my imagination; and I took such a romantic view of a wife's sacred duties that I could not see what it mattered if my husband had a slightly gentler or a slightly less gentle nature, or that he could demand from me anything that I was not willing to give. In this, of course, I was thinking like an abstract philosopher or a solitary who knows nothing of man or of his passions. I took my own affectionate, generous heart to be the common measure of human morality. I made this mistake for many years and it was the prime source of all my sorrows. I hasten to declare it now because it provides the key to my life.

When I got down to the country that time I felt none of my usual relaxation and delight in the beauties of nature. I bore within me a sort of disquiet, a feeling that I was on the edge of some precipice. Was I to leave my dear mother, my cherished studies and my solitary retreats? Was I to lose my independence, in order to take up a way of life which I could not very well imagine but which would certainly entail heavy obligations? I was quite prepared for sacrifices if I knew what they were to be – it was the uncertainty that upset me.

Mademoiselle Desportes had made me promise to send her news, and I did so regularly. But towards the end of the fortnight I learned that her plans had been thwarted. My father, who took everything literally, would not have thought he was doing his duty by his daughter if he had married her off without having carried out to the letter the 'enquiries' laid down in the rule book for this stage of the proceedings. Gardanne had been introduced to us by one of our own relations who knew his background and his way of life. All possible information had been provided This was not enough for my father. From the very beginning of the affair he had written to three or four people in Provence asking them to send him detailed particulars about the doctor and his family. While we were away in the country, his vigilance went further; he laid out small sums of money among the servants and the tradesmen for information about the tastes and habits of his future son-in-law. He even went to call upon the doctor and with the same tactlessness as he had shown during his enquiries – letting the whole world see what he was up to – proceeded to show the poor young man how much he had found out about him. He quoted with approval a compatriot with whom the doctor had quarrelled and ended by handing out unsolicited advice in a patronising manner. At the same time

Gardanne was receiving letters from his home town twitting him about the enquiries which were being made there and he soon heard of the local researches too. On top of all this the school-masterly exhortations of his would-be father-in-law were too much for him. Angry and offended, he went round to Mlle Desportes and complained, with true southern indignation and fire, of the strange behaviour of this man whose most desirable daughter, he said, had the one disadvantage of owning such a father. Mademoiselle Desportes, as proud as he, thought it very wrong that he should be so little in love with her cousin as to cavil at these minor irritations and received him coldly. As soon as I heard all this I seized the opportuntity to escape from my dilemma. I wrote that I hoped on my return not to see the gentleman again. Thus ended a match which they had been in such a hurry to bring about that Gardanne had considered concluding it within a week of my return! I congratulated myself on my escape. My mother, who was a little frightened of the doctor, breathed a sigh of relief not unmixed with regret, while my father tried to conceal feelings of shame and vexation beneath a semblance of great dignity. My cousin preserved her honour by very properly closing her doors against the doctor. Mademoiselle de la Barre was still saying, five years later, that the marriage had been made in heaven, that her friend would never contract another and that the finger of Providence would certainly point the way to reconciliations of which we could have no knowledge.

12

BEREAVEMENT

◦—◦

M Y MOTHER'S HEALTH HAD BEGUN TO DETERIORATE. She had had an attack of paralysis which they pretended for my sake was some sort of rheumatism. She herself was under no illusions. She became serious and taciturn, losing some of her vivacity every day. She liked increasingly to be alone and would often make me go out shopping with the maid while she stayed at home. She often talked to me about getting settled and regretted that I could not accept any of the men on offer. One day in particular she pressed me with tears in her eyes to accept an honest jeweller who had asked for my hand. 'He has the reputation', she said, 'of strict probity; his habits and character are refined; he is wealthy and expects to become more so. He knows that you do not see eye to eye on many things but he has a high regard for you and will be happy to be guided by you. He has already said that he would have no objection to his wife nursing her children. You could dominate him.' 'Ah, Mama, I have no use for a man I could dominate. I cannot marry a great baby.' 'You know, dear, you are very hard to please, for you do not want a strong man either.' 'Try to understand me, Mama. I certainly do not want a man who would give me orders; I should simply learn to resist. But neither do I want to have to control my husband. Either I am greatly mistaken or those little men who are five feet tall with a beard never cease making it clear that they are the masters. If a man like that started trying to make me accept his superiority I should quickly resent it, while if he gave way to me I should feel embarrassed by my own dominance.' 'I understand! You want to control a man in such a way that he thinks himself the master while doing what you want.' 'That is not right either. I hate servitude, but I am not naturally domineering. It would embarrass me. I have enough trouble controlling myself. I want to be loved by someone I can respect, someone to whom I can feel it is an honour to defer, someone who will find his own happiness in pleasing me according to the dictates of his wisdom and his affection.' 'Happiness, my dear girl, is not always built upon a perfect relationship such as you imagine. If there could be no happiness without that, few marriages would be happy.' 'I certainly know of none that I envy.' 'Maybe; but amongst the marriages you do not envy there may be many that are preferable to remaining a spinster all your life. I may be going to die sooner than you think. You will be left alone with your father. He is still young and you have no idea what troubles I see ahead for you. How much happier I should be if I could see you united to a good man before I leave this world!'

These thoughts upset me. My mother seemed to be lifting a veil from a dark and frightening future which I had never even suspected. The very thought of losing her filled me with terror, yet she was talking of it as if it were something that might happen quite soon. I started to tremble, stared at her with wild eyes and burst into tears. 'You must not be afraid,' she said. 'Don't you see that we have to consider every eventuality when we are planning the future? I am not ill, but I am going through one of those recurrent bad patches which could prove fatal one day. It is best to think about these things when one is strong and well. This is an important moment. I must tell you what I think. A good and worthy man offers you his hand. You are over twenty. You will not see so many suitors in the future as you have had during the last five years. I may be gone. Do not turn down a husband who, even if he does not possess all the refinement by which you set so much store – and don't forget that it is a very rare quality, much rarer than you might think – will cherish you and bring you happiness.' 'Yes, Mama,' I cried with a hollow laugh, 'I know! The kind of happiness that *you* have had!' My mother was shaken, silenced. Never again did she press me over this match or over any other. The words had escaped me involuntarily; their effect showed me only too clearly how close they were to the truth.

Strangers must have been able to tell straight away how different my mother was from my father and no one was in a better position than I to appreciate her qualities. But I had never stopped to think how she must have suffered during her marriage. From earliest childhood my home had seemed a peaceful place and I had no reason to suppose that it may have been difficult for her to keep it so. My father loved her and cherished me tenderly. I never saw her look discontented, though she was sometimes reproachful. When she disagreed with my father and could not get him to change his mind she seemed to accept it. It was only in recent years that, becoming uncomfortable with some of my father's opinions, I had begun to join in the arguments myself. I acquired a certain influence and soon used it quite freely. Whether because it was a new experience or out of weakness, my father was more likely to listen to me than to his wife. I became a sort of watchdog to my mother; if he began to snap at her or worry her in my presence I would growl and pull on his coat tails until he let go. The strange thing is that I was just as reserved as she was about him and never said a disrespectful word about him when he was not present. I defended her with the power of reason and persuasion but would never say a word about what had passed once we were alone. He was still my father and he must not be criticised.

But I noticed that he was beginning to be less hardworking. His 'community' business, which had originally been an occasional distraction, now required him to spend more and more time away from home. Bit by bit he became dissolute. He was attracted to parties and the theatre, and he began to gamble. Encouraged by his tavern friends he became addicted to the lottery. In the hope of making a fortune he embarked on commercial ventures which were alien to his art and not successful. The more he lost the habit of work the more he relied on chance and his native talents began to deteriorate. The apprentices, no longer properly supervised, began to skimp their work and as custom fell away some of them had to be dismissed. These changes took place very gradually, but one could see them happening long before realising their significance.

My mother became silent and thoughtful and occasionally she half revealed her anxiety to me. I did not encourage her to talk about something which neither of us could do anything about, but I did my best to make her life easy in any way I could. She began to find our walks very tiring, so I volunteered to go out along with my father. He no longer sought my company for its own sake as in the days gone by, but he was still glad to have me with him and I used to bring him back in triumph to Mama and hand him over to her loving care. This did not always work; there were times when he would deposit me at home and go out again at once, just for a moment he said, and would then forget to come home for supper and not get back until midnight. We wept in silence and if on his return I showed any sign of our discontent he made light of it, turning my remarks aside with a joke, or else retired crossly to his room. Domestic happiness was soon overcast by these gathering clouds but there was never any storm and an outsider would probably not have noticed the deterioration that was taking place every day.

My mother had been suffering greatly for more than a year from a sort of head cold which the doctors could not explain. After trying various cures they recommended exercise, which she did not enjoy, and good country air. The Whitsun holidays of 1775 were just beginning and we had decided to spend them at Meudon. On the Sunday morning I did not wake up bright and early as I usually did when we were off to the country. I was weighed down by heavy sleep with nightmares; I dreamed that we were returning to Paris by water in a storm of rain and that as I was getting off the boat my way was blocked by a corpse which they were carrying ashore. I was in a panic and began to ask who it was when my mother gently woke me and drove the dream away. I threw my arms around her, still frightened, and embraced her passionately as if she had saved me from the direst peril. Then I leapt out of bed, we got ourselves ready and were off. It was a lovely calm day and the little skiff soon landed us at our destination. I recovered my composure in the delights of nature. The voyage did my mother good and she seemed more energetic. It was on the second day that we discovered Ville-Bonne and the sluice-keeper of the Red Mill. We got home on the Tuesday evening. I had promised Agatha that I would visit her in her convent immediately after the holiday, and my mother had intended to come with me. But the two previous days had tired her so she changed her mind at the last moment and asked me to go with my maid. I wanted to stay with her, but she insisted that I keep my promise, adding that I knew very well she liked being alone and that I could take a walk afterwards in the Jardin du Roi if I wished.

So I went to see Agatha. I left her almost at once. 'Why are you in such a hurry?' she asked. 'Are you expected at home?' 'No, but I have a feeling I must go back to Mama.' 'But you told me she was well.' 'Yes, and she is not expecting me back so soon. But something is worrying me and I must get back to her.' So saying I burst into tears despite myself. I dare say the reader will think that I had imagined all this after the event. But I am a faithful historian and I record only what I positively remember having experienced.

Anyone who has followed this account of my personality and of how my ideas developed from childhood onwards will surely admit that I am not likely to have shared popular prejudices of that time any more than I am likely to be superstitious today. I have tried to understand the origins of what we call premonitions and have come to the conclusion that they are a sort of flash of insight, or a cluster of imperceptible impressions impossible to identify, many of which may have been more unconsciously than consciously experienced. In an alert and highly sensitive individual a sudden *aperçu* of this kind can create a state of mind for which there is no logical reason, but which events later clarify and justify. The more lively our interest in some object, the more perceptive and susceptible we allow ourselves to become in regard to that object, the more likely we are to have these psychic insights, if I may so describe them, which we then call premonitions and which the ancients called auguries or warnings from the gods.

My mother was the dearest thing in the world to me; she was nearing her end without showing any signs of it to the outside world. Even I, who watched her so closely, had not detected anything to warn me of the terrible event. But no doubt there were minor changes in her from day to day which caused me anxiety without my realising it. I could not have said that I was anxious; I should not have known what I was anxious about. But I felt troubled, I trembled sometimes when I looked at her and when I was absent from her I had a sort of unease which I could not explain.

I was in such a strange mood when I left Agatha that she begged me to send her news at once. I went straight home despite the maid's suggestion that we should take a walk in the Jardin du Roi. As I approached the house I saw a local girl in front of our door who shouted at me 'Ah, Mademoiselle, your mother is very bad. She came to fetch my mother, who has gone up with her.' I rushed up in panic and there I found my mother sprawled on a chair, head bent, arms drooping, a wild look in her eye and her mouth open. On seeing me she revived a little and tried to speak but could barely formulate the words. Painfully raising one arm she tried to stroke my cheek, tried to smile, tried again to speak. In vain! Paralysis had settled on her tongue, her head and half her body. Spirits of balm, salts in the mouth, massage, all were without effect. I had sent people to fetch the doctor and to find my father and I ran to get two grains of emetic from the nearest chemist. The doctor had now come; my mother was on the bed and remedies were being applied, but the sickness spread with terrible rapidity. Her eyes were closed, her head was sunk immovably upon her breast and a harsh, precipitate breathing portended a general collapse. Yet she could understand what was said to her and when asked whether she was in pain lifted her left hand to her forehead as if to show where she felt it most.

I was feverishly active, giving orders, doing things myself before the words left my mouth, never appearing to leave the bedside and taking care of everything. At ten o'clock at night I saw the doctor draw some of the women and my father aside. I asked what was going on and they told me they had sent for Extreme Unction. I thought I was dreaming. The priest arrived, prayed and did I know not what. I stood stock still at the foot of the bed holding a candlestick, refusing to speak or to move, staring at my darling mother as she died, lost in an ocean of feeling that drowned all my faculties. The candlestick slipped from my grasp and I fell unconscious to the floor. Some time later I found myself in the adjoining room surrounded by members of my family. I turned my eyes towards the door and tried to get up. They held me back. With wild gestures and suppliant cries I begged to be allowed back to my mother. Gloomy silence and a dismal, constant resistance prevented me. I recovered strength, pleaded, raged, but they were unmoved. I had some sort of hysterics and at that moment my father appeared, silent and pale. They appeared to ask him an unspoken question. In reply he raised his eyes in a despairing movement which caused them all to moan and wail. At this I escaped from the people around me and rushed precipitately out of the room. 'Mama!' But she was no longer there. I raised her arms; I could not believe it. I opened and reclosed those eyes that would never look at me again, called to her, threw myself on the bed, pressed my lips on hers, half opened them and tried to breathe life into the dead. I wanted to die myself.

I do not know quite what followed. I found myself next morning at a neighbour's house. Monsieur Besnard arrived, put me in a carriage and took me to his home. When we got there my great aunt kissed me silently, sat me down at a little table and offered me something to drink. She was very insistent and I wanted to please her, but I fainted. They put me to bed where I spent a fortnight between life and death in constant terrifying convulsions. The physical sensation I recall was one of continual suffocation; my breathing was a sort of scream which I am told could be heard in the street. I had suffered a real breakdown from which I was saved only by my strong constitution and the loving care of my relations. These dear people had given up their best room to me and were living in cubby-holes themselves. They seemed to find new strength in looking after me and bringing me back to life. They would not let any domestic serve me but did everything themselves, assisted only by Mme Trude, a young married cousin who came every evening to spend the night with me, slept in my bed and was constantly on the alert to forestall and soothe my frequent convulsions.

A week had passed and still no tears had come; the deepest agony knows no tears. (Bitter, burning tears flow from me as I write, for I now fear a calamity worse even than what I am suffering here. All my prayers have been for the safety of the man I love, and now his fate is more unsure than ever![1] Disaster spreads like a terrible black cloud, blanketing all that I have held most dear. Retracing the past is the utmost I can do to distract my attention from the unbearable present.) In the end it was a letter from Sophie that saved me. Her loving sympathy and understanding achieved what all the baths and the doctors' prescriptions had failed to do; it broke through the barrier which had been holding back my tears. Once I could cry, the sense of suffocation was eased and my convulsions became rarer.

My father and I were both in mourning, but our feelings were very different. His idea of comforting me was to suggest that Providence acted for the best even in tragedies of this kind; that my mother had completed her life's work, the education of her daughter, and that if I was to lose one of my parents it was just as well that Heaven had spared me the one most able to support me. As it turned out, my loss was irreparable even from this point of view, but I did not think that at the time. I thought only how arid and inappropriate was the consolation which he offered me and recognised, for the first time perhaps, the immeasurable distance which stood between my father and myself. It seemed to me that he tore away with his own hands the veil of respect through which I had hitherto looked upon him. I now felt myself to be a complete orphan; my mother was dead and my father would never understand me. A new kind of misery took hold of me and threw me once again into violent despair. Once again I was saved by the tears, the kindness and the love of my dear cousin and of my other relations. But alas! this was only the first of the blows that fate was to deal me. Many more were to follow.

And so those happy, sunny years of childhood were at an end,

---

[1] Madame Roland had probably just learned that Buzot had not embarked for America but had taken refuge in the Gironde.

years of peaceful family life, of carefree affection, of devoted study. It is a consolation now to look back upon those years, like remembering a fine spring morning when the sky is clear and the air as fresh as day, the leaves stirring and the flowers infusing everything that breathes with the enchantment of hope and life. The promise of happiness is happiness.

My mother was only fifty when she was so cruelly taken from me. The strange head cold from which she had suffered so long turned out to be due to an abscess in the brain which was not discovered until after her death. Without this, her second stroke might not have been fatal. We had not had any real warning that she was dangerously ill. We attributed her various indispositions to her time of life and I myself thought that her depressions, which I certainly noticed, were due to the emotional strain from which I well knew she was suffering, rather than to any physical cause.

Our last walks in the country had seemed to revive her. On the day of her death I had left her quite well at three o'clock in the afternoon; at five I found her stricken and by midnight she was dead. What miserable, helpless toys we are in the hands of fate! How terrible that our keenest feelings and our boldest intentions are bound within the limits of so fragile an existence! Here was one of the best and most lovable women who ever lived, snatched away without warning. There may not have been anything very brilliant about her but whoever knew her could see how wise she was, how gentle and true, how utterly reliable and good. I was completely agonised by her sudden death and suffered a nervous breakdown. 'It is good to have a heart,' said Father Legrand when he came to see me at my grandparents', 'but unfortunate to have such a tender one as yours.'

As soon as I began to improve they took the trouble to invite people I knew into the house, so as to draw me out of myself. I seemed not to be living in this world at all, being so obsessed with my grief that I hardly noticed what went on around me, scarcely spoke at all or, if I did, replied to my own thoughts rather than to what had been said to me. They thought I was deranged. Every now and then a sudden realisation of my loss would bring on hysterics. I would shout and scream, throw up my arms and lose consciousness. In quiet intervals I was well aware how unhappy I was making my kind relations and how dependent I was on my cousin's loving care. Then I tried to make amends to them. Father Legrand was clever enough to see that the best way of distracting my attention from my grief was to talk to me about my mother. In this way he gradually brought me to have thoughts and feelings about her which were not related to her loss. As soon as he thought me fit to read a book he brought me Jean-Jacques Rousseau's *Héloise*. This was really my first distraction. I was twenty-one, I had read a lot and I was familiar with many writers, historians and philosophers, but Rousseau made an impression on me at that time comparable to the impact of Plutarch when I was eight. Rousseau was exactly the nourishment I needed. He interpreted feelings which I had had myself before I read him but which he alone could explain.

Plutarch had guided me towards republicanism, awakening my social conscience and inspiring me with enthusiasm for the public service and for liberty. Rousseau showed me the possibility of domestic happiness and the delights that were available to me if I sought them. But though he may have fortified me against the usual run of weaknesses, he could hardly warn me effectively against falling in love!

I was born into a corrupt age and confronted with a revolution which I certainly did not foresee. In these dramatic circumstances there was something in my character which drove me to make great sacrifices and to suffer great wrongs. Death will soon put an end to them all. I would never have thought of devoting the short time that remains to an account of my own life had I not been the object of scurrilous attack by my enemies. My idea here is to present truths which are applicable to others besides myself. I suppress nothing because I believe that the details all serve to create a convincing whole.

It was painful to go back to my father's apartment where everything reminded me of my mother. They had taken the stupid precaution of removing her portrait, as if that was not bound to remind me even more sharply of my loss. I had it put back at once. All the domestic chores were now my responsibility, and I attended to them willingly. They were not very onerous in a household of three people. I have never been able to understand how an active and organised woman can find herself fully occupied by household duties, however large her establishment. The more numerous the household the more there are to share the work. All it requires is wise distribution of duties and a little vigilance. I have been in many different situations in this respect and have been responsible for everything that was done in my home, yet I have never found that it took up more than two hours a day at the outside. One always has leisure if one is busy; it is idle people who have no time for anything. Women who constantly exchange useless visits with one another and who think themselves ill dressed unless they have spent hours in front of the mirror naturally find their days boringly long but too short for their duties. On the other hand I have also seen so-called good housewives who are quite unbearable in company, and even to their husbands, because of their preoccupation with domestic trifles. I know of nothing more tiresome than this or better calculated to make a man look elsewhere for his pleasures. In my opinion a woman ought to be able to keep her linen and wardrobe in good condition, or have it done for her, feed her own babies, manage her own kitchen or even do the cooking herself without complaining about it, and at the same time keep her mind alert, allow herself time to think and talk about other things and give pleasure by her presence as a woman. I have noticed that it is much the same in politics as in the family; the famous housewives who talk the whole time about domestic matters usually leave a lot undone and annoy everyone, just as a busy, chattering politician exaggerates the public problems which he is incompetent to handle.

I became more and more addicted to study. It was my principal consolation. Now that I was still more on my own and often melancholy I felt the need to write. I liked to get my ideas straight and it helped to write them down. With a pen in my hand I was able to control my imagination and follow my reason, whereas without it I too often found myself just dreaming. I had already begun a collection of notes which I now filled out under the heading 'Leisure Writings and Diverse Reflections'. My only thought was to get my various opinions down on paper so that I could compare them later on and form a sort of conspectus of my intellectual progress. I have quite a large bundle of these youthful works piled up in a dusty corner of my library, or perhaps in an attic. I never had the slightest intention of becoming an authoress. I realised very early on that woman who becomes known as a writer loses much more than she gains. Men do not like it and her own sex are always critical. If her works are bad she is jeered at and rightly so. If they are good, then everybody says she cannot have written them herself. If forced to admit that she was responsible for most of it they turn to picking holes in her character, her morals and her talents. All her personal faults are set in the balance against her wit.

Besides, my main concern was with my own peace of mind, and I have never yet heard that the public could play any part in that without destroying it. Nothing is sweeter than being appreciated by one's friends, nothing so empty as the admiration of people whom one is never going to meet. . . .

During the first few weeks of his widowhood my father did his best to stay at home more regularly. But he was bored and since his art was not sufficient to interest him all my efforts to help him were in vain. I tried talking to him, but we had few ideas in common and he was more and more taken up with the sort of topics which he would not have wanted to discuss with me. Often I played piquet with him but it was not very exciting for him playing with his own daughter. Besides, he knew that I hated cards and however hard I tried I could not make him believe that I enjoyed it in any way.

I would have liked to make a pleasant home for him but I did not have the means. The only people I knew well were my grandparents whom we visited but who never came out themselves. He should of course have made his own circle of friends at home, but the trouble was that he had friends outside whom he would not have thought it suitable for me to meet. Perhaps my mother had been wrong to be so exclusive; perhaps she should have created a more lively atmosphere at home which would appeal to her husband? But it would be unfair to blame her, just as it would be wrong to judge my father too severely for the mistakes which brought disaster on him. There is an inevitability in the way sorrows accumulate when they derive from a fundamental cause. One must go right back to that cause if one wants to explain them.

Political thinkers in our times are trying to create a system of universal happiness out of which they hope the happiness of the individual will emerge. I very much fear that they are putting the cart before the horse. It would conform better with nature, and I believe with reason too, if we first examined what makes for domestic happiness and tried to ensure that in every home. The general contentment would then be the sum of all the individual satisfactions and people would have an interest in defending the social system which had procured it. A constitution may enshrine the loftiest principles, but if I observe that a large number of the people who have adopted it are miserably unhappy I must conclude that it is a political monstrosity; and if those who are *not* miserable take pleasure in the unhappiness of the others, then I regard it as an outrage and its authors as either imbeciles or criminals.

When the partners in a marriage are ill assorted, one of the two may be able to keep the peace for a while by his or her devotion and skill. But sooner or later the absence of real understanding must have its effect and cause trouble of some sort. The framework of such a marriage is like our political system; it lacks a solid base and must collapse one day, whatever skill is employed in maintaining it.

My mother could never bring home people of her own type because they would not have suited my father, while the sort of daily acquaintances he enjoyed would have irritated her and would not have fitted in with the way she wanted me brought up. So she had to stick to members of the family and to casual relationships which had no permanent influence. All was well so long as my father was satisfied with his work at home and with the company of his young wife. But he was a whole year younger than she and she began very soon to suffer from ill-health. Various circumstances sapped his will to work. The desire to get rich led him to undertake risky adventures and from then on he was lost. The habit of hard work is an asset to any man in society, and to one who has no cultural tastes it is essential. Such a man loses his self-discipline once he stops working and becomes a prey to his passions. My poor father, widowed at the very moment when he most needed a settled family life, took a mistress in order to avoid saddling his daughter with a step-mother, started to gamble in order to cover his loss of earnings and his expenses and, without ceasing at any point to be an honest man, quietly ruined himself. My relations, who were trusting people and quite unversed in business, assumed that my father would look after my interests and never suggested that an inventory should be made on my mother's death. They would have thought it insulting to him to do so. I myself, though I may have had doubts, did not think it proper to reveal them and resigned myself to the inevitable.

So there I was, all alone, dividing my time between bits of handcraft and study and frequently called upon to make excuses for my father to people who were annoyed to find him so often absent. He now needed only two apprentices and only one ate with him. My maid was a little woman of fifty-five, thin and wiry, sprightly and gay, who liked me because I gave her an easy life. She accompanied me whenever I went out without my father, which meant in effect to my grandparents and to church. I had not become pious again, but having been accustomed to attend divine service for my mother's peace of mind I now felt a similar obligation towards society as a whole and went to church for the edification of my neighbours. On this basis I went with less piety than in the past but at least as much humility and respect. I did not participate in the whole Mass but sat there reading some Christian text. I still had great feeling for St Augustine. After all, there are Fathers of the Church whom one can read with profit even if one is not a believer. It is all good nourishment for the heart and the mind....

13

SERIOUS ADMIRERS

THE NEWS OF MY ILLNESS had become widely known and it was apparently thought rare and even edifying that a girl should nearly die of grief for the loss of her mother. I received tokens of interest from surprising quarters. Monsieur de Boismorel was one of the first. I had not seen him since his visits to my grandmother and I noticed that he was struck by the changes which had taken place in me since that time. He called one day in my absence and had a long session with my father. During the course of this my father, talking no doubt about my literary tastes, showed him the little study where I spent my days. They looked at my books and their curiosity was aroused by my 'Leisure Writings', lying on the table. My father took it upon himself to hand these over to M. de Boismorel.

When I came home and found that my sanctuary had been violated I was furious with anger. My father protested that he would not have done this for anyone less serious and trustworthy than M. de Boismorel, but that did not satisfy me. I felt that there had been an assault on my independence and my privacy; the obviously confidential nature of those notes should have protected them from being shown to anyone without my knowledge. But it was done. The next day I received such a nice letter from M. de Boismorel that I easily forgave him for having profited by my father's indiscretion. He offered me full access to his library, we entered into correspondence and for the first time in my life I knew what it was to be appreciated by someone whose judgement I thoroughly respected.

Monsieur de Boismorel did not live in Paris. His love of the country, combined with his wish not to isolate his mother too far from the delights of the capital, had led him to buy a property below Charenton called Petit-Bercy. It was a lovely house with a garden running down to the banks of the Seine. He often asked us to make this the object of a walk and seemed most keen to receive us. Remembering the reception I had once had from his mother I had no wish to meet her again. But my father insisted and since I did not want to discourage his all-too-rare offer to go on an expedition with me I finally gave way and we set off one day for Petit-Bercy.

The de Boismorel ladies were together in the summer drawing-room. I had heard that the daughter-in-law was quite amiable, so her presence put me at my ease and I was able to manage a friendly smile. The mother did not appear to have become any less proud over the years but she behaved much more civilly to the self-assured young lady who now stood before her than she had to the insignificant child on that earlier occasion. 'How charming she is, your dear daughter, M. Phlipon! You know my son is enchanted with her. Tell me, Mademoiselle, do you not want to get married?' 'Various proposals have been made to me, Madame, but I have not yet thought it necessary to make up my mind.' 'I expect you are difficult to please. Would you have any objection to an older man?' 'I would have to know him before I could venture an opinion for or against.' 'That sort of match is often more solid; a younger man is apt to slip away when you think you are attached to him.' 'And why, my dear Mama,' said M. de Boismorel entering at that moment, 'should you assume that Mademoiselle Phlipon is not capable of securing his entire attachment?' 'She is dressed in good taste,' said Mme de Boismorel to her daughter-in-law. 'Yes, and so modestly,' replied the young woman with the unctuous tone of a true believer; for she was that type, you could see it from the pious expression on her smiling, thirty-four-year-old face. 'How different', she went on, 'from the fancy feathers of the young belles. I am sure you do not like feathers, Mademoiselle.' 'I never wear them, Madame, because I am an artist's daughter and usually go out on foot. Feathers would seem to imply a situation and a fortune which I do not possess.' 'But in a different situation, would you wear them?' 'I have no idea. I attach very little importance to such things. I try to dress with propriety but I would never judge anyone by my first impression of her clothes.' This was rather a severe reply, but I said it so sweetly that no offence was taken. 'A philosopher, evidently,' sighed the young woman, as if she recognised that I was not of her sort.

When I had been thoroughly inspected and they had run out of comments of this kind, M. de Boismorel suggested a visit to his garden and library. The garden had a beautiful view and it contained a superb cedar of Lebanon. In the library I found many fascinating volumes which I asked him to lend me, such as the works of Pierre Bayle and the *Mémoires des Académies*. The ladies invited us to dinner some days later and I could see from the two or three businessmen who had also been invited that the party had been arranged for my father and not for me. But once again M. de Boismorel came to the rescue with the library and the garden, where we had some very agreeable conversation. He had invited his son to join us, a youth of about seventeen, not at all good-looking and singularly lacking in charm. In the evening a lot of smart people turned up on whom I cast my critical eye, coming to the conclusion that they were nothing much despite their titles. There were daughters of a marquis, councillors, a prior and several ancient baronesses, but their conversation seemed just as self-important and dull as if they had been bourgeois churchwardens or district visitors. I was not at all attracted by what I glimpsed of these people and felt more than ever confirmed in my own way of life. Monsieur de Boismorel seemed determined to strengthen the relationship with us, as if he had some project in mind which depended upon it. He lost no opportunity of arranging matters so that the four of us, the two fathers and the two children, would find ourselves together. Thus he made me attend the public session of the Académie française on the next festival of St Louis. This was an occasion when smart society came together to display the rich variety of its manners and its follies. On the morning of the Saint's Day Mass was sung by the actors from the opera in the chapel of the Académie, after which an orator from the fashionable world pronounced a panegyric on the sainted monarch. On this occasion the speaker was Father de Besplas to whom I listened with great pleasure, despite the triviality of this threadbare theme. His speech was full of bold flashes of philosophy and indirect criticisms of the government which he was obliged to cut out when he sent the text to the printers.

Monsieur de Boismorel, who knew him well, tried in vain to get me an unexpurgated copy. Father de Besplas was connected with the Court as almoner to Monsieur[1] and was only too happy to purchase forgiveness for his audacity by agreeing to the total destruction of the offending passages.

In the evening, the formal session of the Académie offered a stage to the foremost wits of the kingdom, to the presiding grandees posing before the public as patrons of intellectual life, to the

---

[1] Comte de Provence, younger brother of the King.

amateurs and aspirants who had come to see and be seen and to all
the pretty women who could be sure of attracting attention. I saw
d'Alembert.[2] I knew of him for his *Mélanges* and his *Discours
encyclopédique* and when I saw his diminutive size and heard his
shrill voice I realised that it was better to know a philosopher by his
writings than in his person. Father Delille gave proof that the same
was true of men of letters; he read out some delightful verses in a
thoroughly unpleasant voice. La Harpe's *L'Éloge de Catinat* won the
prize and richly deserved it.

I have always been very simple and undemonstrative, both in
church when I was young and later at the theatre, and it was the
same at the Académie. I did not take part in the frantic applause
given to good performances when many people were only trying to
show how clever they were to appreciate beauty. But I listened with
rapt attention, taking no notice of anyone who might be looking at
me and when I was moved I cried quite openly without considering
whether this might seem strange to anyone. I soon found that it was
considered eccentric, for when M. de Boismorel gave me his hand
on leaving the hall I saw some men point me out to one another
with a smile, which I was not vain enough to think admiring but
which was certainly not critical, and heard someone speak of my
sensitivity. I felt a mixture of surprise and mild embarrassment and
was very glad when I could escape from the crowd and their staring.

This mention of Catinat gave M. de Boismorel the idea for an
interesting expedition: he suggested that we should visit St-Gratien,
where the great man ended his days in retirement, far from the
Court and public honours. It was a philosophical pilgrimage which
entirely suited my tastes. On Michaelmas Day M. de Boismorel
came with his son to pick up my father and me. We went to the
valley of Montmorency, to the edge of the lake there, and when we
reached St-Gratien we rested under the trees which Catinat had
planted with his own hands. After a light meal we spent the rest of
the day in the delightful park of Montmorency, saw the little house
where Jean-Jacques had lived, and experienced that marvellous
feeling of oneness which comes when two or three like-minded
people are gathered together to admire the beauties of nature. At
one of those moments of repose, when we were contemplating in
silence the majesty of the scene, M. de Boismorel drew from his

[2] Jean le Rond d'Alembert (1717–83): scientist and writer; helped Diderot to
prepare his *Encyclopédie*; admitted to the Académie française, 1754.

pocket a manuscript in his own handwriting and read us a passage which he had copied out from Fréron, which was not well known at that time. It was the description of how Montesquieu, when recognised in Marseilles by the young man whose father he had saved, avoided the gratitude of the family to whom he had done this service. Although I was moved by Montesquieu's self-abnegation I did not altogether admire his refusal to admit that he was the saviour of that family. A generous man certainly does not look for recompense, and it is noble to shun public demonstrations of thanks, but one ought to allow gratitude to be expressed. Sensitive people to whom one has done a service need to be allowed to acquit themselves to some extent of their obligation in this way.

I would not wish to give the impression that I was entirely happy about this association between my father and M. de Boismorel. They were not comparable in any way and this distressed me. De Boismorel's son looked at me a lot and I did not like him; there was more curiosity than genuine interest in the attention he paid me, and the three or four years' difference in our ages was a geat barrier between us. His father was fully aware of this and I learned later that he once said to my father, 'Ah! if only my child were worthy of yours, you might think me strange but I should consider myself fortunate!' I had no such thoughts myself; I felt the difference between us but did not consciously consider it or allow my imagination to play around it. The conduct of M. de Boismorel himself seemed to me what you would expect from an intelligent and understanding man who respected women, had a high regard for me and was concerned to protect my feelings. His letters were typical of the man himself: serious but kind, untainted by prejudice and bearing always the stamp of respectful friendship. Through him I was kept in touch with what was new in the learned world and in literature. I rarely saw him but I heard from him every week. In order to avoid too frequent visits by his servants to our house or too long a journey to Bercy for messengers I might send to him, he arranged to leave books for me with the porter at his sister's, Mme de Favières, where I used to send for them.

Because he loved literature himself M. de Boismorel assumed that I too must be engaged in literary activity. For this reason, or perhaps to test me, he invited me to choose a style and to work on it. I took this at first to be merely politeness, but when he pressed me further I thought I must explain my principles on that subject to him. I told him that I was firmly determined never to push myself forward in any way, that I loved reading for its own sake and as the foundation of my happiness but wanted to avoid any sort of fame as certain to disturb my contentment. When I had gravely expounded this doctrine to him I added some casual verses which rather inadequately expressed my feelings. I remember some lines describing how the gods distribute talents and duties amongst humans:

> When a man sets forth
> On an heroic lifetime mission
> The gods set no boundaries
> To his ambition.

> But from a mere woman
> They do not seem to expect
> Anything more than passive virtue
> And wifely respect.

> Thank your stars that you are admitted
> To all the fields of glory.
> For us, remembering what men have done
> Is the whole story.

Monsieur de Boismorel sometimes replied to me in the same vein; his verse was not much better than mine, but that did not matter. One day he confided in me a plan which he had thought up for stimulating his increasingly idle son.

The young man was naturally friendly with his contemporary and cousin de Favières who was a thoughtless fellow, a parliamentary councillor at twenty-one, keener on his robes of office than on his duties, over-rich and careless in his behaviour. They spent a lot of time together at the Comédie-Italienne or at the Opéra and very little on their respective duties. 'I want you', said M. de Boismorel, 'to write my son a wise and impressive reprimand, reflecting your own deepest feelings, to shame him out of his present lethargy and awaken his higher instincts.' 'Me, sir, me? (I could hardly believe my ears.) How could I possibly start preaching to your son?' 'You may take whatever line you choose. You will not appear in it at all. We will make the letter appear to come from someone who sees a lot of him and knows about his bad behaviour, who has his interests at heart and wants to warn him. I shall decide the right moment to deliver the letter, but on no account must he suspect that I have had anything to do with it. In due course I will tell him whom he should thank for this service.' 'Oh! you must never mention me! Surely you have friends who would do this much better?' 'I do not think so. I ask you to do me this favour.' 'Very well, I will swallow my pride in order to oblige you. I will draft something and you will tell me what you think of it and correct it.' I wrote the letter that very evening. It was quite sharp and ironical in tone, designed to flatter the young man's vanity and make him see that his own happiness depended on his returning to a more serious way of life. Monsieur de Boismorel was delighted with it and had me dispatch it without alteration. I sent it to Sophie so that it might have an Amiens postmark and then waited with great curiosity to see the results of my sermon.

Monsieur de Boismorel wrote to me soon afterwards to tell me what had happened. He had arranged matters so that the arrival of the letter might have its greatest impact; the young man had been touched. He thought at first that the celebrated Duclos was the author and went to thank him. Then he tried another friend of his father's and had no better luck there. There was no doubt that he had begun to work harder.

Not very long after all this, M. de Boismorel went with his son from Bercy to Vincennes where he knew I was staying with my uncle, to bring me a copy of the *Georgics* translated by Father Delille. It was a very hot day. On the way he got sunstroke. He made light of it to begin with, but headaches began, then fever and then a coma and after a few days he died, at the height of his powers. It was barely eighteen months since we had started corresponding and I think I cried more bitterly over his death than even his own son. I never think of him without a deep sense of loss. I had a real regard for him as a good man.

When my grief had subsided a little I wrote a romantic ode in his memory which I sang to my guitar. Nobody ever saw or heard it and now I believe it is lost. I never heard anything more of his family except that once when my father paid a visit there de Boismorel's son, who was called Roberge, said in an off-hand manner that he had found my letters to his father and had put them aside in case my father would like to have them; and that amongst them he had recognised the original of a certain epistle which he had once received. My father of course knew all about this and said very little in reply. But he had the impression that the young man was peeved; from which I concluded that he was a fool and thought no more about him.

A short while later Mme de Favières came to my father's rooms in connection with the purchase of some jewellery and other objects. I was in my little study and could hear what was said in the next room. 'You have a charming daughter, Monsieur Phlipon. My brother tells me she is one of the cleverest women he knows. I hope you will not let her become a wit; that would be horrid. And haven't I heard that she is a little pedantic? I think so. Has she a good figure? Is she nice to look at?' 'There', I said to myself in my corner, 'is an impertinent woman, just like her mother. God preserve me from ever having to meet her.' My father, who knew perfectly well that I could hear what was being said, refrained from calling me, and I did not come out, and that is the only time I have heard the voice of Mme de Favières.

I must say a little more about my excellent cousin Mme Trude.[3] She was one of those good souls whom Heaven has created for the honour of the human species and for the consolation of those who mourn. She was instinctively generous and loving; if she had a fault it was excessive delicacy and piety. She was the type of person who would think herself a failure if anyone doubted for one moment that she could be relied upon.

This was a recipe for becoming completely subordinated to her eccentric husband. He was a sort of clown, half crazy, excitable and boorish in his behaviour. He dealt in looking-glasses, as all the Trudes had done before him for several generations. Energetic by temperament, hard-working in fits and starts and supported by an intelligent wife, he kept quite a good establishment. He was well received in his own family largely for the sake of his wife.

My mother had been very fond of her little cousin, who greatly respected her and became very attached to me. We have seen how she proved this after my mother's death, coming regularly from a great distance to tend me at night until I was out of danger. We became close friends and saw a great deal of each other. But then her husband took it into his head to come often to see me without his wife. I tolerated this at first for her sake, but it soon became unbearable. I did everything I could to persuade him tactfully that being a relation and the husband of my dear friend were not sufficient excuses for these frequent visits. Nor could they any longer be justified by my bereavement and illness.

[3] Wife of Jean-Louis Trude; he was condemned to death by the revolutionary tribunal in June 1794 and his wife barely survived him.

He then began to come less often but when he did come he settled himself in for three or four hours at a time despite all that I could do, even in writing, to make it clear that I was very busy. In the end I had to ask him flatly to leave the house, whereupon he became so bad-tempered at home and gave his wife so much trouble that she begged me to be patient with him for her sake. This imposition was especially hard to bear on Sundays and holidays. When the weather was fine I could sometimes escape and meet his wife at my grandparents'. If I invited them both to my rooms I saw nothing of her but had to sit through the scenes made by her brute of a husband. In the winter I had another solution; immediately after lunch I gave my maid the rest of the day off; she locked and double-locked me in, and I stayed there all alone in peace and quiet until eight o'clock in the evening. Trude came, got no answer, came back again and sometimes wandered about outside the house for two hours on end, in rain or snow, waiting to be let in. It was almost impossible to conceal myself when I had company. I might have absolutely forbidden him my door or tried to make my father break with him (which would have been difficult because he was childless and my father thought it worth his while keeping in with him). But this was the very thing his wife so greatly feared; it would have ended our friendship and exposed her to new humiliations.

There is nothing worse than having to deal with a madman. The only thing to do is to tie him up; everything else is useless. My tiresome cousin was a real scourge to me and it is a tribute to his wife's personality that I restrained myself from throwing him out of the window – though I am sure he would have come in again by the chimney. But I must be fair; Trude was not without a kind of honesty; he was more mad than stupid. It must be said that he knew exactly how far he could go. His crude language was never indecent and although his behaviour was ill-mannered and unreasonable it never offended against modesty or decorum. When his wife went out walking with me he spied upon us, and if any man spoke to us or greeted us he was anxious and angry until he had found out who it was. It may be thought that he was jealous about his wife, and that is true up to a point. But he was much more jealous about me. Despite this extraordinary situation, Mme Trude remained her sweet self and was often in high spirits. She would be in tears one day and invite her friends to a party the next. She gave family dinners from time to time in the winter, followed by dancing; I was always made a great fuss of and for several days afterwards her husband would behave more agreeably towards everybody....

Madame Trude was very keen to visit a favourite relation. It meant an absence of two or three weeks. Her husband objected to the shop being left unattended for so long, but he thought the plan might be feasible if I would agree to come from time to time, in the middle of the day, to serve the customers. My cousin begged me to do her this favour and I could not refuse. So I went seven or eight times, from noon until six o'clock, to take Mme Trude's place in the shop. Her husband was happy and proud, behaved very well, attended to his other business and seemed thoroughly to appreciate what I was doing for them. Thus I must admit that, for all my aversion to commerce, I did spend a portion of my life selling spectacles and watch-glasses. It was not a very pleasant location. Trude's shop was on the rue Montmartre near the rue Ticque-tonne, where, presumably, his successor still operates. The noise of the carriages continually rumbling back and forth in front of the open shop was quite hellish; I should have become deaf if I had stayed there long, as my poor cousin is today. But let us leave this sad *ménage*, whose fate we shall see later, and return to my other cousin.

I used to visit Mlle Desportes once or twice a week, on the days when she regularly received society. I could pen some nice portraits of the people I met there if they were worth the trouble. But by the time I had described the councillors at the Châtelet – such as little Mopinot who wrote epigrams and fancied himself a wit; or de La Presle, a devout peasant whose only faults were Jansenism and an unruly temper; Mme de Blanc-fumé, a dowager lady whose hedonistic appetites lurked beneath a semblance of devotion; a rich old bachelor too repulsive to name; a worthy clerk of the name of Baudin, orderly as clockwork and sonorous as a bell, and a crowd of other individuals no less insignificant – I should have used up all my ink and all my time. But there were two people I did enjoy meeting: Father Rabbe, a fine, respectable, elderly orator of great civility, and Dr Coste, a provincial doctor who liked to play the Perrault (though he built no Louvre)[4] and spoke ill of marriage the way the devil scowls at holy water.

Mademoiselle Desportes had inherited her mother's refinement

---

[4] Claude Perrault (1613–88): a doctor who abandoned medicine in order to study art and was the architect of the Louvre.

and dignified bearing. She had the same knack of developing her little business without appearing to have any hand in it and of treating her rich or titled clients with an air of confidence and equality. But this sort of thing is very different from true commerce, which thrives on active cupidity. And it was not long before Mlle Desportes saw her profits dwindle and was obliged to stop trading and cut down her expenses. My mother had always been impressed by her good character and the respectability of her establishment and had urged me to cultivate her acquaintance. She sent me round there often. Piquet was the main purpose of these gatherings and the main topic of conversation among Mlle Desportes' guests. She knew I did not like cards but often involved me in a game, to test my compliance I think; and I found that having a partner to support me and being allowed to joke about my inattention made it more bearable.

I must now introduce an old man, just arrived from Pondicherry, with whom I had an interesting friendship for more than a year. My father had become friendly with an officer on half pay called Demontchéry whom he met in business, I believe, and who was now some sort of clerk without a job. Demontchéry was a man of thirty-six with the polished manners and graces of one who knows the world. He cultivated my father but seldom came to see my mother, who was unreceptive to his kind of gallant attentions. He openly professed his respect for me and declared that it was his ambition to seek my hand as soon as fortune favoured him. What fortune did, in fact, was to send him off to India, whence he sent news of himself and expressions of his hope of being able to return in improved circumstances. But he was only a captain of sepoys and too good a fellow to know how to make money; and I do not believe that he had advanced very far in this respect when he returned seven years later, rushed round to my father's apartment and found that I had been married a fortnight previously. I do not know what became of him or what I should have thought of him if I had had to form an opinion. During his service in Pondicherry he had made the acquaintance of a M. de Sainte-Lette, a member of the Council of the Indies. In 1776, when the Council sent Sainte-Lette to Paris on some important mission, Demontchéry asked him to carry letters to my father.

Sainte-Lette was over sixty. In his youth he had been a spendthrift and had lost all his money in Paris. He had then gone to America and spent thirteen years as a director of trade with the

Indians in Louisiana. After that, finding himself somehow in Asia, he had been employed in public administration in Pondicherry where he was hoping to earn enough to return one day to live or die in France with his boyhood friend, M. de Sévelinges, of whom I shall have more to say. As soon as he turned up I was struck by his deep, solemn voice, the voice of a man who has seen much and suffered much, and by the expressive clarity of his well-trained mind. Demontchéry had spoken to him about me, which is presumably why he wanted to meet me. My father received him well and he interested me at once. I found his company most agreeable, he sought mine, and throughout the whole of his stay in France he called upon me every four or five days.

People who have seen a lot of the world are always worth listening to and those who are sensitive to their surroundings have always seen a lot more than the rest, even if they have not travelled as much as Sainte-Lette had. He had the sort of knowledge that comes from experience rather than from books. He was more of a philosopher than a scholar; he reasoned from the heart. He had retained from his younger days a taste for light verse, in which he had written many pleasant conceits. He gave me several of these and I passed some of my own scribbles to him. He said to me several times in a prophetic tone, with conviction, 'It is no good denying it, Mademoiselle, you will end up by writing a masterpiece!' 'Then it will have to be under someone else's name,' I replied, 'for I shall cut off my hand before I became an author!'

Sainte-Lette met at my father's someone I had known for several months and who was to influence the course of my life profoundly, though I had no idea of this at the time. Sophie, as I have already said, led a busier social life than I did and did not find it much to her taste. She had sometimes spoken to me about a notable man who had some sort of post in Amiens and who came regularly to her mother's house when he was in town. This was not very often because he spent the winter months in Paris and often undertook long journeys in the summer. She had mentioned him because he stood out among the crowd of nonentities with which she was surrounded. She found his conversation instructive; he always had something new to say and his plain manner, though somewhat austere, inspired confidence. Many people disliked him, she said, because of his severe and often caustic tone, but on the whole he was well thought of. Sophie had spoken to him about me; besides, her family were always talking about the loyal and intimate friendship that had existed between her and me ever since our convent days. The passing of the years had lent it a sort of official respectability. He had also seen my portrait, which Mme Cannet displayed in a prominent position in her home. So he often said 'Why don't you introduce me to your dear friend? I go to Paris every year, could I not deliver a letter to her?'

He eventually obtained this commission in December 1775. I was still in mourning for my mother and in that mood of gentle melancholy which follows violent grief. Anyone coming with an introduction from Sophie was sure of a favourable reception. 'This letter will be delivered', she wrote, 'by the philosopher I have sometimes mentioned to you, Monsieur Roland de la Platière, an enlightened and respectable man whose only faults are excessive admiration for the ancients at the expense of the moderns whom he despises, and a tendency to talk too much about himself.' This description is hardly even a sketch but the comment was not unfair. When he called, I saw before me a man in his forties, tall, careless in posture and with the stiff look of one who sits long at a desk. His thinness, his rather yellow complexion and the prominence of his brow, from which the hair was already receding, did not detract from the regularity of his features but made them more respectable than seductive. When he became animated, reading aloud or enjoying some pleasant thought, a sweet smile and lively expression lit up his face and gave him an entirely new look. He had a deep voice and a clipped way of speaking, as if he was short of breath. His head was full of ideas and his conversation consequently fascinating, but it appealed more to the mind than to the ear, for his diction was rough and unharmonious. An attractive voice is a rare thing; it can have a very powerful effect on the senses, not only by the quality of the sound but by reflecting fine variations of feeling on the part of the speaker.

*

I was interrupted at this point to be told that I am included in the Bill of Indictment against Brissot, together with a whole lot of deputies who have been re-arrested. The tyrants have their backs to the wall; they think that by slaughtering decent men and women they can avoid the fate which is looming before them. Their turn will come. I am not afraid to go to the scaffold in such good company. It is shameful to breathe the same air as these scoundrels.

I shall send this notebook out now and follow it up with another if I am spared.

Today, 4 October, is my daughter's birthday. She is twelve.

*

Beauty of voice, which is quite a different thing from carrying power, is as rare amongst political orators as it is amongst ordinary people. I have looked for it in all three of our national Assemblies and I have not found one perfect example. Even Mirabeau, for all his noble and inspiring delivery, did not sound pleasing and his pronunciation was not perfect. The two Clermonts were nearer to it.[5] By what standard then do I judge voices? I can only reply as the painter did who, when asked where he found the model for his attractive figures, pointed to his own head and replied, 'from in here'; I should point to my ears. I do not go to the theatre very often but even there I have the impression that real beauty of expression is hard to find. Larive[6] is perhaps the nearest, but even he is not perfect. When I was a young adolescent, going through the trauma of trying to please the other sex, I was upset by the sound of my own voice and tried to change it. I can understand that the Greeks, with their exquisite sensibility, set a high value on every aspect of the art of speech; I can also see that our *sans-culottes* today, who despise every form of refinement and are dragging us back to a kind of primitive jungle, are as wholly alien to the plain, practical speech of Sparta as to the graceful eloquence of Athens.

But we left La Blancherie long ago in Orléans or some such place; we must now finish him off. He had returned to Paris shortly after my mother's death and heard the news on calling to see her. I was touched by his consternation and grief. He came back to visit me once or twice and I enjoyed seeing him. My father started off by making it a rule to be at my side whenever any man came to see me, but he soon became bored with the rôle of chaperon and decided that a more convenient plan would be to forbid access altogether to any man who was not in his opinion sufficiently responsible and mature to be left alone with me and my maid. He told me that he was about to order La Blancherie to end his visits. I was upset by

---

[5] Stanislas, comte de Clermont-Tonnerre, and Anne-Antoine-Jules de Clermont-Tonnerre, Bishop of Châlons and later Cardinal. Both were deputies to the Estates-General.
[6] The comedian Jean Mauduit, known as De Larive; member of the Comédie-Française from 1770 to 1788.

this, but did not say a word. I thought of the distress which this would be likely to cause the young man and decided that I would soften the blow by writing to him myself. I was afraid that my father's style might cause offence. To tell the truth, I was interested in La Blancherie and thought that I might easily love him. I think that this was mostly imagination, but it affected me at the time. I wrote him an eloquent letter giving him his marching orders, leaving no room for doubt, but not denying him the knowledge that he had been appreciated, in case he had hoped as much.

This episode cast me into a fairly melancholy mood, though in most respects I was quite happy. Sophie came to Paris and stayed for some time, with her mother and her elder sister Henriette. The latter had calmed down a bit with the passage of time and did not seem so much older than us now, so that she was now more on our level and became my good friend. She had a sparkling imagination which gave pleasure wherever she went.

I often walked in the Luxembourg with friends and with Mlle d'Hangard. One day we met La Blancherie. He greeted me respectfully and I returned his greeting with some emotion. 'Do you know that gentleman?' asked Mlle d'Hangard, who had at first taken his greeting as being addressed to her. 'Yes. Do you?' 'I certainly do, though I have never spoken to him. I often see the Bordenave girls, the younger of whom he wanted to marry.' 'Oh, when was that?' 'I don't know; a year, six months, eighteen months ago perhaps. He got himself an introduction into the house, went there once or twice and made a formal declaration. The girls are rich and the younger one is pretty. He had not a penny and must be looking for an heiress, for he made a similar approach to another girl they know and got thrown out for his pains. We call him the Lover of the Eleven Thousand Virgins. How do you know him?' 'From having seen him several times at Madame l'Épine's concerts.' I bit my lip and said no more. I was piqued at having believed myself to be loved by a man who had no doubt asked for my hand simply because I was an only child, and more piqued still at the thought of having written him a beautiful letter which he did not deserve. I thought I must be more careful next time.

Some months later a little Savoyard came to tell my maid that a gentleman wished to speak to her. She went out and when she came back told me that M. La Blancherie had asked her to beg me to receive him. It was a Sunday and I was expecting my relations. 'Very well,' I said, 'if he comes right away. Go and find him and

bring him in.' La Blancherie arrived. I was standing by the fireplace.
'I did not dare present myself before you, Mademoiselle,' he said,
'after the rebuff which I received. I was extremely anxious to speak
with you and I cannot tell you how moved I was by the dear, cruel
letter you wrote me. My situation has altered since that time and I
am now engaged on a project of which you may have heard.' He
outlined his ideas for a collection of moral and political essays in
the form of letters, along the lines of the *Spectator*, to which he
invited me to contribute on particular subjects. I let him speak
without interruption and even waited a minute or two, after he had
paused briefly, so that he could complete his story. When he had
said all that he had to say I spoke in my turn. I observed calmly and
politely that I had taken the trouble to warn him to discontinue his
visits because the sentiments about me which he had expressed to
my father had led me to suppose that he had a special interest in
continuing, and I wished to mark my appreciation of that interest.
I said that at my age a lively imagination coloured almost all one's
actions and led one sometimes into inconsistency, but that error
was not a crime and that I had recovered well enough from my
misjudgement not to cause him any concern. I said that I admired
his literary projects but could not take part in them in any way
whatsoever, nor indeed in anyone else's plans of a similar nature,
and that I would confine myself to wishing success to all the authors
in the world and to his own plans. I wanted to indicate that he need
not make any similar attempt to be received by me in the future;
and I then asked him to leave. He expressed astonishment, pain,
agitation. Every appropriate plea and argument was deployed. I cut
him short. I said to La Blancherie that I did not know whether the
Bordenave girls, and others to whom he had addressed himself at
about the same time, had spoken to him with equal clarity but that
my own frankness was unlimited and my resolution not to be
questioned. At that I rose, bowed and held out my hand towards
the door in a gesture of dismissal. At that moment cousin Trude
came in and never have I been more glad to see her good, plain
features. La Blancherie retired in silence and I have never seen him
since.

After that interlude, let us return to Sainte-Lette and Roland.
We had reached the end of summer 1776. During the previous
eight or nine months I had met M. Roland several times. His visits
were not frequent but he always stayed a long time, like people who
go to a place for no particular reason but enjoy it very much once

they get there. His conversation was instructive and frank and never bored me and he enjoyed the fact that I listened to him with so much interest. This is something I am good at, even with people less well informed than him, and it has probably made me more friends than my ability to express my own opinions. I had known him after his return from Germany; he was now planning a visit to Italy and as part of the usual precautions which a wise man takes when contemplating a prolonged absence he decided to entrust his manuscripts to me. I was to keep them if anything should happen to him. I was deeply touched by this mark of his special esteem and accepted it with appreciation. The night before he left, he and Sainte-Lette dined with my father and, on leaving, Roland asked permission to kiss me. For some reason, this act of pure politeness always makes a young girl blush, even if her imagination is quite at rest. 'You are fortunate to be leaving,' said Sainte-Lette in his deep, solemn voice. 'You had better hurry up and come back, to ask for the same thing again.'

During Sainte-Lette's stay in France his friend, de Sévelinges, lost his wife. He went down to his friend's home in Soissons to share his grief and brought him up to Paris to take his mind off things. They came to see me together. De Sévelinges was a man of fifty-two, an impoverished gentleman, who had some sort of financial position in the provincial administration and cultivated letters gracefully in his spare time.

Having met him in this way, I kept in touch with him after Sainte-Lette's departure. Sainte-Lette said that it was a joy for him to think, on leaving France, that his friend would not lose the privilege of corresponding with me and he even asked my permission to send him – for return to me later – some manuscripts of my own which I had sent him. This interesting old man then embarked for India for about the fifth or sixth time in his life, but while he was at sea a cerebral ulcer which had previously given him trouble broke open. He arrived in Pondicherry a sick man and died six weeks later. We learned of his death through Demontchéry. De Sévelinges was deeply distressed. He wrote to me from time to time and his thoughtful, elegant letters gave me great pleasure. They showed him to be the type of gentle, sensitive and melancholy philosopher for whom I have always had a soft spot. I remember Diderot's wise observation that great refinement presupposes great intelligence, sensitive feelings and a somewhat melancholy temperament.

My father, who was becoming less sympathetic towards me, now began to think that my intellectual pursuits were costing him too much in postage. I told my little uncle about this and he agreed to allow my correspondence with de Sévelinges to be addressed to him. My manuscripts came back to me with critical comment of which I was very proud. I had not imagined that my writings were worth looking at; to me they were just dreamy speculation, quite wise but commonplace, on topics which I supposed were familiar to everyone. The only original thing about them, I thought, was that they were written by a young girl. It was a long time before I revised this simplistic assessment of my own abilities. Not until I had seen my countrymen under the strain of revolution, and witnessed from close quarters the contentions and pressures of political life did I realise that the platform on which I stood was not so greatly overcrowded. I hasten to say that I took this as proof that the general level was low rather than as showing special merit in myself. It is not cleverness that is in short supply but good judgement and strength of character. And yet these two qualities are essential in a real man. Diogenes was right to take a candle, but perhaps a revolution will do instead. I know of no more acid test, no more merciless judge between man and man.

The Académie de Besançon had offered a prize for an essay on 'How women's education might contribute to the improvement of men'. I took up my pen and wrote an essay which I sent incognito and which, needless to say, did not win the prize. In fact, nobody won it and the subject was proposed again the following year, with what result I do not remember. My line was that it is absurd to try to define a system of education except in relation to the general manners and culture of the state, which depend on the government, and that instead of trying to improve one of the sexes by means of the education of the other, we should concentrate on improving the whole species by the enactment of good laws. Thus, while I was able to explain how I thought women ought to be, I did not think that they could achieve that without a change in the general order of society. This idea, though undoubtedly sound and philosophical, did not meet the requirements of the Académie. I was, of course, reasoning on the problem instead of solving it.

I sent a copy of my essay to M. de Sévelinges after having sent it in. He made some comments on the style only, which were enough to put me off the whole idea. I came to the conclusion that my entire argument was wrong and countered myself by writing a critique of my paper as if it had been written by someone else

[239]

whom I wanted to ridicule. This might be described as equivalent to tickling your ribs to make yourself laugh or slapping your face to warm your cheeks, but it is a harmless way of deriving private amusement. In return, de Sévelinges gave me an academic lecture of his own on the faculty of speech, which he had addressed to the Académie française and about which he had had a nice letter from d'Alembert. I remember that it was full of metaphysics, and a little precious.

Six months to a year went by in this sort of intellectual cross-fire, during which various ideas emerged. De Sévelinges seemed to be worried about my situation and to be bored with living on his own. He dilated on the charms of intellectual friendship and I said that I valued them too. We had long exchanges on this subject. I do not know what conclusions he drew from it all, but one day he called on my father incognito, as if on business. I received him at the door and the funny thing is that I did not recognise him. It was not until he had left, with a highly mortified look on his face, that I thought his features familiar. After he had gone I realised that he must have been de Sévelinges and this was confirmed later by letter. The incident left a very disagreeable impression on me which I cannot describe. Our correspondence faltered and then ceased, as I shall tell.

Sometimes I went to Vincennes. My uncle's canonical retreat was very attractive, the walks delightful and the company most pleasant. But however satisfactory it may have been for him to have his establishment looked after by Mlle d'Hannaches, he was beginning to find that he paid a high price in the vexatious humours and silliness of the pretentious old maid. The château of Vincennes was inhabited by a number of people by grace and favour of the Court. In one wing was a retired royal proctor, Moreau de La Grave, and in another a ghost from the past, Mme de Puisieux to be precise. Further along the corridor there was the comtesse de Laurencin; below, an officer's widow and so on. And of course there was the Governor, Lord Lieutenant Rougemont, whom Mirabeau has described and whose pock-marked face and stupid insolence made a most unpleasant combination. Add to these a group of pensioners, a number of officers with women attached, the Dean and Chapter and the prisoners in the dungeon, and you had a population of some six hundred souls within the precincts of the château. My uncle was welcome throughout but he did not mix very much and received very few people in his own room.

However, it was the custom of an evening, after the promenade, to stop at the pavilion by the bridge, on the parkside, where the ladies were wont to foregather. If I had time I could give some amusing descriptions of these gatherings. But my days are numbered. I have a lot more to tell and must omit a great many things. It would have been nice to say more about the balls they held in the allée des Voleurs, about the comte d'Artois' race meetings and about the follies of Séguin, the duc d'Orléans' treasurer, whose name-day was celebrated with fireworks and who went bankrupt almost at once. I should like also to have described our delightful walks, the splendid view from the top end of the park, looking out over the Marne, which we reached through a breach in the castle wall, and the forest hermits in their rustic haunts who had a fascinating picture in their church of a thousand demons torturing the damned. I should like to have lingered over the readings with my uncle, when we declaimed the tragedies of Voltaire, taking turns with the different parts; and how one day when we had reached a particularly sublime passage Mlle d'Hannaches, who had been quietly spinning wool, suddenly began screaming at the chickens in her shrill, rasping voice, so that we were tempted to shut her in the chicken run. I wish too that I could recall our amateurish concerts after dinner, when the table had been cleared away and the good Canon Bareux, his spectacles on his nose, his music propped up against a muff-box, sawed away on his cello while I scraped on my violin and my uncle piped on his flute. Ah! if they will let me live, I shall return one day to those sweet scenes.

—14—

MARRIAGE

◆◆◆

Paul de Roux, in his introduction to the Mercure de France edition, gives a detailed account of the slow, dispassionate steps by which M. Roland brought himself eventually to marry Marie-Jeanne Phlipon on 4 February 1780. He had met her for the first time in January 1776. It is clear that the relationship was intellectual and philosophical from the start. Monsieur Roland stepped hesitantly into the place vacated by La Blancherie. For a whole year he travelled alone in Italy, and when he returned he found difficulty in countering the objections of his family to what they considered a bad match. In May 1779 the pair were informally engaged, but Roland insisted on 'extreme discretion' and had still made no official move by August of that year. Her father eventually wrote to ask his intentions, but still he could not be drawn. In November, realising that Roland would never call on her at her father's apartment, she took a room in the Convent where she had spent a year as a child, and succeeded in getting him to meet her there on 12 January 1780. At this interview she was evidently able to overcome his scruples and they were married three weeks later.

MEANWHILE, I MUST GO BACK TO MY STORY. My last notebook left us in Vincennes. I was about to write about Carraccioli whom I had met there with the Canon and whose *Letters*, published under the pseudonym of Ganganelli, made quite a stir, although they were little more than a repetition of pieces he had written before. But it would take me too long to follow this through. I do not have enough days left; a summary must suffice.

The manuscripts which M. Roland had left with me told me more about him during the eighteen months he spent in Italy than I could ever have learned from frequent visits. They consisted of travel notes, general reflections, plans for projected works and personal anecdotes. They left a very clear impression of a powerful intelligence, an austere rectitude, strict principles, knowledge and good taste.

Roland had been born into a rich, long-established and highly respected legal family. As a young man he had seen the family fortunes frittered away through incompetence and extravagance. He was the youngest of five sons, all of whom were destined for the Church, and he left home at the age of nineteen in order to avoid becoming either a priest or a businessman, the two callings he most abhorred. His first stop was at Nantes where he apprenticed himself to a ship-builder in order to learn a trade with a view to going out to India. All the arrangements had been made for his journey when he developed some sort of haemorrhage and the doctors said that the sea journey would be fatal. So he went to Rouen where a relation of his, M. Godinot, a factory inspector, suggested that he enter that branch of the public administration. He did so, distinguished himself by his energy and hard work and soon obtained a useful position in that service. Journeys abroad and study occupied his spare time. Before leaving for Italy he had brought to my father's house his favourite brother, Pierre, a Benedictine and Prior of the College of Clugny in Paris, an intelligent and friendly man who came to see me once or twice after his brother's departure. He passed on to me the notes which his brother sent home during his travels and which he published on his return in the form of letters. . . .

When Roland came back I found that he was already a friend. His seriousness, his moral principles and his way of life, all dedicated to his work, made me think of him as a person without sex, as it were, or as a thinker entirely devoted to reason. A sort of confidence was established between us and he enjoyed my company so much that by degrees he needed to come more and more often. It was about five years[1] after we had first met that he declared his feelings towards me. I was not unmoved by this, because I esteemed him more highly than anyone I had met before. But I had noticed that he and his family attached importance to material considerations and felt that I must make my position clear. I replied that his declaration did me honour and that I would be happy to respond to it, but I did not believe I should be a good match for him. I then explained the state of our finances without reserve. The truth was that we were ruined. At the risk of increasing my father's displeasure, I had insisted on extracting some accounts from him and had managed to salvage an income of 600 livres which, together with my wardrobe, was all that was left of the

---

[1] In fact it was only three years.

supposed fortune on which I had been brought up to rely. I pointed out to Roland that my father was reasonably young, that he might well incur debts and be unable to honour them, that he might make a bad marriage and bring more children into the world who would bear my name in poverty, and so on. I said I was too proud to expose myself to the ill-will of his family, which would not consider itself honoured by the alliance, or to the generosity of a husband who could expect nothing but trouble from his union with me. I advised M. Roland, as if I had been a disinterested third party, to give up thinking of me. He persisted, however. I was touched and consented that he should make the necessary approach to my father. He preferred to do this in writing and it was agreed that he should not send the letter until he had gone back to Amiens. We spent the rest of his Paris visit seeing one another every day. I regarded him as the man with whom I was to share my destiny and became sincerely attached to him. As soon as he got back to Amiens he wrote to my father setting out his hopes and plans. My father thought the letter dry. He did not like M. Roland's stiffness and was not at all keen to have a son-in-law whose austerity would seem like a reproach to himself. He wrote a harsh, rude reply which he did not show to me until it had gone off. I decided at once what to do. I wrote to M. Roland that this event had shown only too clearly how well justified had been my fears about my father. I said that I did not want to expose him to any more insults and begged him to abandon his proposal. To my father I said that in view of his conduct I must find another home and that I was retiring to the Convent. As I knew he had some pressing debts I left him my portion of the family silver to cover them. I rented a small flat in the Convent of the Congrégation and settled in there, determined to reduce my needs to match my means. I achieved this. I could tell some entertaining tales about my predicament there, having for the first time to live off my own resources. I reckoned up my expenses, setting aside a sum for tips to the Convent staff. Potatoes, rice or beans, cooked in a pot with a few grains of salt and a little butter, gave variety to my diet without taking up much of my time.

I went out twice a week, once to my grandparents and once to my father's to see to his linen and take away anything that needed mending. The rest of my time I spent in my snow-house as I called it, being right under the eaves and in mid-winter. I did not want to associate regularly with the women pensioners, so I dug myself in with my studies, fortified my heart against adversity and defied fate. Every evening for half an hour dear Agatha came to sit with me, which gave me great comfort. At hours when all were sleeping I took my solitary walk in the Convent garden and there in the silence and peace of the night I could feel my soul resigned and my conscience clear. My courage rose within me; I defied misfortune. Time sped by on the wings of my resolve, my pride, my more than common consciousness of life and beauty. This was where my treasure lay. In melancholy, yes, but even melancholy has its charm and happiness can be dispensed with if one is strong enough and proud.

Monsieur Roland had been astonished and mortified by my father's letter, but he continued to write to me as a man who had not ceased to love me. After five or six months he turned up at the Convent and was indignant when he saw me at the grating despite the fact that I looked healthy and well. He wanted to get me out of this seclusion and again offered me his hand. He had his brother, the Benedictine, urge me to accept. I thought very hard about what I should do. I could not avoid thinking that a man a bit younger than forty-five would probably not have waited several months before urging me to change my mind and I admit that this somewhat lowered the temperature of my feelings. There was little illusion left in them. On the other hand, it could be argued that his return to the charge after such a long time for reflection showed that he appreciated me. And furthermore, the fact that he had evidently overcome his sensitivity to the external disadvantages of an alliance with me seemed to suggest that I could be sure of his esteem. I certainly thought that I should be able to justify it. Finally, if marriage was, as I believed, a very serious tie, in which the woman usually has to take responsibility for the happiness of both parties, was it not better that I should exercise my faculties and my courage in this honourable task rather than waste away in my present isolation?

I could expand here upon many more of the wise reflections (at least, I think they were wise) which led me to take this decision. But I am afraid that there were other considerations which the circumstances ought to have suggested to me but which only experience normally makes one aware of. I became the wife of a truly honourable man, who loved me more the better he knew me. I married in a spirit of solemn rationalism, without reservation, and devoted myself completely to the rôle. In the process of considering my partner's happiness I became aware that there was something missing in my own. I never for a moment ceased to consider my husband one of the most estimable men who ever lived, to whom it was an honour to belong; but I often felt the lack of equality between us. The ascendancy of a dominating character, allied to the weight of twenty years' seniority, made it too one-sided. One of these advantages would have been enough in itself. When we were alone together I went through some really difficult times. When we were out in the world, I could see that I was attractive to a number of people whose admiration I could not safely return. To escape all this I threw myself into working closely and intimately with my husband in everything he did. But this again was an excessive reaction which had unfortunate effects. I accustomed him to being unable to do anything at all without me at any time, and I became exhausted.

I honour and cherish my husband as an affectionate daughter loves a virtuous father to whom she would sacrifice even her lover. But I have now found the man who might be my lover. I have remained faithful to my vows but I have not been able to conceal the feelings which I sacrifice thereby. My husband, over-sensitive both in his affections and in his *amour propre*, was not able to accept the smallest diminution of his ascendancy. He became darkly suspicious, his jealousy irritated me and happiness fled our home. He worshipped me, I sacrificed myself for him and we became profoundly unhappy. If I was at liberty today I would follow him to the ends of the earth to soften his misery and console him in his old age; a character like mine does not leave sacrifices half done. But Roland was indignant at the thought of my making a sacrifice and became exasperated once he realised that this was what I was doing. He resented it and yet could not do without it.

All this throws light, I think, on the workings of the human heart and should be an object lesson to sensitive souls.

We spent the first years of our married life in Paris, where Roland had been summoned by the authorities controlling commerce to help them draw up new regulations for industry. As a convinced libertarian he was strongly opposed to any regulation on trade and commerce. He published some papers which he had written for the Académie on the subject of various arts and crafts and he completed his notes on Italy. I became his copyist and proof-reader. It makes me smile to think of the humility with which I performed these menial tasks, hardly compatible it would seem with my intellectual pretensions. But I did it from the heart.

I had so much respect for my husband that I easily assumed him to be wiser than me and I was so afraid to see a cloud cross his countenance that it was a long time before I had the courage to contradict him on anything.

I was taking courses in natural history and in botany. These were my only recreation from my duties as secretary and housekeeper. As our home was not in Paris we were living in lodgings and since I could see that my husband had to be careful what he ate I took the trouble to prepare all his meals myself. After that we spent four years in Amiens, where I became a mother and nurse and still shared in my husband's work. He had undertaken a considerable part of the preparation of the new *Encyclopédie*. When we were not at work on this we went for walks in the country. I compiled a herbal of all the plants in Picardy and my study of underwater vegetation contributed to Roland's book on peat-cutting. Roland's health gave us cause for concern. He was frequently unwell and I cared for him, and this was another bond. He cherished me for my devotion and I felt closer to him because of the help I was able to give him.

While he was in Italy, Roland had met a young man called Lanthenas[2] whom he liked very much and who had returned to France with him to study medicine. He became a close friend of ours. I would have appreciated him more had not the Revolution, that great acid test of men as I have described it, drawn him into public affairs and exposed his weakness and mediocrity. In private life he was agreeable though not particularly charming. My husband liked him because he was easy to get on with and he became attached to both of us. I treated him like a brother and called him brother. His affection and his sincerity seemed unquestionable. He wanted to come and live with us. Roland was willing, but I opposed it because I suspected that a young man with his affectionate nature would hardly sacrifice his freedom so completely unless he hoped secretly for a reward which my principles would not allow and which he could never have obtained from me. He was a good and loving brother but could never have meant more to me than this, and for that very reason I was able to accept the

---

[2] François Lanthenas (1754–99): a doctor and friend of the Rolands; became a member of the Convention and Roland made him a head of division in the Ministry of the Interior. But he quarrelled with the Rolands, partly out of jealousy of Buzot. Survived the Revolution.

open and uninhibited intimacy which grew up between the three of us. But Lanthenas evidently shared with the common herd the weakness of being thankful for small mercies so long as no one else enjoyed greater ones. As soon as he learned that I was susceptible to another love he became miserable and jealous. Nothing makes a man more disagreeable and unfair. I was offended by this and too proud to forgive him. He walked out in a rage, imagining the worst. Even his political opinions were affected. It was not in him to become an extremist like the Montagnards but he was no longer prepared to support my views, still less those of the man I loved. He claimed to stand between the right whose fanaticism he deplored, and the left whose excesses he could not sanction. He fell between the two and was despised by both sides.

Sophie got married while we were in Amiens to the chevalier de Gomiecourt, who lived about six leagues out on his farm. Henriette, who was fond of M. Roland and whose family had wanted her to marry him, entirely approved of his having chosen me instead, which was typical of her generosity. She married old de Vouglans, a widower whose doctor and confessor had advised him to take a second wife although he was seventy-five. Both sisters are now widows. Sophie has become religious again, but she had a lung infection which makes her very lethargic and there is concern about the future of her two sweet children if anything should happen to her. We are not so close as we were; life has kept us apart and our opinions have developed along different lines. Henriette is still lively and affectionate, without domestic ties. She came to see me in my captivity and offered to take my place in prison to save my life.

When we first married, Roland wanted me to see less of these dear friends. I acceded to his wishes and did not start visiting them more often again until time had given him more confidence in me and removed any fear of competing affections. This was a great mistake on his part. If you deprive a sensitive woman of the comforts of friendship with members of her own sex you deprive her of essential support and expose her to temptation. This has been only too clearly proven!

We had moved to Lyons in 1784 and settled down at Villefranche, in M. Roland's paternal home, where his mother, who was eighty-five, and his elder brother the Canon still lived.[3] I

---

[3] Dominique Roland, born 1722, guillotined in Lyons, 22 Dec. 1793.

could write many interesting pages about life and manners in a small country town and about the domestic complexities of a household in which a venerable old lady with a very bad temper lived with her two sons, the one accustomed to dominate and the other fanatical for his independence.

For two months in winter we lived in Lyons itself, which I knew very well and of which I should have much to say if I had the time. It was a superb town, both in situation and in construction. It had flourishing commerce and industry, fascinating antiquities and art collections and great wealth of which even the Emperor Joseph was envious. Today it is nothing but a vast tomb sheltering the victims of a government a hundred times more horrible than the despotism on whose ruins it was founded.

We used to go to the country in the autumn, and after the death of my mother-in-law, Mme de la Platière, we spent the greater part of the year there. The Clos la Platière, lying in the parish of Thézée, some two leagues from Villefranche, is a rather arid region redeemed by its vineyards and woodland. It is the last wine-growing district before you come to the high mountains of Beaujolais. In this rustic setting I was able to indulge my simple tastes in every detail of country life. All that I learned of medicine and of science in general was applied to the relief of my neighbours. I became the village doctor, all the more cherished for giving succour rather than demanding fees. The pleasure I had in being useful made my attentions doubly welcome. How freely the countryman gives his confidence to anyone who will do him a good turn! They say he is ungrateful; certainly I did not expect anyone to feel obliged to me, but I was much loved and when I was absent much missed. There were some pretty scenes too. Good women would come on horseback from three or four leagues away to beg me to ride over and save from death some poor devil whom the doctor had given up. In 1789 I saved my own husband from dying of a terrible illness which all the doctor's prescriptions could not have overcome without my supervision. I spent twelve days without sleep on that occasion, never once taking off my clothes, and followed this by six months of anxious vigil during his dangerous convalescence. Yet I was never ill myself, such is the strength and energy imparted by a courageous heart!

Then the Revolution came and engulfed us. We were lovers of humanity; we worshipped liberty. We thought that the Revolution would regenerate society and put an end to the grinding misery of the oppressed classes whose sufferings we had so long deplored. So we welcomed it with enthusiasm. This attitude upset a lot of people in Lyons who, being commercially minded, were unable to understand how one could provoke and applaud changes which only benefited other people. For that reason alone they quarrelled with M. Roland and his 'philosophy'; and by the same token other people supported him. He was elected a member of the municipal council,[4] where his inflexible sense of honour and justice made him both friends and enemies. As a deputy representing the city's interests in the Constituent Assembly he went to Paris where we spent nearly a year. I have described how we already knew several members of this Assembly and how we formed special ties with those who, as we did, valued liberty for its own sake. All these people who founded the Revolution are now at risk like us and are likely to suffer the same fate as other true humanitarians of the past such as Dion, Socrates and Phocion, amongst many others in antiquity, or Barnevelt[5] and Sidney in modern times.

My husband took me to England in 1784 and to Switzerland in 1787. We met many interesting people in both countries and have kept in touch with several of them. Less than a year ago I had news of Lavater, the celebrated pastor from Zurich and of Gosse of Geneva, such a wise man, who must surely be distressed to learn how we are being persecuted. I do not know what has happened to Dezach, last heard of travelling in Germany, who was formerly a professor in the University of Vienna and whom I saw often in London. He and Roland used to cross swords in the discussions organised by Banks, the President of the Royal Society, who gathered together all the learned men of his country as well as distinguished foreigners passing through London. ...

My father, of whom by now we had no reason to feel very proud, did not in fact marry again or let himself in for any very heavy new commitments. We paid off a few of his debts and persuaded him to retire from business by offering him a pension. But despite all his disastrous mistakes (which included squandering my grandmoth-

---

[4] Roland had already acquired the reputation of a radical when he was elected to the municipal council in Nov. 1790. He became chairman of the finance committee of the municipality and was sent to Paris early in 1791 to demand the nationalisation of the city's debts, amounting to 39 million livres.

[5] Jean Barnevelt (1549–1619): one of the founders of the Republic of the United Provinces, executed by order of the Prince of Nassau.

er's little inheritance) and despite his dependence on our help, he was bitterly resentful of everything we did for him and quite unfair to people who were only trying to help him. He died in the hard winter of 1787/8 from a catarrhal condition which had been troubling him for some time.

My dear uncle died in Vincennes in 1780 and shortly after that we lost my husband's much-loved brother. He had been with us on our journeys to Switzerland, after which he had become a prior and curé at Longpont; he was nominated as an elector for his canton, preaching liberty as enthusiastically as he practised his evangelical duties and acting as advocate and medical consultant to his parishioners. He was altogether too wise for a monk and was persecuted by the more worldly and ambitious of his Order. He took this very hard and it certainly hastened his end. So everywhere, at all times, the good succumb. Is there not another world where they may live again? If there is not, what is the point of having been born into this one?

Poor, blind slanderers! Look into the course of Roland's career! Check his records. Check mine. Enquire among the people who have known us, search us out in the towns where we have lived, in the countryside where there are no secrets. The more of the truth you discover the more disappointed you will be. That is why you are determined to get rid of us!

Roland has been reproached for having applied for titles of nobility. Here is the true story. His family had enjoyed noble status for several centuries by reason of their functions, which were not hereditary. Their rank was recognised so long as they had the wealth to support the cost of insignia, coat of arms, chapel, livery, etc. Once the wealth disappeared the family continued to thrive respectably at a more modest level. Roland had the prospect of ending his days in the one property which remained in the family, which still belongs to his elder brother. He had become a father and he felt that he had the right, because of his own services to the state, to leave to his descendants the same advantages his ancestors had enjoyed but which he would have scorned to buy. He therefore presented his title with a view to obtaining letters of recognition of nobility or of ennoblement. This was at the beginning of 1784 and I do not know of any man at that time and in his situation who would have thought it wrong. But when I came to Paris I saw at once that the situation was not favourable for his application. The new superintendents of trade were jealous of his long-established position in that part of the administration, where he knew so much more than they did. They were also bitterly opposed to his opinions on freedom of trade. They knew that they could not refuse him the certificate confirming his work in the department, which he needed to support his application, but they could and did so word it as to ensure its lack of success. I decided that it was better to let the matter lie dormant and did not pursue the application. It was at that time that I secured Roland's transfer to Lyons, in a post which brought him back into contact with his own family and his native town. I knew of course that he wanted eventually to retire there. So, all you ephemeral patriots, who without revolution would have been nothing at all, let us see the records of what *you* have done for the State and judge how they compare with Roland's!

For thirteen years we led a very full life, travelling, working ceaselessly and meeting a great variety of people in public life. Our experiences, especially during the last few years, are closely bound up in the history of these times. All this would have been material for the fourth and most interesting volume of my memoirs. But the fragments contained in my Portraits and Anecdotes will have to serve in its place. I cannot go on writing in the midst of all these horrors which are tearing my country apart. I cannot live amongst its ruins. I prefer to be buried beneath them. Nature, open your arms to me! Righteous God, receive me!

At the age of thirty-nine.

FINAL THOUGHTS

These pages were written by Mme Roland when she had resolved to let herself die of starvation. On 3 October the Convention outlawed the Girondin deputies who were on the run, charged forty-one others and ordered the arrest of a further seventy-six. It was the annihilation of the Girondin Party. When she heard the news, Mme Roland decided to put an end to her life. She wrote a farewell note to her daughter, composed these Final Thoughts and started to starve herself to death. It is not known how long she kept this up, but on the 14th she was in the prison hospital. In the end she decided to stay alive long enough to attend the trial of the Girondins, in the hope of being able to give evidence on their behalf. Her dream was to take poison in full court after a passionate declaration. But Bosc refused to produce the poison. In any case, she never had the satisfaction of speaking on behalf of her friends. The trial began on 24 October, she was cited as a witness and taken to the Palais de Justice where she waited the whole day without being called. The accused were sentenced to death six days later without any defence witnesses having been heard.

To be, or not to be: it is the question.[1]
The question will soon be answered for me.

IS LIFE A BLESSING WHICH IS BESTOWED UPON US? I believe it is. But I also believe that there are conditions attached which we must observe. We are born to seek happiness and to serve the happiness of our fellow mortals. The social order merely extends the range of this objective and indeed of all our faculties; it adds nothing new.

So long as we can see a course ahead in which we may do good and set a good example it behoves us not to abandon it. We must have the courage to persist even in misfortune. But when a term has already been set to our life-span by our enemies, we are surely entitled to shorten the period ourselves, particularly when nobody on earth will gain anything from our battling on. When I was first

---

[1] The misquotation is hers.

arrested I flattered myself that I could contribute to my husband's reputation and help to enlighten the public in any trial that they might set up. But they were too clever to give me the chance. They still ran the risk of powerful opposition from those of our friends who were beyond their reach and they had to be circumspect. But now they have nothing to restrain them. The Terror triumphs; all opposition is crushed. Insolence and crime rage furiously together and the people bow down in mindless homage. A vast city, gorged with blood and rotten with lies, wildly applauds the foul murders which are supposed to be necessary for its safety.

Two months ago I coveted the honour of going to the scaffold. It was still possible to speak and I thought that a demonstration of vigorous courage might set a useful example. But now all is lost. The present generation, brutalised by the high priests of slaughter, treats all those who love humanity as conspirators and makes heroes of the dregs. I feel soiled and degraded to be living amongst these vile, cowardly monsters.

I know that the empire of evil never lasts long. Sooner or later the wicked get their deserts. If I was unknown, tucked away in some silent corner, I might find it possible to ignore the horrors that are tearing France apart and to wait patiently for better times, keeping virtue alive in private. But here in prison, a proclaimed victim, every hour that I remain alive gives tyranny new scope for boasting. I cannot beat them, but I can at least defraud them.

Forgive me, honoured husband, for casting away a life which I had consecrated to you. If I had been allowed to comfort your sorrows I would gladly have stayed to do so, but this is now for ever denied me. All that you lose in my death is a shadow, a useless object of harrowing disquietude. Forgive me, dear child, my sweet young daughter! The thought of you softens your mother's heart, daunts her resolution. I would never have failed you if they had let me be with you to guide you. But they have no pity, even on the innocent. Whatever they do to me, you will always have my example to follow, and I feel I can say, here at the very gate of the tomb, that it is a rich legacy!

And you, whom I dare not name![2] One day we shall be united in death and together lament our common woes. Here on earth, despite your passionate love, you never overstepped the bounds of virtue and I cannot think that you will grieve to see me go before

[2] Buzot.

[254]

you to realms where we may love with impunity and be united for ever. No dismal prejudice will plague us there, no arbitrary prohibitions, no hateful tyranny of any kind. I shall await you there and rest. But you, you should stay here below so long as there remains any honourable refuge. Stay, that you may denounce the injustice which has condemned you. But if relentless misfortune hunts you down, let not some mercenary hand prevail against you. Die freely as you have lived! Let your last act confirm my faith in your deathless courage!

All you whom Heaven in its goodness gave me as friends, look to my orphan child! Let not the young plant, torn from its native soil, lie by the wayside, sullied perhaps and trampled by passers-by! And you good people who have given her a comforting home, may she flourish there and reward you with her charms! Do not grieve that I have resolved to end my days. You know me well enough to believe that neither fear nor weakness has dictated my decision. If there were any chance that I could appear before the court and denounce the tyrants I would seize upon it. But we know only too well that these sham trials are designed to deprive the victim of any opportunity to speak. Should I allow my executioners to choose the moment of my death? Should I expose myself to the insolent abuse of the mob? Of course I should face them, if there were any possibility of it having any effect. But they are mad with the lust for blood, cannibals and cowards, beyond the reach of reason....

What of the advance of foreign troops? What prospect of a new revolution? I do not care. I should be no happier to receive salvation at the hands of the Austrians than to be killed by the present rulers of France. Both are equally the enemies of my country and it is an honour to be hated by both.

If only they had had my courage, those miserable creatures, not worthy of the name of men, who allowed themselves to be terrorised on 2 June into voting for the proscription of the Twenty-Two.[3] They should have allowed themselves to be arrested there and then; it would have created such a scandal that the departments would

---

[3] Madame Roland, who had been arrested the previous day, heard the tocsin sound a new insurrection on 2 June. Next day she read in the newspaper that the Convention, under threat from the artillery of the Commune, had voted for the arrest of the leading Girondin deputies, including Buzot. A fortnight later she learned that Buzot, who had fled from Paris, was trying to raise the departments of Normandy against the Convention and that Roland was in hiding in Rouen.

have been alerted and the republic might have been saved. Even if it had cost them their lives, they would have had the privilege of serving their country. But the cowards temporised with crime and when their turn came, which of course it did, they died shamefully, unwept, despised by posterity. I can see that that was a turning-point. Instead of yielding to intimidation and trooping out of the Assembly like a flock of sheep marked for the slaughter they should have fallen upon the monsters and destroyed them.

Liberty? Liberty? Liberty is for proud hearts who fear not death and are ready to die; it is not for this corrupt nation which, the moment it was rescued from debauchery and tyranny, fell into brutal licence and wallowed in blood. Nor is it for those feeble individuals who think only of saving their own skins when the whole nation is weeping, with civil war raging and fear and destruction everywhere.

Eternal Creator, Supreme Being, soul of the universe, the source of all that is great and good, I believe in thee because I cannot accept that I am simply a product of this terrible material world. I know that I am of thine essence and I return to thee!

I earnestly entreat all to whom I have been dear to take care of my good and faithful maid. Her attachment to me over the last thirteen years has been touching. She has stood by me in all my struggles, wept with me in all my sufferings. If I could come back into this world a second time, I would ask for nothing better than to serve and comfort her in her old age! Look after her, my friends! You could pay no sweeter tribute to my memory.

One advantage of my decision to end my life is that I can ensure that my property goes where it belongs – to my daughter[4] Even if they seize her father's fortune she will still have the right to whatever is mine, including what is under seal. She could also claim the 12,000 livres which I brought in as dowry. This is recorded in the marriage contract of February 1780, now in the possession of Durand, a notary in the Place Dauphine. Apart from this there is a small property, consisting of a wood and some meadow, which I bought in accordance with my marriage settlement with funds derived from various things belonging to me by inheritance. All this is recorded in the contract which was entrusted to Dufresnoi, a

---

[4] A law of 10 March 1793 ordered the confiscation of property only of those who had been condemned to death.

notary in the rue Vivienne, in 1791, and in a document of which there are duplicates in my apartment at Thézée and at Villefranche: the whole amounting to some 13,000 or 14,000 livres.

I also possess a thousand livres in paper money. Out of this sum I would like the harp which my daughter is using and which is rented from Koliker in the rue des Fossés-St-Germain-des-Prés, to be bought for her. He is a decent man and it should be possible to come to an agreement with him. He might be willing to reduce the price of 100 écus which he quoted me. In any case I would prefer this money to be spent in that way rather than kept as cash. The most important thing in life is to be virtuous, but to have skills as well is a very great advantage. Music in particular not only sweetens solitude and unhappiness but provides a protection against temptation in times of prosperity. I would like the harp lessons to be continued for a few months more. After that, provided that she does not waste her time, the child should have enough skill to entertain herself without further instruction. There is an excellent piano under seal in the apartment; it was bought with my savings and the receipt is in my name. It must at all costs be claimed. But I hope that she will pay greatest attention to drawing, which should be her principal accomplishment.

I have been able to write to her uncle and godfather[5] and I hope he will take the necessary steps, if he is at liberty, to see that she gets what belongs to her. In that case my daughter, being reasonably well-off, should be able to make adequate provision for her maid and I hope that those who are looking after her will see that this is done. My elderly Besnard relations, living on the Île St-Louis, entrusted certain sums of money to my husband, on which we were paying them a regular income. It is possible that they will not know the formalities necessary for establishing their right to this money and I hope that they will be given every assistance. I also hope that they will be able to see their great-niece from time to time; she took the place of a child for them and all their hopes will rest on her.

I have never had any jewellery, but I have two rings of little value which my father gave me. I leave them as souvenirs, the emerald to my daughter's adopted father and the other to my friend Bosc.

I have nothing to add to what I have recently said to the generous woman who has agreed to be a mother to my child. My feelings of gratitude towards her and her husband will be carried with me

---

[5] Dominique Roland: he was arrested and executed shortly afterwards.

beyond the grave and cannot be expressed in this world.

I pray that my daughter will remember the advice which I gave her in my final letter, and that the memory of her mother will keep her constant in virtue.

Farewell my child, my husband, my maid, my friends! Farewell glorious sun that ever filled my heart with contentment as it filled the skies with light. Farewell lone countryside, where I have sighed and dreamed, and you, rustic villagers, who blessed my presence as I eased your toil, lightened your misery and nursed you in your sicknesses! Farewell my peaceful study, where I ever strove after truth and beauty and learned to control my senses and to despise vanity.

Farewell, dear —; no, I am not saying farewell to you. Leaving this world brings me nearer to you.

POSTSCRIPT
FROM PAUL DE ROUX'S INTRODUCTION TO THE FRENCH EDITION

◦—◦

Next day, a few hours after the execution of the Girondin deputies, Mme Roland, accused of 'conspiring against the unity and the indivisibility of the Republic and attempting to introduce civil war', was transferred to the Conciergerie. She was interrogated on 1 and 2 November. Judgment was passed on the 8th. Fouquier-Tinville, the public prosecutor, based the whole case on the accused's correspondence with the insurgents of Calvados. Madame Roland had at first asked that Chauveau-Lagarde should defend her, but decided at the last moment that she did not want him to compromise himself in a lost cause. She was therefore defended by an obscure lawyer, officially appointed. After his pleading she rose to speak but was at once interrupted by the president who declared that the accused could not abuse the right of speech 'to glorify crime, that is to say, Brissot and company'. She is said then to have turned towards the public and cried 'I call on you to witness the injustice they do to me.' To which the crowd replied with cries of 'Long live the Republic! Down with traitors!' A contemporary reports also that when the sentence of death was pronounced she said to the judge, 'You find me worthy to share the fate of the great men whom you have assassinated. I shall do my best to mount the scaffold with the same courage as they.'

The execution took place on the afternoon of the same day. Madame Roland had asked Sophie to come and watch the tumbril pass by at the corner of the Pont-Neuf, so that she might bear witness afterwards to her fortitude in face of death. Madame Grandchamp wrote: 'She had to share her last hours with a forger of banknotes called La Marche. She insisted on dining with him, encouraged him to eat and managed several times to make him smile. When they were taken to the tumbril, La Marche went in front of her. Despite her visible emotion at that point she said "You are ungallant, sir. A Frenchman should never forget his duty to a woman." On the scaffold, after they had cut off his hair, she looked at him carefully and said, "That suits you; you have a truly classical head." When the executioner had done the same to her she started to walk away; he stopped her, to tie her hands. "Pardon me," she said, "I am not used to it." '

Sophie Grandchamp did not fail her friend in their last rendezvous. 'I left for the appointed place an hour before her departure from the Conciergerie. There was a great crowd pressing towards the spot. I forced my way through them and took hold of the parapet as near to the steps as I could. There was a general shout: "Here she comes! Here she comes!" I saw the fateful wagon from far away. As soon as I could distinguish the features of my friend I never took my eyes off her again. She was radiant, calm, smiling. I could see her talking to her unfortunate companion and trying to put some courage into him. His pallor and dejection were in striking contrast to her confident bearing and glowing complexion. As she approached the bridge, she searched for me in the crowd. I could see her look of satisfaction when she recognised me. When she passed, she gave me a smile.' (Other contemporaries have recorded the famous phrase which she is said to have uttered before the Statue of Liberty, in the Place de la Révolution: 'O Liberty! What crimes are committed in thy name!')

When Roland learned of his wife's death, on 10 November 1793 he left his hiding-place in Rouen, went out into the country and killed himself. The following summer, between 19 and 22 June 1794, Buzot too, who was on the run, killed himself to avoid arrest. His body was found in a field near Bordeaux, half eaten by wolves.

PRINCIPAL DATES

1754   17 March. Birth of Marie-Jeanne Phlipon (Mme Roland).

1765   Marie-Jeanne enters a convent for 12 months and meets the Cannet sisters, who are to be lifelong friends.

1766   She spends a year with her paternal grandmother on the Île St-Louis before returning to her parents' apartment near the Pont-Neuf.

1772–5 She loses her faith.

1774   Accession of Louis XVI, whose wife was Marie Antoinette, daughter of Maria Theresa, Empress of Austria.

1776   Marie-Jeanne meets Jean-Marie Roland de la Platière (1734–93).

1780   4 Feb. She is married to M. Roland.
After one year in Paris they settle in Amiens.

1781   4 Oct. Birth of their daughter.

1784   Roland appointed Inspector of Lyons. The family move to Villefranche.

1787   Roland enters into correspondence with the journalist/politician Brissot. Beginning of the Rolands' involvement in national politics.

1788   The Paris *parlement* calls for the summoning of the Estates-General, which had not met since 1614.

1789   5 May. The Estates-General meet at Versailles.
17 June. The Third Estate adopt the title of National Assembly and call for constitutional reform.
20 June. The 'oath of the tennis court'.
July. Riots in Paris.
14 July. Fall of the Bastille.
26 Aug. Declaration of the Rights of Man.
5–6 Oct. March of the market women to Versailles.

1789   The royal family are brought to Paris.

10 Oct. Louis XVI declared 'King of the French' and installed in the Tuileries.

The National Assembly assumes the title 'Constituent Assembly' and spends the next eighteen months preparing a new Constitution.

1790   Roland elected to the municipal council of Lyons.

He is sent to Paris to procure the nationalisation of the city's debt.

1791   The Rolands installed in Paris. Her small salon becomes a meeting-place for deputies of the left (Girondins, Jacobins, etc.).

20 June. The King's flight to Varennes. He is intercepted, brought back to Paris and suspended from his functions.

17 July. The 'massacre of the Champ de Mars'.

14 Sept. The King accepts the new Constitution and is restored to his functions.

1 Oct. First meeting of the Legislative Assembly.

Dominance of the Girondin Party, who call for war with Prussia and Austria.

Roland is admitted to the Jacobin Society and becomes its secretary.

1792   10 March. Dismissal of the Narbonne ministry.

Gen. Dumouriez called upon to form a new cabinet. He invites the Girondins to nominate two ministers: Roland nominated as Minister of the Interior, Clavière as Minister of Finance. A third patriot, Gen. Servan, becomes Minister of War a month later.

20 April. The Assembly declares war on Austria.

10 June. Roland writes the King a vigorous protest (drafted by Mme Roland) against his refusal to sanction two decrees.

13 June. The three patriot ministers are dismissed.

20 June. The mob invade the Tuileries.

July/Aug. Increasing disorder in Paris and throughout France.

4 Aug. Insurrectionary Commune formed in Paris.

17 Aug. Storming of the Tuileries. The King suspended from his functions. Roland and the other dismissed ministers reinstated. Rise of Danton and increasing

1792   dominance of the Paris Commune.
2 Sept. Verdun surrenders to the Prussians.
2–6 Sept. Massacres in the Paris prisons.
20 Sept. Battle of Valmy. Prussian army defeated.
The Convention (taking over from the Legislative Assembly) abolishes the monarchy.
6 Nov. Army of the Convention advances into Belgium.

1793   Roland and his wife under increasing attack from the left, notably Danton, Marat, Robespierre and the extremists of the Paris Commune.
21 Jan. Execution of the King.
22 Jan. Roland resigns from the Ministry of the Interior.
War declared against Britain, Holland and Spain.
10 Mar. Revolutionary tribunal set up.
Revolt in the Vendée – suppressed in December by troops of the Convention.
26 Mar. Gen. Dumouriez deserts to the Austrians.
Committee of Public Safety set up.
29 May–2 June. Overthrow of the Girondins in the Convention.
1 June. Arrest of Mme Roland.
Flight of Roland and Buzot.
3 June. Arrest of the principal Girondin deputies.
24 June. Mme Roland released and re-arrested.
16 Oct. Marie-Antoinette executed.
24 Oct. Trial of the Girondin deputies. All executed on 31 Oct.
1/2 Nov. Interrogation of Mme Roland.
8 Nov. Execution of Mme Roland.
10 Nov. Suicide of Roland.

1794   June. Suicide of Buzot.